AMC'S BEST DAY HIKES NEAR
WASHINGTON, D.C.

Four-Season Guide to 50 of the Best Trails in Maryland, Virginia, and the Nation's Capital

3rd Edition // Jennifer Adach & Beth Homicz

Appalachian Mountain Club Books // Boston, Massachusetts

AMC is a nonprofit organization, and sales of AMC Books fund our mission of protecting the Northeast outdoors. If you appreciate our efforts and would like to become a member or make a donation to AMC, visit outdoors.org, call 800-372-1758, or contact us at Appalachian Mountain Club, 10 City Square, Boston, MA 02129.

outdoors.org/books-maps

Distributed by National Book Network.

Front cover photograph of a hiker at Theodore Roosevelt Island © Michael Martin.
Back cover photograph of a hiker at Bull Run Mountains Natural Area Preserve © Jennifer Adach
Title page photograph of hikers at Sky Meadow State Park © Jennifer Adach
Interior photographs by Beth Homicz, Jennifer Adach, and Annie Eddy, unless otherwise noted
Maps by Ken Dumas © Appalachian Mountain Club
Cover design by Jon Lavalley
Interior design by Abigail Coyle

Library of Congress Cataloging-in-Publication Data

Names: Adach, Jennifer, author. | Homicz, Beth, author.
Title: AMC's best day hikes near Washington, D.C. : four-season guide to 50
    of the best trails in Maryland, Virginia, and the Nation's Capital / Jen
    Adach & Beth Homicz.
Description: Third edition. | Boston, MA : Appalachian Mountain Club Books,
    [2023] | Includes bibliographical references and index. | Summary: "A
    collection of 50 of the greatest hikes in and around America's capital,
    including past some of the country's most famous monuments and around
    Civil War battlefields"-- Provided by publisher.
Identifiers: LCCN 2022048687 (print) | LCCN 2022048688 (ebook) | ISBN
    9781628421590 (trade paperback) | ISBN 9781628421545 (epub) | ISBN
    9781628421552 (mobi)
Subjects: LCSH: Hiking--Washington Metropolitan Area--Guidebooks. |
    Trails--Washington Metropolitan Area--Guidebooks. | Washington
    Metropolitan Area--Guidebooks.
Classification: LCC GV199.42.W17 M38 2023 (print) | LCC GV199.42.W17
    (ebook) | DDC 796.510975--dc23
LC record available at https://lccn.loc.gov/2022048687
LC ebook record available at https://lccn.loc.gov/2022048688]

The paper used in this publication meets the minimum requirements of the American National Standard for Information Sciences-Permanence of Paper for Printed Library Materials, ANSI Z39.48-1984. ∞

Outdoor recreation activities by their very nature are potentially hazardous. This book is not a substitute for good personal judgment and training in outdoor skills. Due to changes in conditions, use of the information in this book is at the sole risk of the user. The authors and the Appalachian Mountain Club assume no liability for accidents happening to, or injuries sustained by, readers who engage in the activities described in this book.

Interior pages and cover are printed on responsibly harvested paper stock certified by The Forest Stewardship Council®, an independent auditor of responsible forestry practices.
Printed in the United States of America, using vegetable-based inks.

5 4 3 2 1   23 24 25 26 27

MIX
Paper from responsible sources
FSC® C005010
www.fsc.org

In the memory of Ernest and Carol Adach

—Jennifer Adach

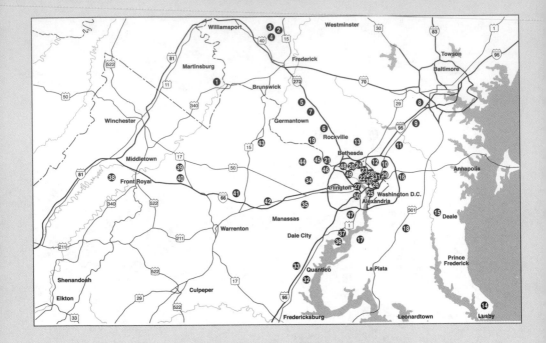

KEY TO ICONS

Steep or difficult terrain

Kid-friendly

Dog-friendly

Wheelchair accessible (Sometimes only part of the hike is accessible.)

Waterfall

Pond, stream, spring, or other water feature

Snowshoeing

Cross-country skiing (Sometimes only part of a trail is skiable or a ski trail is adjacent.)

Scenic views

Designated tentsite

Designated swimming area (nearby)

Picnic area (nearby)

Visitor center (nearby)

Public transportation available

$ Fee

Fishing

Horseback riding

Bicycle trails

CONTENTS

2 // WASHINGTON, D.C.   99

3 // VIRGINIA   155

NATURE AND HISTORY ESSAYS

AT-A-GLANCE TRIP PLANNER

Trip number	Trip name and location	Difficulty rating	Round-trip distance	Elevation gain	Estimated time
SECTION 1 // MARYLAND					
1	Harpers Ferry to Maryland Heights *Harpers Ferry, WV/Maryland*	Strenuous	6.5 mi	1,670 ft	4–4.5 hrs
2	Gambrill State Park *Frederick, MD*	Strenuous	8.2 mi	1,472 ft	3.5–4 hrs
3	Catoctin Mountain Park and Cunningham Falls State Park *Thurmont, MD*	Strenuous	8.2 mi	1,560 ft	4.5–5 hrs
4	Annapolis Rock and Black Rock Cliff *Myersville, MD*	Moderate	7.2 mi	840 ft	3.5 hrs
5	Sugarloaf Mountain *Dickerson, MD*	Moderate–Strenuous	5.3 mi	1,375 ft	3–3.5 hrs
6	Seneca Creek State Park: Clopper Lake *Gaithersburg, MD*	Moderate	4.5 mi	400–500 ft	2.5–3 hrs
7	Black Hill Regional Park *Boyds, MD*	Moderate	6.8 mi	320 ft	3–3.5 hrs
8	Patapsco Valley State Park *Elkridge, MD*	Strenuous	8.6 mi	1,032 ft	3.5–4 hrs
9	Wincopin Trails *Jessup, MD*	Easy	3.6 mi	310 ft	1.5–2 hrs
10	Greenbelt Park *Greenbelt, MD*	Moderate	5.3 mi	350 ft	2–2.5 hrs
11	Patuxent Research Refuge *Laurel, MD*	Easy	2.1 mi	35 ft	1.5 hrs (longer with a stop at the nature center)
12	Lake Artemesia and Northeast Branch Trail *College Park and Berwyn Heights, MD*	Easy	3.5 mi	20 ft	2 hrs
13	Matthew Henson Trail *Veirs Mill and Colesville, MD*	Moderate	4.5 mi	235 ft	2.5–3 hrs
14	Calvert Cliffs State Park *Lusby, MD*	Moderate	4.8 mi	330 ft	2–2.5 hrs
15	Jug Bay Wetlands Sanctuary *Lothian, MD*	Easy–Moderate	5.3 mi	208 ft	3 hrs

Trip highlights	Trip features
Challenging, historic hike with gorgeous river confluence vistas	🐕 💧 👟 🏕️ ⬆️ $
Rugged hike with outstanding views	🐾 👟 ⛺ ⬆️
True mountain trails, pristine waterfall, rustic setting	🚶 🐕 ♿ 〰️ 🎣 🎿 👟 🏕️ ⬆️
Two stunning overlooks	🚶 🐾 👟
Challenging hike, wildflower-rich trails, farmland views	🐾 💧 👟 🏕️ 🚲
Mature hardwoods, excellent lakeshore views	🚶 🐾 💧 🏕️ ⬆️ $ 🎣
Butterfly hot spot, ruined mill, lakeshore trail	🐾 🐕 ♿ 💧 🏕️ ⬆️
Tranquil Cascade Falls	🐾 〰️ 💧 $ 🚲
Hidden gem offers robust hiking and stream views	🚶 🐾 💧
Excellent loop hike through secluded second-growth forest	🚶 🐾 💧 ⛺ 🏕️ 🚌 🐎 🚲
Hands-on nature center, wonderful array of flora and fauna, bald eagles	🚶 🐾 💧 ♿ ⬆️ 🎣
Birding trail, fishing piers, lake and river views; good for all ages	🚶 🐾 💧 🚌 🎣 🚲
Peaceful trail with flora- and fauna-sighting opportunities	🚶 🐾 ♿ 💧 🏕️
Miocene-epoch cliffs rich in shark teeth and other ancient fossils	🚶 🐾 💧 🏕️ $
Wildlife from snails and lizards to turtles and otters	🚶 💧 🏕️ $

Trip number	Trip name and location	Difficulty rating	Round-trip distance	Elevation gain	Estimated time
16	Watkins Regional Park *Largo, MD*	Easy	2.2 mi	45 ft	2.5–3 hrs, including farm and nature center
17	Piscataway Park *Accokeek, MD*	Easy	4 mi	Minimal	2 hrs
18	Cedarville State Forest *Brandywine, MD*	Easy	4.1 mi	230 ft	2–3 hrs
19	Blockhouse Point Conservation Park *Potomac, MD*	Easy	2.7 mi	330 ft	1–1.5 hrs
20	Capital Crescent Trail *Bethesda, MD and Georgetown, Washington, D.C.*	Moderate	7.8 mi	–310 ft downslope	3 hrs
21	Billy Goat Trail at Great Falls *Great Falls, MD*	Strenuous	5.2 mi	435 ft	4–4.5 hrs

SECTION 2 // WASHINGTON, D.C.

Trip number	Trip name and location	Difficulty rating	Round-trip distance	Elevation gain	Estimated time
22	Rock Creek Park: Western Ridge and Valley Trails *Northwest Washington, D.C.*	Moderate	6.1 mi	840 ft	2.5–3 hrs
23	Rock Creek Park: Pulpit Rock and Boulder Bridge *Northwest Washington, D.C.*	Moderate	1.5 mi	130 ft	1 hr
24	Around Georgetown *Northwest Washington, D.C.*	Moderate	6.9 mi	800 ft	3.5 hrs
25	National Mall *Southeast, Southwest, Northwest Washington, D.C.*	Easy–Moderate	3.8 mi	–70 ft downslope	3 hrs
26	East Potomac Park and Monuments *Southwest Washington, D.C.*	Easy–Moderate	6.6 mi	30 ft	3–4 hrs
27	Theodore Roosevelt Island *Arlington, VA, and Washington, D.C.*	Easy	2.3 mi	Minimal	2–2.5 hrs
28	U.S. National Arboretum *Northeast Washington, D.C.*	Easy–Moderate	8.2 mi	800 ft	4.5–5 hrs
29	Kenilworth Park and Aquatic Gardens *Northeast Washington, D.C.*	Easy	2.5 mi	Minimal	1.5–2 hrs
30	Kingman and Heritage Islands *Northeast and Southeast Washington, D.C.*	Easy	2.2 mi	Minimal	1–1.5 hrs
31	Anacostia Park and Riverwalk *Southeast Washington, D.C.*	Easy	5.2 mi	Minimal	2–2.5 hrs

SECTION 3 // VIRGINIA

Trip number	Trip name and location	Difficulty rating	Round-trip distance	Elevation gain	Estimated time
32	Crow's Nest Natural Area Preserve *Stafford, VA*	Easy	5.8 mi	405 ft	2.5–3 hrs

Trip highlights	Trip features
Family fun: farm animals, wetland trail, carousel, nature center	
Shoreline views, explorations of cultural and natural history	
Home to the headwaters of Maryland's largest freshwater swamp	
History, views of the Potomac River	
Views of C&O Canal, Potomac River, and old railway crossings	
Spectacular hike to Mather Gorge overlooking Potomac River with rock scrambling	
Natural oasis of 1,700 wooded, hilly acres with challenging trails	
Two iconic sites of Rock Creek Park	
Secluded, shady hike through charming historic neighborhoods	
Art spaces, landscaped gardens, iconic memorials, Capitol Hill	
Memorials to great leaders, four bodies of water, cherry trees	
Secluded, woodsy riverine island with cityscape vistas	
Bonsai, azaleas, 15 collections of flora from around the globe	
Human-made ponds teeming with waterlilies and lotuses	
Manmade islands offer a habitat for nature	
Paved path explores both sides of the Anacostia River	
Unique preserve with diverse flora for visitors to explore	

Trip number	Trip name and location	Difficulty rating	Round-trip distance	Elevation gain	Estimated time
33	Prince William Forest Park *Triangle and Quantico, VA*	Moderate–Strenuous	7.9 mi	600 ft	3 hrs
34	Washington and Old Dominion Trail, Gerry Connolly Cross County Trail *Vienna, VA*	Moderate–Strenuous	12 mi	230 ft	4.5–5 hrs
35	Bull Run Occoquan Trail *Manassas, VA*	Moderate	7.8 mi	470 ft	4 hrs
36	Mason Neck State Park *Lorton, VA*	Easy	4.5 mi	196 ft	2–2.5 hrs
37	Gunston Hall: River Trail *Lorton, VA*	Easy	2.5 mi	86 ft	1.5 hrs
38	Signal Knob *Fort Valley, VA*	Strenuous	10.6 mi	2,680 ft	7–7.5 hrs
39	Sky Meadows State Park *Delaplane, VA*	Moderate	5.8 mi	1,000 ft	3 hrs
40	G. Richard Thompson Wildlife Management Area *Delaplane, VA*	Strenuous	8.8 mi	1,750 ft	4.5–5 hrs
41	Virginia Outdoors Foundation's Preserve at Bull Run Mountains *Broad Run, VA*	Easy	2.2 mi	250 ft	1–1.5 hrs
42	Manassas National Battlefield Park *Manassas, VA*	Moderate	5.4 mi	900 ft	3–3.5 hrs
43	Banshee Reeks Nature Preserve *Leesburg, VA*	Moderate	5.2 mi	215 ft	2.5 hrs
44	Meadowlark Botanical Gardens *Tysons Corner, VA*	Easy	0.8 mi	70 ft	1 hr
45	Riverbend Park and Great Falls Park *Great Falls, VA*	Moderate	6.8 mi	1,100 ft	4–4.5 hrs
46	Scott's Run Nature Preserve *McLean, VA*	Strenuous	3.1 mi	710 ft	2–2.5 hrs
47	Huntley Meadows Park *Alexandria (Hybla Valley), VA*	Easy	2.1 mi	Minimal	1 hr
48	Turkey Run Park *McLean, VA*	Easy–Moderate	2.3 mi	200 ft	2–2.5 hrs
49	Potomac Overlook Regional Park *Arlington, VA*	Easy	1.7 mi	200 ft	1–1.5 hrs
50	Arlington National Cemetery and Marine Corps War (Iwo Jima) Memorial *Arlington, VA*	Easy–Moderate	4 mi	600 ft	3–4 hrs, including sightseeing

Trip highlights	Trip features
More than 15,000 protected acres, numerous trail options	
Paved hike/bike path; historic Colvin Run Mill	
Remote trail through rural lands	
Wide array of winged predators, including bald eagles	
Wild birds of the Potomac wetlands	
Rugged loop with lovely views, greatest elevation gain	
Stunning blend of wildflower meadows and woodlands	
2,200 feet above sea level; Virginia's best display of trilliums	
Closest mountain range to D.C.	
Rolling hills, forested solitude, historic landmarks	
Secluded, wild, little-known Virginia ramble	
Easygoing trails, wildflowers, wetlands, Korean bell garden	
Dynamic views of the Potomac's Great Falls	
Strenuous hike and scramble overlooking Potomac River	
Freshwater marsh supporting more than 200 species; prime birding	
Rugged ramble along the Potomac River	
Neighborhood gem with interpretive nature displays	
Metro-friendly hike offers classic views amid hallowed hills	

PREFACE

Writing this new edition of *AMC's Best Day Hikes near Washington, D.C.* was especially poignant at times. During the recent COVID-19 pandemic, the outdoors reopened for many folks—and opened for the first time for others. Tents and backpacks flew off shelves, and people laced up hiking boots to reacquaint themselves with nature.

Let's keep those hiking boots on. For this third edition, we've moved a little closer to home, adding neighborhood gems such as the Potomac Overlook Regional Park (Trip 49), Rock Creek Park's Pulpit Rock and Boulder Bridge (Trip 23), and Wincopin Trails (Trip 9). The Anacostia Riverwalk (Trip 31) and Kingman and Heritage Islands (Trip 30) deliver new ways to explore the city. These close-by trips give hikers of all skill levels a chance to squeeze in a quick outing after a long day.

But sometimes you want to get away. Head to the beach and explore southern Maryland's Calvert Cliffs State Park (Trip 14). Aim for the heights and tackle Signal Knob (Trip 38) or Catoctin Mountain (Trip 3). Journey south to explore Crow's Nest Natural Area Preserve (Trip 32), new to this edition.

And even though residents have been known to complain about the influx of tourists and wish they would stand to the right on the Metro escalator, many still marvel at the sight of the monuments at night. If you're a local, become a tourist and reexplore the National Mall (Trip 25) and East Potomac Park (Trip 26).

The past few years have brought challenges—and for some, losses—but they also forged many of our relationships to the land and helped us find the healing and strength that a day in the woods can bring. Let's lace up our boots and get outside.

—Jennifer Adach, April 2022

ACKNOWLEDGMENTS

Part of the joy in working on a book such as this is the opportunity to explore new corners of Washington, D.C. It delights me to no end to keep uncovering all that the area has to offer. A huge thank-you to the public servants and volunteers who dedicate their time to make this region an active and exciting one and to maintain the trails that we love to explore.

I'd be remiss if I didn't thank the amazing team at AMC Books, particularly Tim Mudie, who provided valuable support in making this book a reality.

A huge thank-you to Beth Homicz and Annie Eddy for laying the groundwork (and for putting in the hiking miles) for the previous edition of this book.

Writing this book was a particular challenge because my mother, my biggest publicist, passed away while I was working on it. I imagine that she'd be proud of the end result. A special thanks to all family members and friends who offered support and were there to lend a hand. It means more than I could ever say. To my sister, Katie, for being there. And, finally, to Michael—taking that GPS class was my luckiest day. I couldn't have done this without you.

I didn't start hiking until I was 30, so my outdoors life started late. To everyone who dreams about adventure, this book is for you—it's never too late to get started.

—Jennifer Adach

INTRODUCTION

WELCOME TO WASHINGTON, D.C.

Washington, D.C., is an outdoors town. The region around the nation's capital affords a rich, pleasing, and challenging variety of terrain and ecology, with abundant wildlife, extraordinary vistas, and sites that speak to the United States' historical roots. Parks of all sorts—arboretums, meadows, forests, mountains, aquatic gardens, wildlife management areas, canals, Colonial-era streetscapes, funky urban art spaces, waterfront wharves, and Civil War battlefields—are within an enjoyable 90-minute drive; many of them are just a short Metrorail ride from downtown. Most of the 50 hikes included here offer a year-round water feature, be it a creek, a waterfall, a bay, or a river. Moreover, several of these havens welcome hikers at no charge. Even the most overworked and underpaid political operative, legislative staffer, or White House intern can manage to squeeze in an occasional getaway to green spaces and quiet places. The nearness of such oases makes Washington, D.C., a truly vibrant outdoors destination.

The District of Columbia is cradled in a bowl at the falls point of the Potomac River, upstream from which large watercraft cannot pass. These waters are brackish, a mix of salt water and freshwater. In Colonial days, many settlements were established at river falls points: Fredericksburg and Richmond in Virginia, for example, at the falls of the Rappahannock and James rivers, respectively, where the Piedmont plateaus wend their way down to the tidal waters. All waterways in the region flow into Chesapeake Bay and, eventually, to the Atlantic Ocean.

This blend of geographic and hydrologic features offers a wonderful spectrum of level strolls within the boundaries of the nation's capital, such as along the National Mall and through East Potomac Park; interesting, shady inclines, such as those in Rock Creek Park and Georgetown; and iconic riverwalks, such as the one along the Anacostia River. But as you venture from D.C. into the Piedmont region of Virginia, Maryland, and West Virginia, the terrain and geology—and the whitewater rapids—are stunning and varied from the falls upstream. Riverbend Park, Billy Goat Trail at Great Falls, and the confluence of the Shenandoah and Potomac rivers at Harpers Ferry, for instance, all provide a window into primeval times and the power of water rushing through chasms in ancient rock.

Rolling from the tidewater up to the base of the Appalachian Mountains—represented by Virginia's Blue Ridge Mountains and Maryland's Catoctin Mountain ranges—the Piedmont offers rich clay soils, verdant hills, excellent horse pastures, and wildflowers galore. The well-worn Appalachians beckon hikers ever upward with their serene and rustic beauty, their rich offerings of fauna and fall colors, and their marvelous vistas. These gifts await you at Maryland's Catoctin Mountain Park, Virginia's Sky Meadows State Park and G. Richard Thompson Wildlife Management Area, and other sites featured in this book. Three hikes included here—Annapolis Rock and Black Rock Cliff (Trip 4), Harpers Ferry to Maryland Heights (Trip 1), and Sky Meadows State Park (Trip 39)—traverse short segments of the revered, rugged Appalachian Trail, which stretches 2,190 miles from Georgia to Maine.

The Washington, D.C., region also bears the memories—some would say the ghosts—of the shared human history familiar to most of us, if sometimes vaguely recalled from school days. From Harpers Ferry in West Virginia to Arlington National Cemetery and Mount Vernon—and even Washington, D.C., itself—the area provides visitors with countless opportunities to walk through sites that hum with the vibrations of iconic American experiences.

When it comes to family-friendly parks, gardens, and trails, be sure to check out standbys (and standouts!) such as Meadowlark Botanical Gardens (Trip 44), Watkins Regional Park (Trip 16), and Huntley Meadows Park (Trip 47). Don't miss Jug Bay Wetlands Sanctuary (Trip 15) and Banshee Reeks Nature Preserve (Trip 43), which offer sheer enjoyment and learning for young and old alike.

HOW TO USE THIS BOOK

With 50 hikes to choose from, you may wonder how to decide where to go. The locator map at the front of this book will help you narrow down the trips by location, and the at-a-glance trip planner that follows the table of contents will provide more information to guide you toward a decision.

Once you settle on a destination and turn to a trip in this guide, you will find a series of icons that indicate whether the hike is a good place for children, whether it is fully or partly wheelchair accessible, whether dogs are permitted, whether the location is good for winter sports, whether the site can be reached via public transportation, whether it has a water feature, and whether fees are charged.

Information on the basics follows: location, difficulty rating, distance, elevation gain, estimated time, maps, global positioning system (GPS) coordinates for parking lots, and contact information. The ratings are based on the authors' perception and are estimates of what the average hiker will experience. You may find the hikes to be easier or more difficult than stated. The estimated time is also based on the authors' perception. Consider your own pace when planning a trip.

The elevation gain is calculated from measurements and information from United States Geological Survey (USGS) topographic maps, landowner maps, and Google Earth. Information is included about the relevant USGS maps as well as where you can find trail maps.

A boldfaced summary provides a basic overview of what you will see on your hike.

"Directions" explain how to reach the trailhead by car and, for some trips, by public transportation. When you enter the given GPS coordinates into your device, it will provide driving directions. Whether or not you own a GPS device, it is wise to consult an atlas before leaving home.

In the "Trail Description," you will find instructions about the trails on which to hike and where to turn. You will also learn about the natural and human history along the route as well as information about flora, fauna, and any landmarks and objects you may encounter.

The trail maps that accompany each trip are helpful, but it would be wise to also take an official trail map with you. They are often available online, at the trailhead, or at the visitor center.

Each trip includes a "More Information" section that provides details about the locations of bathrooms, access times and fees, the property's rules and regulations, and other relevant facts.

A "Nearby" section describes attractions that can be found near the site of the hike.

TRIP PLANNING AND SAFETY

While elevations in and around Washington, D.C., are relatively low compared with other regions of the East Coast, and the hikes detailed in this guide aren't particularly dangerous, you'll still want to be prepared. Some of the walks traverse moderately rugged terrain along rocky hills, and others lead to sandy beaches, ponds, and fields where you'll have extended periods of sun exposure and find areas where walking is slow in soft sand. Heat and humidity are pervasive in summer months, so make sure you have adequate water and sun protection.

You will more likely have an enjoyable, safe hike if you plan ahead and take proper precautions. Before heading out, consider the following:

Select a hike that everyone in your group is comfortable taking. Match the hike to the abilities of the least capable person in the group. If anyone is uncomfortable with the weather or is tired, turn around and complete the hike another day.

Plan to be back at the trailhead before dark. Before beginning your hike, determine a turnaround time. Don't diverge from it, even if you have not reached your intended destination.

Check the weather. If you are planning a ridge or summit hike, start early so that you will be off the exposed area before the afternoon hours, when thunderstorms most often strike, especially in summer. Hikers at coastal locations should be prepared for wind year-round, especially during winter, when windchill is a concern. Temperatures—and humidity—can soar in summer months, so ample water is a must, even on short walks. Compared with inland locations, the climate is generally cooler along the immediate coast during warm months and milder in winter. Significant storms—including heavy winter snowfalls, spring rains, and tropical storms in late summer and fall—may cause flooding, potentially dangerous ocean tides, and other hazards. When exploring beaches or other areas along the coast, be sure to check tide tables in advance and keep an eye on the water at all times.

Bring a pack with the following items:

- Water: Two quarts per person is usually adequate, depending on the weather and the length of the trip.

- Food: Even if you are planning just a one-hour hike, bring some high-energy snacks, such as nuts, dried fruit, or granola bars. Pack a lunch for longer trips.

- Map and compass: Be sure you know how to use them. A handheld global positioning system (GPS) device may also be helpful, but it is not always reliable.

- Headlamp or flashlight, with spare batteries

- Extra clothing: Rain gear, wool sweater or fleece jacket, hat, and mittens

- Sunscreen
- First-aid kit, including adhesive bandages, gauze, nonprescription painkillers, and moleskin
- Pocketknife or multitool
- Waterproof matches and a lighter
- Trash bag
- Toilet paper
- Whistle
- Insect repellent
- Sunglasses
- Cell phone: Be aware that cell phone service is unreliable in rural areas. If you are receiving a signal, use the phone only for emergencies to avoid disturbing the backcountry experience for other hikers.
- Binoculars (optional)
- Camera (optional)

Wear appropriate footwear and clothing. Wool or synthetic hiking socks keep your feet dry and help prevent blisters. Comfortable, waterproof hiking shoes or boots provide ankle support and good traction. Avoid wearing cotton clothing, which absorbs sweat and rain and contributes to an unpleasant hiking experience. Polypropylene, fleece, silk, and wool all wick moisture away from your body and keep you warm in wet or cold conditions. To help avoid insect bites, you may want to wear pants and a long-sleeve shirt.

When you are ahead of the rest of your hiking group, wait at all trail junctions until the others catch up. This avoids confusion and keeps people from getting separated or lost.

If you see downed wood that appears to be purposely covering a trail, it probably means the trail is closed due to overuse or hazardous conditions.

If a trail is muddy, walk through the mud or on rocks, never on tree roots or plants. Waterproof boots will keep your feet comfortable. Staying in the center of the trail will keep it from eroding into a wide hiking highway.

Leave your itinerary and the time you expect to return with someone you trust. If you see a logbook at a trailhead, be sure to sign in when you arrive and sign out when you leave.

After you complete your hike, check for deer ticks, which carry the dangerous Lyme disease.

Poison ivy is always a threat when hiking. To identify the plant, look for clusters of three leaves that shine in the sun but are dull in the shade. If you come into contact with poison ivy, wash the affected area with soap as soon as possible.

Wear blaze-orange items in hunting season. For Virginia hunting season, see dgif .virginia.gov/hunting/regulations, and for Maryland hunting season, see dnr.maryland.gov /huntersguide/Pages/allspecies.aspx.

Biting insects are present during warm months, particularly in the vicinity of wetlands. They can be a minor or significant nuisance, depending on seasonal and daily conditions. One serious concern is the eastern equine encephalitis virus (commonly referred to as

EEE), a rare but potentially fatal disease that can be transmitted to humans by infected mosquitoes. The Mid-Atlantic's many swamps provide ideal mosquito habitats; the threat is generally greatest in the evening hours, when mosquitoes are most active.

A variety of options are available for dealing with bugs, ranging from sprays that include the active ingredient N,N-diethyl-meta-toluamide (commonly known as DEET), which can potentially cause skin or eye irritation, to more skin-friendly products. Head nets, which often can be purchased more cheaply than a can of repellent, are useful during especially buggy conditions.

LEAVE NO TRACE

 The Appalachian Mountain Club is a national educational partner of Leave No Trace, a nonprofit organization dedicated to promoting and inspiring responsible outdoor recreation through education, research, and partnerships. The Leave No Trace program seeks to develop wildland ethics—ways in which people think and act in the outdoors to minimize their impact on the areas they visit and to protect our natural resources for future enjoyment. Leave No Trace unites four federal land management agencies—the U.S. Forest Service, National Park Service, Bureau of Land Management, and U.S. Fish & Wildlife Service—with manufacturers, outdoor retailers, user groups, educators, organizations such as AMC, and individuals.

The Leave No Trace ethic is guided by these seven principles:

1. *Plan Ahead and Prepare.* Know the terrain and any regulations applicable to the area you're planning to visit, and be prepared for extreme weather or other emergencies. This will enhance your enjoyment and ensure that you've chosen an appropriate destination. Small groups have less impact on resources and on the experiences of other backcountry visitors.

2. *Travel and Camp on Durable Surfaces.* Travel and camp on established trails and campsites, rock, gravel, dry grasses, or snow. Good campsites are found, not made. Camp at least 200 feet from lakes and streams, and focus activities on areas where vegetation is absent. In pristine areas, disperse use to prevent the creation of campsites and trails.

3. *Dispose of Waste Properly.* Pack it in, pack it out. Inspect your camp for trash or food scraps. Deposit solid human waste in cat holes dug 6 to 8 inches deep, at least 200 feet from water, camps, and trails. Pack out toilet paper and hygiene products. To wash yourself or your dishes, carry water 200 feet from streams or lakes and use small amounts of biodegradable soap. Scatter strained dishwater.

4. *Leave What You Find.* Cultural or historical artifacts, as well as natural objects such as plants and rocks, should be left as found.

5. *Minimize Campfire Impacts.* Cook on a stove. Use established fire rings, fire pans, or mound fires. If you build a campfire, keep it small and use dead sticks found on the ground.

6. *Respect Wildlife.* Observe wildlife from a distance. Feeding animals alters their natural behavior. Protect wildlife from your food by storing rations and trash securely.

7. *Be Considerate of Other Visitors.* Be courteous, respect the quality of other visitors' backcountry experience, and let nature's sounds prevail.

AMC is a national provider of the Leave No Trace Master Educator course. AMC offers this five-day course, designed especially for outdoor professionals and land managers, as well as the shorter two-day Leave No Trace Trainer course at locations throughout the Northeast.

For Leave No Trace information and materials, contact the Leave No Trace Center for Outdoor Ethics, P.O. Box 997, Boulder, CO 80306. Phone: 800-332-4100 or 303-442-8222; fax: 303-442-8217; web: lnt.org. For information on the AMC Leave No Trace Master Educator training course schedule, see activities.outdoors.org.

From serene and rustic Catoctin Mountain to shining Chesapeake Bay, the topography of Maryland offers rich variety and memorable appeal. Maryland is one of the smaller states in the nation in terms of landmass, yet it's nearly as wide east to west as its big northern neighbor, Pennsylvania. The hikes described in this section cover a large share of that geographic range.

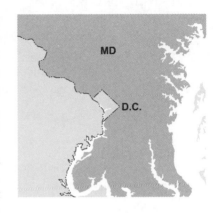

The winding western shore of Chesapeake Bay a few dozen miles east and south of Washington, D.C., offers more than a day at the beach. Calvert Cliffs State Park (Trip 14) rewards intrepid hikers with miles of sandy cliffs safeguarding Miocene-epoch fossils and sharks' teeth. Piscataway Park (Trip 17) offers views of Mount Vernon and a working farm. Jug Bay Wetlands Sanctuary (Trip 15) appeals to all ages with its wide variety of wildlife.

Peaceful retreats ring the bustling metro area of Washington, D.C. These include Watkins Regional Park (Trip 16), a family-friendly destination with a nature center, a farmstead housing peacocks and other critters, and even a carousel. Lake Artemesia and Northeast Branch Trail (Trip 12) in College Park is a wonderful hike for bird-watching and just a short walk from the Metro. Matthew Henson Trail (Trip 13) is a suburban-to-rural universally accessible trail with chances to observe deer and other shy fauna.

Greenbelt Park (Trip 10) provides surprising seclusion and good hiking for a nature spot just outside the Capital Beltway, the interstate highway ring around Washington, D.C. A bit farther to the northeast, Patuxent Research Refuge (Trip 11) offers an easy lakeshore hike, a wildlife center, and peaceful fishing. Capital Crescent Trail from Bethesda into Georgetown (Trip 20) is an appealing rail-trail mix of urban hustle and steampunk style, with plenty of shady stretches and river views tossed in.

North and west of the nation's capital, stretching upward into higher elevations, savor the rugged beauty of Catoctin Mountain Park (Trip 3). Sugarloaf Mountain (Trip 5), a privately owned monadnock, or standalone mountain, that Franklin D. Roosevelt once coveted for a presidential retreat, showcases outcroppings of ancient quartzite. Don't miss

Facing page: The canal along Billy Goat Trail in Great Falls, Maryland offers lush beauty in early spring—and opportunities to spot goslings getting a taste of the water.

Patapsco Valley State Park (Trip 8), one of the more demanding Maryland trips in this guide, which rewards hikers with the lovely Cascade Falls.

Closer to the capital, Seneca Creek State Park (Trip 6) and Black Hill Regional Park (Trip 7) offer more-moderate trails within wide stretches of unspoiled lands. Billy Goat Trail at Great Falls (Trip 21) is a popular challenge for most any hiker looking for a good climb, and it's only a few miles beyond the Capital Beltway.

If you're interested in historical sites, make tracks for the Harpers Ferry to Maryland Heights hike (Trip 1), which starts and ends just inside the West Virginia panhandle (and briefly joins the Appalachian Trail). This trip delivers stunning views of the point where the Shenandoah River and the Potomac River join. Closer to home, Blockhouse Point Conservation Park (Trip 19), new to this edition, offers a short route packed with history.

(*Note*: Maryland's Department of Natural Resources maintains the system of state parks, forests, and wildlife sanctuaries, which is among the best in the nation. All the state parks listed in this section have well-maintained trails, and most have historical sites and excellent visitor centers.)

1 HARPERS FERRY TO MARYLAND HEIGHTS

This hike from downtown Harpers Ferry to Maryland Heights across the Potomac is as challenging as it is gorgeous.

Features 🐕 💧 🎋 🏕 ⬆ 💲

Location Harpers Ferry, WV, via Maryland

Rating Strenuous

Distance 6.5-mile loop

Elevation Gain 1,670 feet

Estimated Time 4–4.5 hours

Maps USGS Harpers Ferry; Potomac Appalachian Trail Club Map 7: AT in WV and N. VA–Potomac River & Harpers Ferry to VA 7; National Park Service map available on-site; online: nps.gov/hafe/planyourvisit/hikes.htm

GPS Coordinates 39° 19.033′ N, 74° 45.426′ W

Contact Harpers Ferry National Historical Park, National Park Service, nps.gov/hafe, 304-535-6029

DIRECTIONS

From the I-495 (Capital Beltway) inner loop, take Exit 38 (from the outer loop, take Exit 35) onto I-270 north toward Frederick. At Exit 32, take I-70 west and then immediately take Exit 52 for US 340 west (also US 15 south). Continue on US 340 west toward Charles Town, West Virginia, for 19.5 miles. Turn left on Shoreline Drive to enter the Harpers Ferry National Historical Park Visitor Center (entrance fee applies). From here, board the shuttle bus, which will take you directly into the town.

TRAIL DESCRIPTION

Harpers Ferry, West Virginia, is the site of the abolitionist John Brown's infamous attempt to incite an insurrection of people who were enslaved. In October 1859, Brown and 21 men, including three of his sons, raided the U.S. arsenal here, hoping to seize rifles and other firearms and distribute them to people who were enslaved and abolitionists, who could then fight for freedom. Robert E. Lee, representing the federal government he would soon disavow, led the U.S. reprisal. Ten of Brown's men were killed, five fled, and the rest were captured. The state of Virginia (West Virginia didn't come into being until 1863) tried and hanged the prisoners at nearby Charles Town.

This 6.5-mile hike visits sites of both historical significance and pristine beauty, offering incomparable vistas. It starts at the National Park Service shuttle bus stop, visits old-town Harpers Ferry, passes John Brown's Fort, crosses the Byron E. Goodloe Memorial

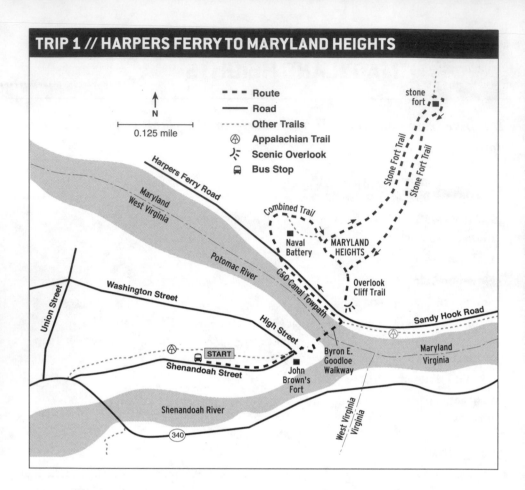

Pedestrian Walkway into Maryland, follows the Chesapeake & Ohio (C&O) Canal towpath west, and ascends Maryland Heights to the ruins of a Union stone fort.

From the shuttle bus stop, face Shenandoah Street and turn to the right to follow this street into the historical center of the town. Look for John Brown's Fort on the right. This structure was the guardroom and fire engine house of the original river-powered United States Armory and Arsenal at Harpers Ferry, the building into which Brown and his cohorts retreated for their final stand. Continue over the Byron E. Goodloe walkway, crossing the border into Maryland, and descend the spiraling steps to the C&O Canal towpath.

Turn left on the towpath and pass the stone remnants of lock 33, the old unloading point for goods bound for Harpers Ferry. Tread the preserved path where workers once struggled to maintain the water levels and keep the barges moving. The C&O Canal began operation in 1836, but after years of decline, a flood in 1924 spelled its end. (See "Centuries of Perseverance: The Chesapeake & Ohio Canal," on page 92.) Stay on the towpath for 0.25 mile and then cross a small bridge to Harpers Ferry Road. Cross the street and then pass the gate to start following green-blazed Combined Trail as it begins the tough ascent to Maryland Heights.

A hiker takes in the view of Harpers Ferry from the overlook.

As Combined Trail makes its way uphill, excellent views offer opportunities to stop and take a break. The trail eventually bends to the right, bringing you away from the river views and into the surrounding trees. The trail forks about 1.4 miles into the hike. Both paths are on course with the route, but bearing to the right offers a chance to see the remains of an old naval battery. Rejoin Combined Trail and arrive at an intersection marked by an informational sign.

Turn left onto blue-blazed Stone Fort Trail, which leads to the Union stone fort atop 1,000-foot Maryland Heights. The climb isn't over yet—to reach the plateau, the trail steeply gains more than 500 feet in 0.5 mile.

Upon reaching the plateau, the route winds through a level area, with circular earthen platforms that mark Civil War campsites, and passes a long stone-and-earth breastwork, one of two parallel rifle pits erected in June 1863. These fortifications were built too late to prevent one of Lee's masterstrokes as a Confederate general—a three-pronged attack on Harpers Ferry in September 1862 that netted 10,000 prisoners. The inexperienced Union defenders surrendered in droves, enabling the Confederate detachment to rejoin the main force just in time for the Battle of Antietam.

Follow the trail uphill and cross a stone wall; turn left and continue to the northwest corner of the interior fort. The parapet here is the largest earthwork constructed on

Maryland Heights. The trail then turns to the right—follow the blue blazes on the rocks a short distance ahead into the stone fort. A row of large foundation stones offers an excellent view, especially in winter months.

Follow the blue blazes southward down the mountain on Stone Fort Trail. In 0.5 mile, reach the former site of a giant Parrott rifle, which weighed 9,700 pounds and took 300 men to haul up the mountain. It was mounted on a 360-degree swivel and could hurl its 100-pound projectiles more than 2 miles toward the opposing high grounds of Loudoun Heights (in Virginia) and Bolivar Heights (in present-day West Virginia). Go left where Stone Fort Trail splits, and pass the pits of old collapsed powder magazines. Walk downhill on the spine of the rocky ridge and turn left where Stone Fort Trail meets red-blazed Overlook Cliff Trail. Continue downhill on Overlook Cliff Trail on a series of winding switchbacks to the cliff-top overlook above Harpers Ferry. It is a stupendous, worth-every-muscle-ache vista of the two rivers, the railroad bridge, and the historic downtown. After enjoying the scenery, retrace your steps on Overlook Cliff Trail to rejoin Combined Trail. Follow the trail downhill to return to the gravel C&O towpath and from there to Harpers Ferry.

MORE INFORMATION

The historic sites at Harpers Ferry are open daily (except Thanksgiving, Christmas, and New Year's Day), from 8 A.M. to 5 P.M. Visit nps.gov/hafe for an interactive map of Lower Town and a page devoted to the park's hiking trails or call 304-535-6029.

NEARBY

Hiking all three of the heights—Bolivar, Loudoun, and Maryland—would make for an extremely ambitious outing. For additional exciting adventures, check out whitewater rafting trips on the Shenandoah and Potomac rivers. The town of Harpers Ferry offers numerous delights from food to shopping to make a visit even more enjoyable.

2

GAMBRILL STATE PARK

Gambrill State Park offers stunning views and steep climbs in a vigorous outing a short drive away from Washington, D.C.

Features

Location Frederick, MD

Rating Strenuous

Distance 8.2-mile loop

Elevation Gain 1,472 feet

Estimated Time 3.5–4 hours

Maps Potomac Appalachian Trail Club, Maps 5 & 6, Appalachian Trail across Maryland and the Entire Catoctin Trail; online: dnr.maryland.gov/publiclands /documents/gambrill_map.pdf

GPS Coordinates 39° 27.728′ N, 77° 29.685′ W

Contact Gambrill State Park, Maryland Department of Natural Resources, dnr.maryland.gov/publiclands/pages/western/gambrill.aspx, 301-271-7574

DIRECTIONS

From the Capital Beltway (I-495), take I-270 north for 29.0 miles. Take Exit 32 to merge onto I-70 west toward Hagerstown. Drive 4.9 miles and then take Exit 49 for US 40 Alt toward Braddock Heights/Middletown. Turn right onto US 40 Alt East/Old National Pike and drive for 0.7 mile. Turn left onto Blentlinger Road, and then turn left onto US 40 West/Baltimore National Pike/West Patrick Street. Follow US 40 West/Baltimore National Pike for 2.4 miles. Turn right on Gambrill Park Road. Follow Gambrill Park Road for a little less than 2 miles. Turn left into the High Knob parking area.

TRAIL DESCRIPTION

With 16 miles of trails, Gambrill State Park offers hikers stunning mountain views and challenging climbs. The park was named after James H. Gambrill Jr., a conservationist from the Frederick area who spotted the beauty of this location and advocated for it to be a park. A group formed under his lead purchased the land and donated it to Frederick. In turn, the city of Frederick donated it to Maryland to be developed into the park seen today.

That development was made possible by the Civilian Conservation Corps (CCC) that came to the region in 1933—one of the CCC camps was nearby—and built much of the infrastructure to make Gambrill possible, including roads, picnic sites, overlooks, and parking lots.

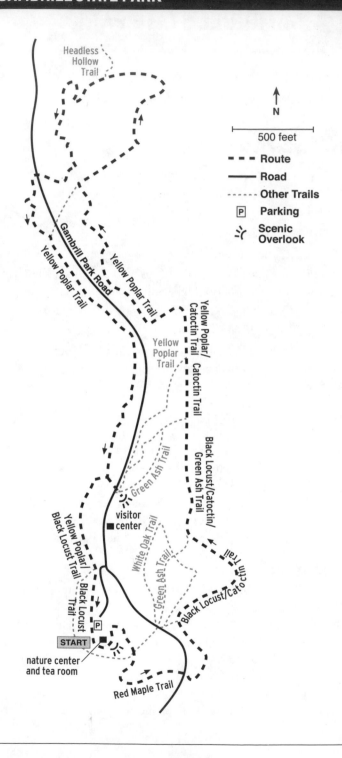

Headless
Hollow
Trail

N

500 feet

- - - Route
––– Road
····· Other Trails
P Parking
Scenic
Overlook

Gambrill Park Road

Yellow Poplar Trail

Yellow Poplar Trail

Yellow
Poplar
Trail

Yellow Poplar/
Catoctin Trail

Catoctin Trail

Black Locust/Catoctin/
Green Ash Trail

Green Ash Trail

visitor
center

White Oak Trail

Green Ash Trail

Black Locust/Catoctin Trail

Yellow Poplar/
Black Locust Trail

Black Locust
Trail

P

START

nature center
and tea room

Red Maple Trail

Gambrill was correct—this is beautiful land. The High Knob area, from which this hike starts, has overlooks that deliver valley views. Mountain laurels festoon the trails when in bloom. The park itself is on one of the ridges of Catoctin Mountain.

This hike starts from the High Knob area, dips down into the Rock Run area, and then loops around the park. The climbs and descents can be rocky and steep—be careful with footing but also make sure to enjoy the adventure.

From the parking lot, look for picnic shelter 4 to spot the start of the hike. Follow the path past the shelter and then bear right to begin the initial descent down this rocky start. The trail, blazed green and black, works its way steeply downhill—dropping more than 300 feet in 0.5 mile. Stay straight through the intersection with Yellow Poplar Trail, marked with a "Red Rock Run" sign, and arrive at the intersection with Red Maple Trail. Turn left here to follow the red-blazed trail. Look for small plaques along the way that provide information on the types of trees that can be found in the park.

Cross Gambrill Park Road, turn left to briefly follow a gravel road, and then bear slightly left to follow the trail off the road. A dizzying array of trail blazes marks this next stretch as numerous trails wind together briefly and then spin off the route. At the next intersection, turn right to start following Catoctin and Black Locust trails—the blazes are now blue and black. Soon, Green Ash Trail merges with this path, adding green to make a trio of blazes. This also heralds the start of a long, steady climb during the next mile and a half. During the ascent, Green Ash and Black Locust trails depart to the left—stay straight on Catoctin Trail, now just with a blue blaze.

Catoctin Trail climbs for a short distance before Yellow Poplar Trail swoops in to share the path, at which point the route is blazed both blue and yellow. Follow this path for a short distance before the trail splits as Catoctin Trail departs to the right. Turn left here to follow yellow-blazed Yellow Poplar Trail. The path splits again rather quickly—a signpost with a yellow arrow marks the way. Follow the arrow and the yellow blazes to the right. The trail works its way through a rocky stretch and then crosses a gravel path—keep following the yellow blazes.

At 3.5 miles into the hike, Yellow Poplar Trail intersects with a power line path. Turn left here to follow the narrow path along the power lines. Arrive at an intersection that marks Upper and Lower Yellow loops for the Yellow Poplar Trail—turn right to follow Upper Yellow Loop of this trail. (Turning left here would shorten the hike by 2.5 miles.)

The trail makes a quick descent and then starts to climb again. Pass a rugged section with several flat rocks, and follow the trail as it swings to the left. The climb slowly starts to ease. Reach another intersection and turn left to keep following the yellow-blazed trail. The trail loops around, almost creating the feeling that it is going in circles, as it passes through mountain laurels.

The hiking eases out from here, as Yellow Poplar Trail rolls along the ridge. Cross Gambrill Park Road and continue to follow the yellow blazes. At 6.0 miles into the hike, pass the intersection with Lower Yellow Loop—stay straight. Walk another 1.3 miles and arrive at the intersection with North Frederick Overlook, signified by a black blaze outlined in white. Follow this short side path across Gambrill Park Road and immediately arrive at the overlook.

After admiring the views, cross the road again. Several trails link up here. Pass the first intersection and then go straight at the next intersection to start following the route—now blazed yellow and black, as Yellow Poplar Trail and Black Locust Trail share this path.

As the route nears the parking lot, it splits again. Follow Black Locust Trail straight ahead as it works its way around the parking area and then arrives at Middletown Overlook. An interpretive sign provides details about the sights to the south and west, but keen eyes and a clear day could yield distant views of the valley below and the mountains beyond, including Maryland Heights (Trip 1). When ready to end the hike, follow the steps back up to the parking lot.

MORE INFORMATION

The High Knob area has various wooded picnic sites and picnic shelters—the picnic shelters are available for reservation. Also available for reservation is the Tea Room. Now frequently the site of special events, the Tea Room was built by the CCC in the 1930s to house community events. It also hosts open houses throughout the year—check the park's website for current dates. Camping is available in the Rock Run area. Reservations for this campground can be made online (dnr.maryland.gov/publiclands/Pages/western/Gambrill/Camping.aspx) or by calling 888-432-2267.

Middletown Overlook at Gambrill State Park provides valley views—a fitting culmination to the hike.

The High Knob Nature Center offers exhibits on the CCC and on wildlife in the park. Budding geologists can download the park's self-guided tour to walk among the rocks throughout the park. Trail maps are also available at the nature center's bulletin board. To learn more, visit dnr.maryland.gov/publiclands/Pages/western/Gambrill/Nature-Center.aspx.

Park hours are 8 A.M. to sunset from April through October, and 10 A.M. to sunset from November through March.

NEARBY

Explore more of this area by visiting nearby Catoctin Mountain Park and Cunningham Falls State Park (Trip 3). The historical downtown of Frederick offers numerous brewpubs, restaurants, and shops to entice visitors.

Catoctin Mountain Park and Cunningham Falls State Park offer true mountain trails only an hour from Washington, D.C., with a pristine waterfall as the featured attraction.

Features 🚶 🐕 ♿ 〰️ 📍 🎿 ❋ ⛺ ↑

Location Thurmont, MD

Rating Strenuous

Distance 8.2-mile loop

Elevation Gain 1,560 feet

Estimated Time 4.5–5 hours

Maps USGS Blue Ridge Summit, USGS Catoctin Furnace; free NPS map of Catoctin Mountain Park on-site; online: nps.gov/cato/planyourvisit/hiking.htm

GPS Coordinates 39° 38.029′ N, 77° 26.980′ W

Contact Catoctin Mountain Park, National Park Service, nps.gov/cato, 301-663-9388; Cunningham Falls State Park, Maryland Department of Natural Resources, dnr.maryland.gov/publiclands/pages/western/cunningham.aspx, 301-271-7574

DIRECTIONS

From the I-95/I-495 (Capital Beltway) inner loop, take Exit 38 (from the outer loop, take Exit 35) onto I-270 north to Frederick and merge onto US 15 north. Take US 15 approximately 18 miles north to Thurmont and then take the exit for MD 77 west (east leads into town). Drive 2.5 miles, turn right onto Park Central Road in Catoctin Mountain Park, and then immediately turn right again into the visitor center parking lot.

TRAIL DESCRIPTION

Catoctin Mountain, the easternmost ridge of the Blue Ridge Mountains, offers serious mountain hiking only an hour from Washington, D.C. The extensive trail system delivers stunning vistas and vigorous climbs.

From the trailhead at the visitor center, follow the orange-blazed trail to the right toward the park headquarters and Chimney Rock. This trail parallels the road for the next mile before reaching the park headquarters and the intersection with the trail leading up to Chimney Rock—now it is time to climb. Follow the trail to the left as it starts uphill, passing an intersection with a trail that leads to Crows Nest Campground.

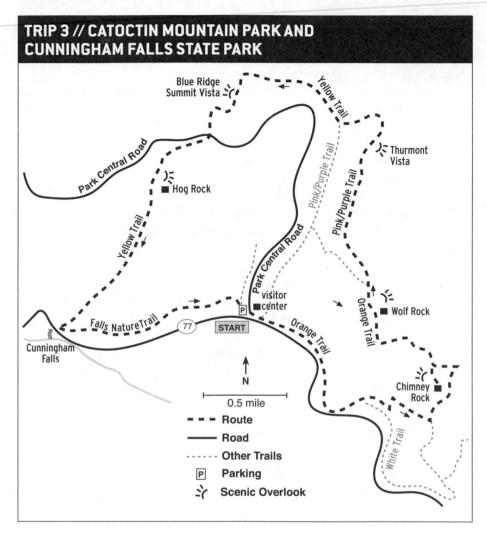

The trail switchbacks, often steeply, before reaching an intersection with Crows Nest Trail. Turn left to continue the steady ascent and arrive at Chimney Rock 3.0 miles from the start of the hike.

Reach Chimney Rock via a steep access trail that cuts left. From here, visitors have a year-round, awe-inspiring view of the mountains and valleys to the west. The overlook also features several flat, exposed quartzite pedestals.

After a strong dose of Catoctin Mountain beauty, return to the main trail and turn left to follow the orange blazes toward Wolf Rock, the next goal of the hike. In 0.5 mile, reach 1,400-foot Wolf Rock—a large shelf of quartzite rocks, part of the Weverton Formation deposited 550 million years ago. The fissured rocks resemble giant fists punching into the sky. In winter, climb the rocks and head to the left for a great view. (Leaves mask the vantage in spring and summer.) Watch for poison oak and poison sumac growing between rocks.

(*Note*: Pets are not allowed on the Chimney Rock overlook or on the formations of Wolf Rock, although leashed pets are permitted in Catoctin Mountain Park.)

After admiring the scenery from Wolf Rock, continue along the orange-blazed trail. Pass an intersection with a trail that leads back to the visitor center. Stay straight to follow pink and purple blazes to Thurmont Vista, which is a little less than a mile away and offers valley views with the town of Thurmont below.

From Thurmont Vista, the pink-and-purple-blazed trail bends to the left and descends. At a four-way intersection, turn right to start following the yellow-blazed trail toward the Blue Ridge Summit Vista.

Enjoy the sights from the overlook and then continue on the trail to the Hog Rock parking lot. Cross Park Central Road and follow the yellow-blazed trail toward Hog Rock, which offers the final vista of the hike. Pass the intersection with Hog Rock Nature Trail and arrive at Hog Rock. When ready to resume, pass another intersection with Hog Rock Nature Trail and stay straight to follow the yellow-blazed trail on an often steep and rocky descent to the intersection with Falls Nature Trail and with MD 77.

Go straight to cross MD 77—take care when crossing this hairpin turn in the road—and then go left toward the parking area for the boardwalk to visit Cunningham Falls. Follow the accessible boardwalk to the falls.

At 78 feet, Cunningham Falls is the largest cascading waterfall in Maryland. It was named for a local photographer whose scenic shots popularized the location. After a brief rest here, follow the boardwalk back to the parking lot and carefully cross MD 77 again. Reenter Catoctin Mountain Park and turn right to start following yellow-blazed Falls Nature Trail. The trail rolls along the side of the ridge for 1.3 miles. Follow it down well-graded steps and cross a small feeder stream on a little wooden walkway to wrap up your journey—the parking lot is just a few steps away.

MORE INFORMATION

Catoctin Mountain Park is open year-round, dawn to dusk; admission is free. Camping, picnicking, wildlife viewing, fly fishing, and cross-country skiing are all available. Leashed pets are allowed on trails but not on the Chimney Rock overlook or on Wolf Rock. Visit nps.gov/cato or call 301-663-9388 for more information. Planning is under way to potentially reroute some of the trails in the coming years. Check the park's website for the latest information or stop by the visitor center to learn more.

NEARBY

Cunningham Falls State Park is home to various trails and worth another visit to the area. Cat Rock is a short, steep, and rewarding hike—this rocky path climbs through pines and gains more than 700 feet in 1.3 miles to reach Cat Rock itself. A more epic adventure awaits with the 26.6-mile Catoctin National Recreation Trail. The northern trailhead is in Catoctin Mountain Park, and the southern trailhead is in Gambrill State Park (Trip 2). The African American Cemetery Trail is a shorter and accessible outing. This 0.5-mile unpaved ADA-style path has interpretive signs that detail the lives and experiences of the 271 men and women who were enslaved and worked at Catoctin Furnace. To learn more about this trail, visit dnr.maryland.gov/publiclands/DocumentsCFSP_African-American -Cemetery-Trail.pdf.

Vistas abound on this hike, offering a rugged challenge for hikers. *Photo by Sandra Shaklan.*

Also nearby, with access from Catoctin Hollow Road, is a nineteenth-century furnace and the ruins of an ironmaster's house. The furnace, nicknamed Isabella, was built in the 1850s, but an earlier version, built in 1774, produced pig iron for the cannons of George Washington's Continental Army. North of the furnace, directly off Catoctin Furnace Road, is the Catoctin Wildlife Preserve Zoo, housing 450 animal species. South Mountain State Park, at a mountain pass important during the Battle of Antietam in the Civil War, is 10 miles west of the Catoctin and Cunningham Falls parks.

And it's not a state secret that Camp David lies in the northern portion of Catoctin Mountain Park. The presidential retreat, first known as Shangri-La and later renamed for President Eisenhower's grandson, hosted the Camp David Accords, a 1978 agreement between Egypt and Israel, and is the site of Evergreen Chapel. Trails may close depending on certain high-level visitors.

4 ANNAPOLIS ROCK AND BLACK ROCK CLIFF

One of Maryland's most popular day hikes, this out-and-back trip on the Appalachian Trail offers stunning views from two outlooks.

Features 👤 🐕 ❋

Location Myersville, MD

Rating Moderate

Distance 7.2 miles round-trip

Elevation Gain 840 feet

Estimated Time 3.5 hours

Maps USGS Myersville; Potomac Appalachian Trail Club, Maps 5 & 6: Appalachian Trail across Maryland and the Entire Catoctin Trail; Maryland Department of Natural Resources: Appalachian Trail from Maryland Department of Natural Resources; also available at Appalachian Trail Conservancy, 799 Washington Street, Harpers Ferry, WV 25425

GPS Coordinates 39° 32.133′ N, 77° 36.245′ W

Contact South Mountain State Park, Maryland Department of Natural Resources, dnr.maryland.gov/publiclands/Pages/western/southmountain.aspx, 301-791-4767

DIRECTIONS

From I-495 (Capital Beltway), take I-270 north for 29.1 miles. Take Exit 32 to merge onto I-70 west. After 11.5 miles, take Exit 42 onto MD 17 north. After 0.7 mile, turn right to continue on MD 17 north. After 0.4 mile, turn left onto US 40 west. Drive 3.0 miles; the parking area is on the left.

TRAIL DESCRIPTION

As the Appalachian Trail (AT) passes through Myersville, Maryland, its fortuitous proximity to the road allows day-hikers to take advantage of two impressive viewpoints on the South Mountain Ridge—Annapolis Rock and Black Rock Cliff—with less than 1,000 feet of climbing. Falling within the region designated as South Mountain State Park, this trek attracts a mix of long-distance hikers, day-trippers, and families with young children. South Mountain Ridge lies along a migration route for eagles, hawks, and owls; keep an eye out for these winged travelers.

The parking area by the side of US 40 is fairly expansive but fills up on weekends as day-trippers flock to this popular trailhead, so plan on arriving early. Begin on the paved

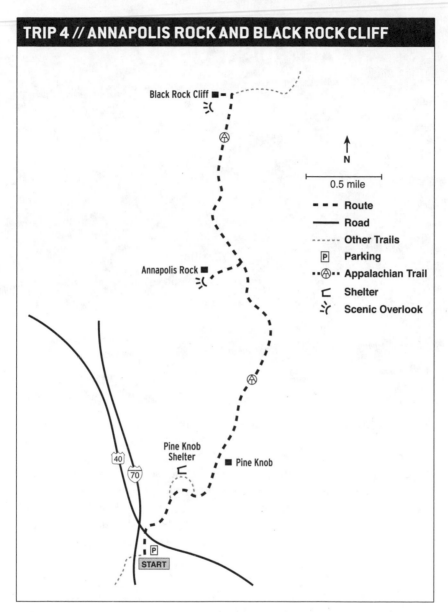

Black Rock Cliff ■

N

0.5 mile

- - - Route
—— Road
----- Other Trails
P   Parking
■⊕■ Appalachian Trail
⊏   Shelter
ξ   Scenic Overlook

Annapolis Rock ■

Pine Knob
Shelter

40

70

Pine Knob ■

P

START

section of the connector trail, past the Appalachian Trail sign. When the old section of road terminates at a highway barrier, turn left at the blue-blazed post. Follow the rocky path as it curves around to the narrow, covered pedestrian bridge over I-70. Do not cross the bridge; turn right immediately before it, following the sign that indicates a distance of 2.2 miles to Annapolis Rock.

The level trail follows noisy I-70, separated from the traffic by some elevation and a chain-link fence. Walk under the US 40 bridge and then curve to the right, away from the traffic, as the trail rises steeply into the forest. Pass a placard welcoming you to the Appalachian Trail as the route curves left. Soon after, an unmarked splinter trail departs to the right; stay straight, following the AT's white blazes.

A hiker observes the view from Black Rock Cliff. This vista, just off the Appalachian Trail, offers one of the most scenic overlooks in South Mountain State Park. *Photo by Annie Eddy.*

The AT crosses a utility cut under power lines before returning to the cover of trees. At 0.5 mile, the first connector trail for the Pine Knob shelter branches off to the left, followed shortly by the second connector trail to the same shelter. Pass both of these side trails, continuing on the AT. The elevation gain is steep for the next half-mile as the trail becomes rockier. Ascend over logs crossing the trail and then turn right and left on switchbacks. Pass an unmarked trail that departs to the right and stay on the AT as it curves to the left.

At 1.1 miles, the AT levels out as it crests South Mountain Ridge. Ferns blanket the forest floor and fringe the treadway, and the ground rises on either side, giving the ferns the appearance of height. The trail descends briefly, levels out into a sandy track bordered by rocks, and then begins to climb again, more gently now. A large rock outcropping on the right, 100 yards from the trail, offers an obstructed view down into the forest below the ridge. Pass through another grove of ferns as the view begins to gradually open up on the right before the AT curves back into the woods.

At 2.3 miles, arrive at the intersection with the connector trail to Annapolis Rock. Turn left onto that trail, following blue blazes, to descend 0.25 mile to the viewpoint. Pass the caretaker's campsite on the right. Soon after, a sign welcomes you to Annapolis Rock Backpacking Campground, with paths leading to campsites on either side and to a privy on the right. As you approach the cliff, a fence separates the trail from a reforestation area. The lookout offers a sweeping vista to the west. Greenbrier Lake, the site of a popular day-use beach within Greenbrier State Park, is visible to the southwest.

Return to the intersection with the AT and turn left to continue 1.0 mile north to Black Rock Cliff. The trail remains level for some time. To the left, the sky is visible through the trees where the ground slopes away. An unmarked turnoff to the left leads 100 yards to a smaller but still impressive vista. Continue toward Black Rock Cliff, passing a reforestation area posted with a No Camping sign. Soon after, at 3.6 miles, a sign marks the turnoff for the connector trail to Black Rock Cliff. Take a left on the connector and proceed 75 yards to the outlook, which offers an excellent view to the west, looking over scree and dead trees to the distant farms, fields, and bustling highway.

To finish the hike, turn right (south) from the Black Rock Cliff connector trail, retracing your steps along the white-blazed AT back to the US 40 parking area.

MORE INFORMATION

Hunting is permitted in South Mountain State Park, although not within 150 yards of the AT. Pets are allowed. For more information, visit dnr.maryland.gov/publiclands/Pages /western/southmountain.aspx or call 301-791-4767.

NEARBY

History buffs should stop at nearby South Mountain State Battlefield, the site of Maryland's first major Civil War battle. The aftermath of the Battle of South Mountain precipitated the Battle of Antietam, the bloodiest day in U.S. history. Washington Monument State Park on South Mountain boasts hiking trails, mostly part of the AT, around the nineteenth-century monument.

5 SUGARLOAF MOUNTAIN

Sugarloaf Mountain offers a challenging and popular hike close to D.C., with dozens of wildflower-rich trails.

Features

Location Dickerson, MD

Rating Moderate to Strenuous

Distance 5.3-mile loop

Elevation Gain 1,375 feet

Estimated Time 3–3.5 hours

Maps USGS Buckeystown, USGS Urbana; free map at trailhead; online: sugarloafmd.com/trail-maps

GPS Coordinates 39° 15.092′ N, 77° 23.611′ W

Contact Stronghold on Sugarloaf Mountain, sugarloafmd.com, 301-869-7846

DIRECTIONS

From the I-495 (Capital Beltway) inner loop, take Exit 38 (from the outer loop, take Exit 35) onto I-270 north toward Frederick. Take Exit 22 onto MD 109 south (Barnesville/Hyattstown exit) and drive 3.0 miles to the intersection of Comus Road. Turn right onto Comus Road (west) and drive 2.5 miles to the Sugarloaf Mountain entrance. Turn right at the gates and follow the road uphill to the West View parking lot.

TRAIL DESCRIPTION

Sugarloaf Mountain is a monadnock, or a mountain that stands alone after the bedrock surrounding it has eroded away. A dominant 150-foot quartzite cliff rises from Sugarloaf's western edge, with jumbles of talus rock—rock split from the cliff by water freezing in joints and fissures—scattered beneath it. The geological history of the mountain is complemented by an unusually diverse ecosystem, where plants indigenous to the Mid-Atlantic coastal plain, Piedmont, and mountain region can all be found.

Obtain a trail map at the donation box just beyond the gated entrance at the base of the mountain. This hike begins with a sharp ascent from the West View lot and descends the other side of the mountain before following Blue Trail as it circles the northern ridge. All trails are named for the color of their blazes.

From the West View lot, locate Green Trail just beyond the covered wooden shelter. This trail rises 325 vertical feet over 0.25 mile. Begin a gradual climb and then a sharper ascent over granite rocks that lead to a series of steep stone steps toward the 1,282-foot summit, taking in the must-see view of Frederick Valley and the bluish Catoctin Mountain on the

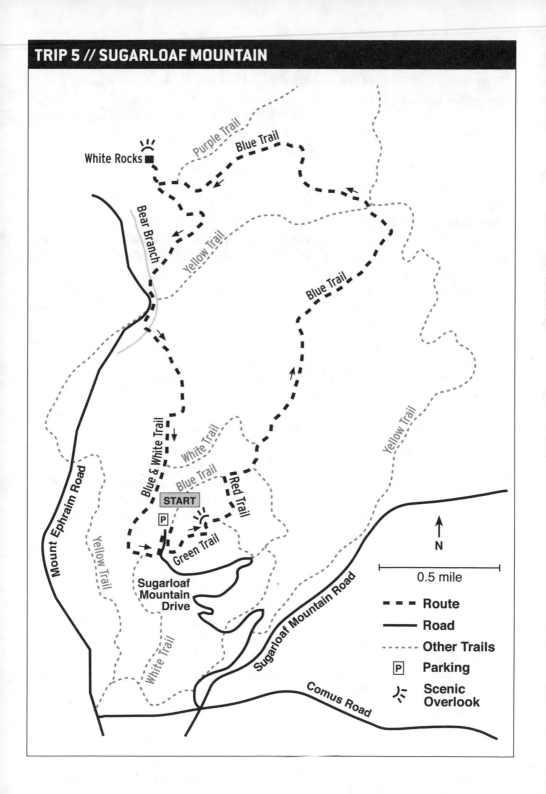

White Rocks

Purple Trail

Blue Trail

Bear Branch

Yellow Trail

Blue Trail

Blue & White Trail

White Trail

Yellow Trail

Blue Trail

Red Trail

START

P

Green Trail

Mount Ephraim Road

Yellow Trail

Sugarloaf Mountain Drive

White Trail

Sugarloaf Mountain Road

Comus Road

N

0.5 mile

- - - Route

—— Road

- - - Other Trails

P Parking

Scenic Overlook

horizon. The Catoctin range abruptly ends to the south at Point of Rocks, near the Monocacy Aqueduct (circa 1833), built largely from stone quarried at Sugarloaf.

Start down Red Trail opposite the view from the summit. At the trailhead is a small forest of *Chionanthus*, or fringe trees, which are usually found in tropical or subtropical climates. Pass Orange Trail on the right and begin a steep descent on Red Trail. In spring, showy jack-in-the-pulpit, yellow corydalis, black cohosh, and wild geranium bloom on the forest floor. The high elevation also nurtures a canopy of black birch, red maple, tupelo, chestnut oak, and hickory. At 0.5 mile from the start, arrive at the intersection with Blue Trail and a northwesterly view of McCormack View. Turn right here to start following Blue Trail.

Blue Trail (also called Northern Peaks Trail) is a 5-mile circuit that loops back to the West View parking lot. Continue downhill and turn left where White Trail merges with Blue Trail. White Trail quickly splits off again—bear to the right at the split to stay on Blue Trail. After a brief level stretch, climb steeply to the left and onto the crest of the northern ridge to hike the narrow summit. In summer, look for blueberry and huckleberry bushes (with edible berries) and deerberry bushes (with hard, inedible berries). Violet, cut-leafed toothwort, yellow corydalis, and the rare early saxifrage bloom in spring, followed by black cohosh in June. Continue downhill and onto level ground before climbing over moss-tinged granite rocks. This section is especially beautiful in early spring, when shadbushes unfurl creamy white blossoms against the gray-pink rock.

At the peak of this small rise, climb the large pile of rocks for a view of the western wooded slopes. The trail then plunges 100 feet to a five-way intersection, Yellow and Purple trails. Yellow Trail turns sharply to the left; Purple Trail goes straight. Blue Trail is in the middle—bear slightly to the left to continue following it, meandering uphill before navigating a challenging set of switchbacks to a 1,015-foot summit, the highest point on the northern ridge and the trip's approximate halfway mark. This is the most isolated portion of the trail. An ancient-looking cairn sits on the summit. Head downhill in the direction of the White Rocks overlook, following the spine of the ridge. In spring, look for jack-in-the-pulpit and bulbous pink lady's slipper.

Pass Purple Trail on the right and turn right on a spur path to White Rocks, where two overlooks offer views to the west of Lilypons Water Gardens; Adamstown, Buckeystown, and Frederick; and Catoctin and South mountains. Return to Blue Trail and go right toward Mount Ephraim Road. The trail descends, ascends, and winds to the left.

Reach Mount Ephraim Road at a valley and wade through a small, shallow tributary of Bear Branch. Pass another stream flowing underneath the road; follow the road to the left and then right. Turn left onto Blue Trail and begin a gradual ascent adjacent to the Bear Branch tributary. The deep, rocky streambed carves its right of way below a steep mountainside, bringing color in the form of cinnamon fern, skunk cabbage, spicebush, Indian cucumber root, and the rare and beautiful whorled pogonia. American beeches and dogwoods are common on this stretch, as are resident birds, such as ovenbirds, wood thrushes, and red-eyed vireos. The trail turns abruptly to the right about 0.5 mile after Mount Ephraim Road and begins ascending. White Trail again merges with Blue Trail—follow the combined trail as it makes its way alongside a boulder-strewn ridge before turning left (uphill) to the parking lot.

Hikers strike a pose while admiring the view from the White Rocks overlook.

MORE INFORMATION

Sugarloaf Mountain is open to the public. It has no admission fee, but hikers can leave a suggested donation in a box by the entrance. The trails are marked with numbered signposts roughly every 0.5 mile. Leashed dogs are permitted, and picnic areas are available. Sugarloaf also offers bicycling and rock-climbing opportunities. The mountain's Strong Mansion can be reserved for social events. Visit sugarloafmd.com or call 301-869-7846 for more information.

NEARBY

Lilypons Water Gardens (lilypons.com) has 300 acres of seasonally colorful aquatic plants and holds public events. Also nearby is Monocacy Natural Resource Management Area (dnr.maryland.gov/publiclands/Pages/parkmaps/monocacy_map.aspx), which contains miles of wildflower-rich hiking trails.

6 SENECA CREEK STATE PARK: CLOPPER LAKE

This hike travels beneath towering mature hardwoods—following Great Seneca Creek to Clopper Lake and then circling the lake, providing excellent shoreline views across open water.

Features

Location Gaithersburg, MD

Rating Moderate

Distance 4.5-mile loop

Elevation Gain 400–500 feet

Estimated Time 2.5–3 hours

Maps USGS Seneca; Maryland Trail Guide (shopdnr.com/trailguides.aspx); online: dnr.maryland.gov/publiclands/Pages/central/Seneca/Trails.aspx

GPS Coordinates 39° 9.054′ N, 77° 14.858′ W

Contact Seneca Creek State Park, Maryland Department of Natural Resources, dnr.maryland.gov/publiclands/Pages/central/seneca.aspx, 301-924-2127

DIRECTIONS

From the I-495 (Capital Beltway) inner loop, take Exit 38 (from the outer loop, take Exit 35) onto I-270 north toward Frederick. Take Exit 12 for Watkins Mill Road. Turn left onto Watkins Mill Road and follow it for a little less than a mile. Turn right onto MD 117 West/Clopper Road. Follow Clopper Road for 0.8 mile. Turn left on Seneca Creek Road into the park, and then immediately turn right into the visitor center parking lot.

TRAIL DESCRIPTION

Seneca Creek State Park is a 14-mile stretch of preserved land running along both sides of Great Seneca Creek. With 6,300 acres, the park starts just outside Gaithersburg's town limits and continues south to Riley's Lock, the creek's confluence with the Potomac River, near McKee-Beshers Wildlife Management Area. The Clopper Lake area is in the northern section of the park. The park's trail system is extensive: the 25-mile Greenway Trail follows Great Seneca Creek for its entire distance, and the Schaeffer Farm area has 10 miles of loops popular with mountain bikers and equestrians. Traveling under the tall ceilings of old-growth deciduous trees and viewing several crumbling nineteenth-century mills provides a pleasantly humbling experience.

Park at the park offices off Clopper Road. The Grusendorf Log House (circa 1855) stands nearby on land that once made up the estate of Francis C. Clopper, who, along with his

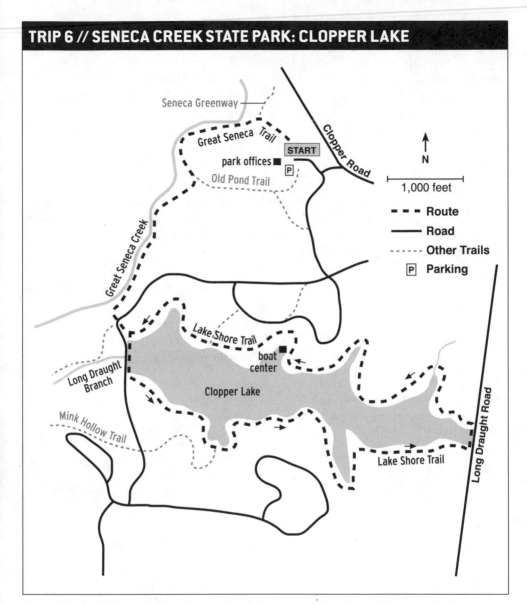

descendants, built several mills on Great Seneca Creek. One of these mills, just to the north near Clopper Road, made woolen clothes for Union soldiers in the Civil War; another, near the creek's confluence with the Potomac River, cut the red sandstone used to construct the Smithsonian Castle in Washington, D.C.

At the intersection of the entrance road and the parking lot, start on 1.2-mile Great Seneca Trail. The orange-blazed trail immediately descends 100 feet, running parallel to MD 117 through a draw (a small valley running across or streambed) with power lines, a tunnel of dense shrubbery, and a series of knolls supporting great sycamores and oaks. Throughout this hike, practice plant identification skills by trying to distinguish sycamores with their mottled bark that may reveal the cream-colored bark underneath from maples with their hard, close-grained bark.

Reach an intersection with Seneca Greenway Trail and turn left. Seneca Greenway Trail and Great Seneca Trail combine here to share the path along Great Seneca Creek. The 0.6-mile stretch along the creek travels through a lush deciduous forest and is frequently muddy from floods. The branches of massive oaks, sycamores, maples, and beeches form a lofty, leafy ceiling 40 feet overhead. At a point where a beaver-dammed island splits the water into two channels, the trail bends left under a few large maples and passes through an aromatic pine grove. Enter an open draw, cross a wooden bridge over seasonal runoff, and return to deep-green pines.

Great Seneca Trail/Seneca Greenway Trail emerges into a second draw, recrossing the power lines. Downy woodpeckers enjoy the poles, and spring and summer wildflowers attract spicebush and tiger swallowtail butterflies. Pass the intersection with Old Pond Trail and follow the trail over a bridge that spans a trickling tributary. A wide lane runs along the power lines for several hundred yards, parallel to the edge of the forest, and then plunges back into the woods. The moss-covered trail winds left and right on a high ridge over Great Seneca Creek before veering sharply left for an 80-foot ascent to a park road. The road marks the end point of Great Seneca Trail.

Cross the road in the direction of Clopper Lake (southeast). Turn right onto blue-blazed Lake Shore Trail, which encircles the 90-acre lake. It's worth exploring the full

Autumn sunshine casts reflections through the hardwoods lining the shores of Clopper Lake, in Seneca Creek State Park. *Photo by Mr. TinMD, Creative Commons on Flickr.*

loop, which clocks in at 3.7 miles. Stream-fed fingers, which you'll cross via wooden walkways, reach out from Clopper's north and south sides. This hike offers excellent opportunities to see red-shouldered hawks, ospreys, and barred owls fishing for dinner, as well as great blue herons roosting in the treetops. The tree diversity—maples, oaks, sycamores, pines, cedars, hickories, beeches, and yellow poplars—makes for a great variety of reds, oranges, and yellows rimming the lake in autumn against a backdrop of evergreens. (*Note*: Park officials have rerouted the trail away from the immediate shore to higher ground in some areas to restore the natural lakeside environment. Head for higher ground whenever the trail forks; the first tree on the correct route is always clearly marked with a blue blaze.)

Spur paths lead to picnic areas as the trail begins to approach the boating center. Continue following Lake Shore Trail as it loops around Clopper Lake. Pass an intersection with Connector Trail and continue straight on Lake Shore Trail. Arrive back at the intersection with Great Seneca Trail/Seneca Greenway Trail where the loop began. Turn right and retrace the trail back along Great Seneca Creek to return to the visitor center and parking area.

MORE INFORMATION

The park entrance is at 11950 Clopper Road in Gaithersburg, Maryland. Visitors pay no fee weekdays or from November through March. On weekends and holidays from April through October, the entrance fee is $3 per person for Maryland residents and $5 per person for out-of-state visitors. The Clopper Lake Boat Center has canoes, kayaks, and paddleboats available for rent and offers nature tours on a pontoon boat in summer. The center offers several fishing programs throughout the summer, and bait is available for sale. Check the U.S. Geological Survey gauging station on MD 28 for water levels, which should be at 2.1 feet or higher. More information about fishing at Clopper Lake can found on the Maryland Department of Natural Resources website (dnr.maryland.gov/fisheries/pages /hotspots/clopper.aspx).

Seneca Creek State Park also boasts a 32-acre disc golf course. Find scorecards and golf discs in the visitor center. For more information about the park, visit dnr.maryland.gov /publiclands/Pages/central/seneca.aspx or call 301-924-2127.

NEARBY

Magruder Branch Stream Valley Park, Black Hill Regional Park (Trip 7), and Little Bennett Regional Park all offer great hiking opportunities nearby. For an excellent map of Seneca Creek State Park, visit shopdnr.com/SenecaCreekStatePark.aspx.

7 BLACK HILL REGIONAL PARK

Black Hill Regional Park, surrounding 500-acre Little Seneca Lake, is a butterfly hot spot with meadows that attract hundreds of monarchs during their semiannual migrations in April and September.

Features 🐕 ♿ 🌢 🏕 ⬆

Location Boyds, MD

Rating Moderate

Distance 6.8-mile loop

Elevation Gain 320 feet

Estimated Time 3–3.5 hours

Maps USGS Germantown; online: montgomeryparks.org/parks-and-trails/black-hill-regional-park

GPS Coordinates 39° 12.025′ N, 77° 17.301′ W

Contact Black Hill Regional Park, montgomeryparks.org/parks-and-trails/black-hill-regional-park, 301-528-3480

DIRECTIONS

From the I-495 (Capital Beltway) inner loop, take Exit 38 (from the outer loop, take Exit 35) onto I-270 north toward Frederick. At Exit 16, turn right onto Father Hurley Boulevard, which becomes MD 27/Ridge Road. Turn left onto MD 355 (Frederick Road) and go 1.0 mile. Turn left onto West Old Baltimore Road and go 1.5 miles; then turn left onto Lake Ridge Drive into the park. Follow Lake Ridge Drive 1.5 miles to the visitor center near Little Seneca Lake.

TRAIL DESCRIPTION

Black Hill Regional Park's 500-acre Little Seneca Lake was built in 1984 by damming Little Seneca Creek to provide an emergency water supply for residents of the D.C. metro area. In the nineteenth century, the creek was used to power several lumber and grist mills, and the ruins of one of those mills are visible near where the creek enters the lake. The trails here traverse rolling terrain with lots of elevation change, but little is precipitous. Expect to encounter meadows, fields giving way to forest, thick deciduous woods, and stands of conifers. A dizzying number of monarch butterflies visit the park in late spring and early fall during their migrations to and from Mexico.

Upon exiting the visitor center, follow the path downhill through the Monarch Wayside garden and then turn right onto paved Black Hill Trail. The meadow is planted with

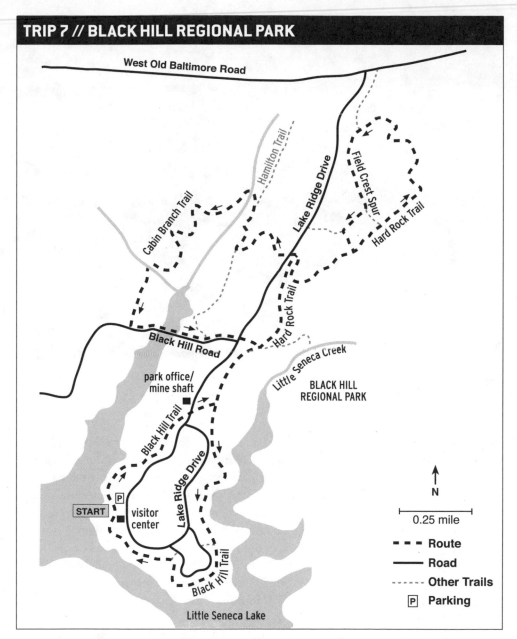

milkweed, the host plant for larval monarch butterflies. Black Hill Trail skirts Little Seneca Lake past wide-crowned Chinese elms, with picnic pavilions on the right. Where the trail reaches Lake Ridge Drive at 0.6 mile, stop at the park office on the left to see a mine shaft from the Black Hill Gold Mine (circa 1850). Local resident George Chadwick transformed the mine into a bomb shelter during the Cold War and used fieldstone from the mine to build the current park office.

Cross Lake Ridge Drive and follow a grassy clearing, visible between two thin strips of trees. Pass a greenhouse and reach natural-surface Hard Rock Trail where it splits in two,

Black Hill Regional Park's diversity of wildflowers makes it a favorite destination for migrating and breeding butterflies, such as this clouded-sulphur (*Colias philodice*) variety. *Photo by Domingo Mora, Creative Commons on Flickr.*

looping south around the tip of the peninsula. Turn left on the rocky trail through sycamores and yellow poplars and hike to a four-way intersection. Turn right for a quick side trip down a steep gravel road to a bridge over Little Seneca Creek. On a small side path to the right, just beyond the bridge, are the remains of Water's Mill, built by Zachariah Water in 1810. The mill became one of the few in the area to press flaxseed into linseed oil. It closed in 1895. The river power in this area was vital to the local farm economy until the railroad made it possible to bring in cheaper flour and cornmeal from the Midwest.

Return across the bridge. Take the first right before the gravel trail and then a second right to return to Hard Rock Trail heading north. Cut across a pipeline clearing and walk parallel to a streambed on the right, almost reaching Lake Ridge Drive before making a U-turn and crossing the stream. Follow the stream south on the opposite slope, and come back to the pipeline clearing before turning left and heading gradually uphill on a sprawling bed of loose rocks. Pass two grass connector trails on the left and reenter the forest.

Follow the trail between stone ruins and curve to the left. Exit the forest at a meadow with a group of bluebird nesting boxes in the center. Stay straight on what is now Field Crest Spur (watch out for an old sign indicating that Field Crest Spur branches right) and enter a large meadow serving as a monarch way station, where milkweed provides opportunities for breeding and feeding. Pass a maintenance area on the left and take the second left onto a connector trail, which leads back to Hard Rock Trail.

Turn right, and as the trail rises from the streambed at 3.3 miles, turn right again across Lake Ridge Drive, and start on Cabin Branch Trail. At the intersection, turn right onto the combined Cabin Branch and Hamilton trails; then turn left to cross a stream. The trails will split—follow Cabin Branch as it travels south parallel to the main stream and over a series of hills carved by small feeder streams. At 4.5 miles, reach a pipeline clearing and turn left, proceed over a third tributary stream, and immediately turn right. Leave the forest as the trail cuts through a thickly growing tunnel of shrubs before reaching a mowed swath near Black Hill Road.

Turn left onto Black Hill Road and cross a dammed causeway over the lake. Continue on the road past the start of Hamilton Trail on the left and cross Lake Ridge Drive again. Go past the gate, follow the connector trail, and then turn right onto Hard Rock Trail. Pass the grass connector trail you previously took from the park office and head south, passing several side paths that lead to playgrounds and parking areas. Stay with the forested high ground above the lake. At 6.1 miles, the trail meets paved Black Hill Trail and leads past various exercise stands. Continue on Black Hill Trail as it loops around the main parking area before returning to the visitor center.

MORE INFORMATION

The park is open year-round, sunrise to sunset. The visitor center is open from 11 A.M. to 5 P.M. on Fridays, Saturdays, and Sundays. The park offers several nature programs—check the website to see a list of upcoming programs and events. The boat rental facility near the visitor center offers pontoon boat tours Saturday and Sunday from May to September. Rent rowboats, canoes, paddleboards, pedal boats, and kayaks during the same period. For rates and information, visit montgomeryparks.org/parks-and-trails /black-hill-regional-park/black-hill-boats-little-seneca-lake or call 301-528-3466.

Many parts of the park are ADA accessible. Black Hill Trail and Crystal Rock Trail are paved; all other trails are natural surface. A hard-surface trail with gentle inclines can be reached from the visitor center and picnic area.

NEARBY

For more hiking options, continue on Black Hill Trail past the mill site, where the trail becomes asphalt and turns south for 2.0 miles along the eastern shore of Little Seneca Lake. End at Wisteria Drive and return to the park. Another good option is Hoyle's Mill Trail, which travels through South Germantown Recreational Park to Seneca Creek State Park (Trip 6).

The waters of Cascade Falls, on the ridge east of the Patapsco River, are one of the highlights of this hike.

Features

Location Elkridge, MD

Rating Strenuous

Distance 8.6-mile loop

Elevation Gain 1,032 feet

Estimated Time 3.5–4 hours

Maps USGS Relay; waterproof Maryland Park Service trail maps available at Avalon Visitor Center; online: dnr.maryland.gov/publiclands/Pages/central/PatapscoValley/Trail-Maps.aspx

GPS Coordinates 39° 13.595′ N, 76° 43.463′ W

Contact Patapsco Valley State Park, Maryland Department of Natural Resources, dnr.maryland.gov/publiclands/pages/central/patapsco.aspx, http://dnr.maryland.gov/publiclands/Pages/central/PatapscoValley.aspx, 410-461-5005

DIRECTIONS

From I-95/I-495 (Capital Beltway), go north on I-95 to Exit 47 (BWI Airport) and then go east on I-195. Take Exit 3 to Elkridge and turn right at the stoplight onto US 1 south. Take the next right onto South Street and then immediately turn left into Patapsco Valley State Park. Pass through the contact station ($2 per vehicle for in-state residents; $4 per vehicle for out-of-state; on weekends and holidays April through October, fees are $3 per person in-state and $5 per person out-of-state). Travel under the Thomas Viaduct and I-95. Turn left at the intersection with Gun Road. Turn right to park in the first parking lot on River Road.

TRAIL DESCRIPTION

Patapsco Valley State Park extends along nearly 32 miles of the Patapsco River in Maryland, from Elkridge in the east to Woodbine in the west. The river valley encompasses more than 16,000 acres and is divided into multiple recreation areas. This hike explores the eastern section, made up of the Avalon, Hilton, Glen Artney, and Orange Grove areas, all named for long-gone mill towns.

Although the mills are no longer here, the river valley remains a transportation corridor. Maryland Area Regional Commuter (MARC) trains rumble across the breathtaking, 704-foot Thomas Viaduct, which was the largest bridge in the nation at the time of its completion in 1835 and remains the oldest stone arch railroad bridge still in use.

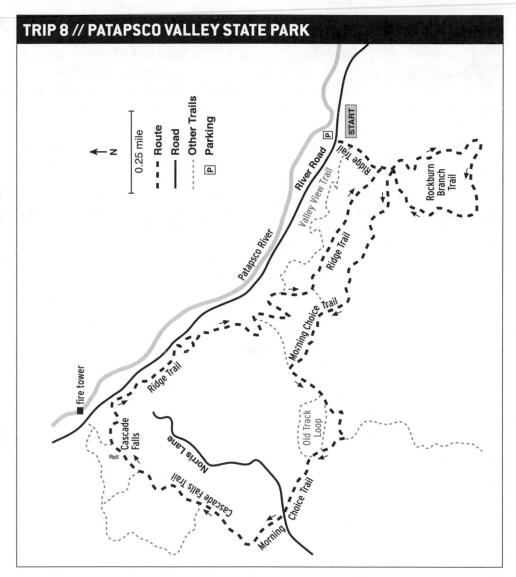

This hike starts from the Avalon area parking lot on the southern side of the Patapsco River and encompasses five major south-side trails. The trailhead for Ridge Trail is directly across the road from the parking lot—cross carefully and start following the orange-blazed trail on a steady climb as it enters the woods. Arrive at an intersection with an unmarked trail and turn left to keep following the orange blazes. The trail will quickly reach another intersection—stay straight here.

Arrive at an intersection with Rockburn Branch Trail. Turn left to start following this 1.2-mile, purple-blazed route, enjoying the mature open forest and pleasant peeks into stream valleys. This loop trail intersects with yellow-blazed Morning Choice Trail, heading northwest. Follow Morning Choice Trail as it passes through big-leafed pawpaw thickets before reaching a large, open field. The path skirts the edge of the field before diverting back into tree cover beneath a large shagbark hickory. Pass a connector trail that leads to Ridge Trail, and take a moment to view the remains of a house.

Continue on Morning Choice Trail to an open field that marks the edge of the Belmont Conference Center property; the center is just visible uphill to the left. Reenter the woods and, after a slight uphill climb, plunge down across the source of a creek and then ascend a draw (small valley sloping toward a streambed) to a series of wide curves. Turn sharply left and pass Old Track Loop on the right. Continue underneath a massive grove of tulip trees. The trail will soon split—both branches are Morning Choice Trail. Follow the branch to the right, passing a bamboo thicket. Old Track Loop soon comes in from the right, briefly sharing the same path as Morning Choice Trail before darting back into the woods. Continue on yellow-blazed Morning Choice Trail, passing a connector trail to the left. The trail crosses Norris Lane and then heads downhill. Near the bottom of the descent, the trail splits. Bear right to start following blue-blazed Cascade Falls Trail.

Rather quickly, Cascade Falls Trail splits at an intersection. Turn right to stay on the blue-blazed path as it follows Cascade Falls Trail downstream, paralleling the stream and crossing it several times. The path becomes rockier as it makes its way along, and spurs lead off to the water's edge. Keep an eye on the blue blazes to stay on the main route.

Arrive at the falls, where the stream course is strewn with large boulders and the water drops 15 feet into a pool. (Also, note the intersection with Ridge Trail—this is the path to follow after the viewing the falls.) Several good spots are available for taking a break to enjoy the views.

When you are ready to resume hiking, go back to the well-marked intersection with Ridge Trail and follow the orange blazes. This section of Ridge Trail offers a challenging ridge run that undulates down and up the sides of steep draws and turns back on itself in tight switchbacks. Mountain laurel, dogwood, and pawpaw crowd the treadway.

Pass a connector trail that comes in from the left—and then soon pass another that shoots off into the woods to the right. Valley View Trail crosses paths with Ridge Trail several times in the next stretch—keep following the orange blazes to maintain the course.

Familiar ground will soon emerge as Ridge Trail meets back up with the intersection to Rockburn Branch Trail. Follow Ridge Trail as it works its way around and downhill to the parking lot.

MORE INFORMATION

The park is open from 9 A.M. to sunset, year-round. Dogs are welcome on all the trails. Besides hiking, Patapsco Valley State Park is perfect for road biking (paved trails extend along either side of the Patapsco River), mountain biking (especially on Rockburn Branch Trail), swimming and fishing (at numerous points on the river), and photography (Ilchester Rocks Trail and the Thomas Viaduct provide excellent vantages for photographing trains). Additional use fees may apply. Visit dnr.maryland.gov/publiclands/Pages/central/patapsco.aspx or call 410-461-5005 for more information.

Those looking for an accessible alternative can explore Grist Mill Trail. This asphalt trail parallels the Patapsco River for a mile and a half and delivers lovely river views. In total, Grist Mill Trail extends for 5.0 miles, running from River Road in the park to

Cascade Falls, which once must have attracted the valley's mill workers just as it attracts today's sightseers, is the perfect spot to stop for lunch. Along with the Thomas Viaduct, Bloedes Dam, and the old suspension bridge, it is one of the best-known sites in the park. *Photo by Stephen Mauro.*

Ilchester Road in Ellicott City. Visit dnr.maryland.gov/centennial/pages/centennial-notes /gristmill.aspx to learn more about this trail.

NEARBY

Ellicott City, county seat of Howard County, lies to the southeast along the banks of the Patapsco. This former mill town, dating to pre–Revolutionary War days, features attractive homes, shops, and public buildings and even hosts a ghost tour of the village, which has been called one of the most haunted small towns on the East Coast. The hilltop mansion Mount Ida (circa 1833), home to the Historic Ellicott City nonprofit and the Patapsco Female Institute, is open for public tours one Saturday each month from June to November, for a small fee. Severe flash flooding in the summer of 2016 caused extensive damage to the historic district, but rebuilding efforts are well under way. Paved Trolley Line #9 Trail follows a shady 1.25-mile segment of the now-defunct trolley right of way that shuttled passengers from Ellicott City to Baltimore from the 1890s until its decommissioning in the 1950s. See visitoldellicottcity.com and visithowardcounty.com for more information.

9 | WINCOPIN TRAILS

Wincopin Trails pack quite a lot in 4 miles, including water views and historical mill remains.

Features

Location Jessup, MD

Rating Easy

Distance 3.6-mile loop

Elevation Gain 310 feet

Estimated Time 1.5–2 hours

Maps Map available on sign at the trailhead; online: howardcountymd.gov/sites/default/files/2021-11/Wincopin%20Trail.pdf

GPS Coordinates 39° 9.000′ N, 76° 50.051′ W

Contact Howard County Department of Recreation and Parks, howardcountymd.gov/rap, 410-313-4700

DIRECTIONS

From I-95 north, take Exit 35B and merge onto MD 216 west toward Scaggsville. Follow MD 216 west for 4.9 miles and then turn right onto Leishear Road. After 0.8 mile, turn right onto Gorman Road. Follow Gorman Road for 0.7 mile and then turn left onto Murray Hill Road. Drive 0.9 mile and then turn right onto Vollmerhausen Road. Drive 1.3 miles and turn right into a paved parking lot. The trails begin at the corner of the lot near the information board.

TRAIL DESCRIPTION

Wincopin Trails can qualify as one of Maryland's hidden gems. This small trail system only has 4 miles of trails, but it offers a peaceful escape just minutes from I-95 in Howard County, Maryland. The trails are nestled between the Little Patuxent and Middle Patuxent rivers. In spring, hikers with keen eyes can spot wildflowers such as perfoliate bellwort, early saxifrage, and wild sarsaparilla.

This walk has a few steep climbs and can pack a little punch for those seeking an enjoyable day in the woods. The trails are helpfully marked with the same colors as their names—no navigation challenges here.

From the parking lot, start down Red Trail, which begins as a paved path but quickly transitions to a dirt one. In a little more than 0.3 mile, turn left to follow Green Trail. Green Trail makes a gentle rolling descent for the next few tenths of a mile before dropping down and making a hairpin turn to the right as it runs along the Little Patuxent River. Pass

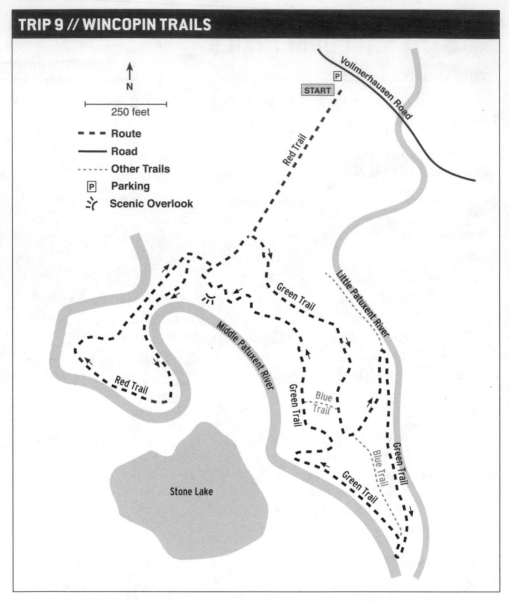

the remains of a stone finishing plant. This area used to be an industrial site where gabbro, a coarse-grained igneous rock, was quarried.

Green Trail swings to the right, now following the Middle Patuxent River. At this point, look to the left to see remains of a bridge support, which offers a good view of the water below. Take time to enjoy the scenery from the overlook and from the trail itself before the route gets down to business about 1.6 miles into the hike with a steep climb back up to the ridge.

Near the top of the climb, Blue Trail comes in from the right and merges with Green Trail for a few tenths of a mile. Blue Trail diverts to the right—bear left to continue on Green Trail. After this point, spur paths on the left lead to scenic overlooks that are worth

Hikers enjoy a snowy day exploring Wincopin Trails.

a short detour or two. In just a few more steps, Green Trail arrives at an intersection with Red Trail, about 2.3 miles into the hike. Turn left here to start following Red Trail.

Red Trail quickly splits into a loop. Bear left to follow the loop as it makes a sharp descent back to the river. The trail briefly travels along the river before bending to the right and climbing back up to the ridge. Return to the start of the loop and stay to the left to follow Red Trail back to the parking lot.

MORE INFORMATION

Wincopin Trails are open daily, from 7 A.M. to sunset. The parks are administered by the Howard County Department of Recreation and Parks (howardcountymd.gov/rap), 410-313-4700. The trailhead is at 9299 Vollmerhausen Road in Jessup, Maryland.

NEARBY

Wincopin Trails is just a short distance away from Savage Park, home to more trails, including Patuxent Branch Trail, which extends for 10.4 miles along the path of the Patuxent River. Hikers looking to refuel can explore Historic Savage Mill, once the site of a major textile manufacturing center (1810 to 1947). The building, now listed on the National Register of Historic Places, was renovated in the 1980s and currently houses various small businesses.

10 GREENBELT PARK

Greenbelt Park, just inside the Capital Beltway, offers an excellent loop hike traversing a secluded second-growth forest.

Features

Location Greenbelt, MD

Rating Moderate

Distance 5.3-mile loop

Elevation Gain 350 feet

Estimated Time 2–2.5 hours

Maps USGS Washington East; map in National Park Service brochure on-site; online: nps.gov/gree/planyourvisit/maps.htm

GPS Coordinates 38° 59.637′ N, 76° 53.700′ W

Contact Greenbelt Park, National Park Service, nps.gov/gree, 301-344-3944

DIRECTIONS

From I-95/I-495 (Capital Beltway), take Exit 23 to MD 201 (Kenilworth Avenue) south and exit immediately onto MD 193 (Greenbelt Road) east. Go 0.3 mile and turn right at a traffic light onto Walker Road, which enters Greenbelt Park. Go past the park police station to an intersection. Turn right at the intersection, and then immediately turn left into the Sweetgum parking and picnicking area.

By Metrorail, take the Green Line to the final stop at the Greenbelt station. Then take Metrobus C2 for a short ride to the park entrance at the intersection of Greenbelt Road and Walker Drive. Visit wmata.com for the latest schedule information.

TRAIL INFORMATION

Greenbelt Park is just 10 miles from the National Mall. This urban oasis is bounded by Baltimore–Washington Parkway to the east, the Capital Beltway to the north, and Kenilworth Avenue to the west. Once denuded for farming, the land has been recovering since the early 1900s and now supports a forest of mixed pine and deciduous trees. The small creeks in the park flow into the Anacostia River, which in turn feeds the Potomac River and Chesapeake Bay. The site was initially part of a never-finished "green belt" separating Greenbelt, Maryland—the first federally planned community—from Washington, D.C.

Perimeter Trail, a 5.3-mile route, hugs the park boundaries, sometimes running close to the highways and buildings but mostly traveling through green spaces and along gentle watercourses. Benches are provided at least every half-mile. From the Sweetgum picnic area, follow the road on which you entered the parking lot. Pass the start of Azalea Trail.

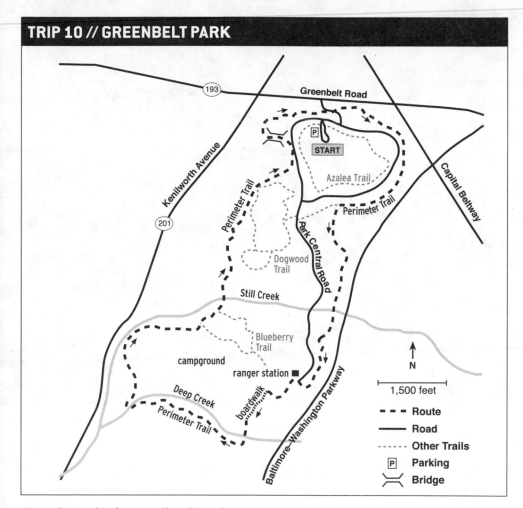

Cross the road to locate yellow-blazed Perimeter Trail. Turn right to follow Perimeter Trail clockwise and note the first of many mile markers indicating distance traveled. In 50 yards, cross the road near the park entrance. Look for loblolly pines, whose developing cones glow yellow-green in spring. Pass oak and beech trees, as well as maintenance sheds, behind the park headquarters. At the 0.2-mile marker, head up a slight hill past a jumble of fallen pines. At the 0.4-mile marker, traffic comes into view on I-495 below and to the left.

Follow Perimeter Trail along the shoulder of the park road, back into a wooded area of beech, laurel, and oak trees, and then downhill to an intersection with a trail leading to the parking area for Dogwood Trail. Bear left to stay on Perimeter Trail. Continue down the hill along the north branch of Still Creek, where large oaks grow near the streambed, and large tulip trees, some with trunks 40 inches in diameter, dot the area. During most of the year, more than half a dozen species of colorful stem-and-cap and polypore mushrooms grow throughout the park. As the narrow trail crosses Still Creek, it comes within 25 yards of Baltimore–Washington Parkway. Climb uphill to the right, where a secondary trail comes in. Continue to follow the yellow blazes to the left past a bench.

Greenbelt Park is home to more than half a dozen species of mushrooms, of both the stem-and-cap and polypore varieties. *Photo by Stephen Mauro.*

About 2 miles into the hike, cross the end of Park Central Road. To the left, a paved bike trail begins, and straight across is a secondary road that leads to the ranger station and a camping area. Take a quick side trip to read the kiosks at the ranger station describing the origin of the town of Greenbelt (just to the north) and how the park is helping remove pollutants from Still Creek. Return to Perimeter Trail, following signs past large yellow poplars to the artificially developed wetlands buffer area that slows water flow and filters pollution. Hike downhill through rugged terrain over exposed roots, passing numerous holly trees. The trail turns into a boardwalk through the wooded, low wetlands. After crossing Deep Creek, at the end of the boardwalk, turn right at the trail fork. (Even though it flows intermittently, Deep Creek is responsible for significant erosion in this area.)

After passing the point where Perimeter Trail comes very close to the park's southern boundary fence, roughly 2.5 miles into the hike, begin to traverse a relatively isolated portion, heavily wooded with more oaks and poplars but fewer evergreens. For the next half-mile, hike just to the left of the gullies cut by Deep Creek, and then turn sharply right to follow the trail as it passes over both the creek and a maintained gravel path. Remain on the dirt treadway as it wanders slightly uphill past oaks, beeches, and poplars. The mile markers that were scarce in the Deep Creek area return, here plotted every 0.2 mile.

Perimeter Trail follows the course of Still Creek (50 to 150 yards to the left), crosses a gravel road, and heads uphill along the side of a ridge. After passing two intersections that connect with the Blueberry Trail loop, cross Still Creek on an elevated wooden bridge. Continue uphill, past the intersection with the Dogwood Trail loop and adjacent to apartments along the park's boundary. Following Perimeter Trail gets tricky as it passes between Park Central Road on the right and the apartment complex on the left. Watch carefully for the yellow blazes after crossing the wooden bridge—the trail soon turns right and goes uphill. Cross two more wooden bridges over intermittent streams, hike past the park police station surrounded by willow oaks, and follow the trail back to the Sweetgum parking lot.

MORE INFORMATION

Greenbelt is administered by the National Park Service (NPS). Hiking, horseback riding, bike riding, and picnicking are free, but fees are charged for overnight camping. The NPS ranger station near the campground is open on weekdays and weekends but is sometimes unstaffed when rangers are on patrol. Park facilities include bathrooms, picnic areas, a baseball field, and children's playgrounds. Other trails include the 1.1-mile Azalea Trail loop around the Sweetgum picnic area, near the park entrance; 1.4-mile Dogwood Trail in the center of the park; and 1.0-mile Blueberry Trail, near the campgrounds. For more information, visit nps.gov/gree or call 301-344-3944.

NEARBY

NASA's Goddard Space Flight Center, a short distance east of Greenbelt Park, provides visitors a taste of the kinds of research and experimentation performed by America's space agency in the fields of Earth science, astrophysics, heliophysics, planetary science, engineering, communication, and technology development. On-site are a solarium, a lunar reconnaissance orbiter prototype, an outdoor rocket garden, a Gemini capsule model, child-sized space suits to try on, and more. Additional information is available at nasa.gov/goddard.

11 PATUXENT RESEARCH REFUGE

Grassy meadows and aquatic plants, hardwood forests and holly trees, Canada geese and bald eagles: find all of these at Patuxent Research Refuge, the only national wildlife refuge with a specific mission of wildlife research. Hands-on exhibits help hikers of all ages learn how scientists care for wild creatures.

Features 👥 🐕 💧 ♿ ⛺ 🎣

Location Laurel, MD

Rating Easy

Distance 2.1-mile loop

Elevation Gain 35 feet

Estimated Time 1.5 hours (longer with a stop at the nature center)

Maps USGS Laurel; map available at the refuge's visitor center; online: fws.gov/refuge/patuxent-research/map

GPS Coordinates 39° 01.628′ N, 76° 47.944′ W

Contact Patuxent Research Refuge, fws.gov/refuge/patuxent, 301-497-5772

DIRECTIONS

From I-95/I-495 (Capital Beltway), take Exit 22A and follow Baltimore–Washington Parkway (MD 295) north toward Baltimore. Drive 3.5 miles on the parkway and then take the Powder Mill Road/Beltsville exit and turn right (east) onto Powder Mill Road. Drive 1.8 miles and turn right onto Scarlet Tanager Loop, at the brown National Wildlife Visitor Center sign. Follow this one-way entrance road 1.4 miles to the parking lot. When departing, keep right to follow the one-way exit road.

TRAIL DESCRIPTION

Patuxent Research Refuge, named for nearby rivers in the Chesapeake Bay watershed and established in 1936 as an experiment station, is the only national wildlife refuge with a primary mission of wildlife research. Thanks largely to the refuge's leadership, the bald eagle has been brought back from the brink of extinction, and whooping crane populations have grown significantly; the latter's numbers had diminished precariously to 21 birds worldwide by the 1930s, but have grown to more than 600.

This trip explores the South Tract section of the refuge. Before setting off on your hike, a stop in the National Wildlife Visitor Center is recommended. Say hello to the massive polar bear (taxidermic, of course) and other wild critters on display, a reminder that the

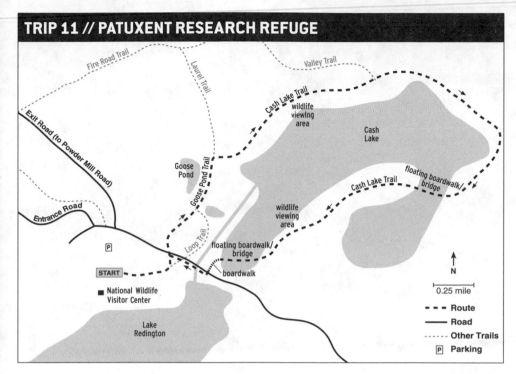

U.S. Fish & Wildlife Service manages more than 500 national wildlife refuges, representing very different climates and habitats. Enjoy the eight-minute introductory video and then pop into the glass-walled viewing pod to try your hand at some scopes and radio tracking equipment. Check out the live-scale exhibition on habitats (good for kids), the endangered-species hall, and the Hollingsworth Gallery of wildlife art.

Exit the visitor center through the northeast doors and step onto Loop Trail to begin the hike. This trail is paved and accessible. You'll immediately see the first of numerous wayside signs focusing on aspects of wildlife management. This one discusses conservation landscaping and invites you into a small, wild garden; others along the trail explore utility-line right-of-way open spaces, meadow management, and habits of wild birds. Just past two benches, at a fork, bear left to continue on Loop Trail and cross the tram roadway. At the next intersection, turn left onto Goose Pond Trail (which begins with a wood-chip surface and becomes rugged later on) and continue straight until you reach Goose Pond on the left. Look for nesting boxes atop poles, protected by conical predator guards to keep eggs and young birds safe. During nesting season, generally mid-March to mid-May, you can also see nesting baskets of straw-filled netting suspended over the water for use by Canada geese.

Just past the pond, turn right onto Cash Lake Trail, which veers into a forest predominantly made up of hardwoods. The tree trunks aren't blazed, but the treadway is well maintained and easily visible. Several good-sized American holly trees grow in the understory here. Soon, reach the wildlife-viewing area for the near shore of Cash Lake, just off the main trail to your right. Make a detour to enjoy this quiet spot by the water's edge, where aquatic plants abound. The lake, created in the late 1930s by President Franklin

White-tailed deer enjoy the peace of Patuxent Research Refuge, where many species of wildlife thrive under benevolent management. *Photo by Chesapeake Bay Program, Creative Commons on Flickr.*

Roosevelt's Civilian Conservation Corps, is one of more than 40 impoundments, or artificial bodies of water, on the refuge. Scientists manage the water levels in the lake and in Goose Pond as needed to support wildlife populations. Back on Cash Lake Trail, approach the fishing pier and cross one of the spillways that drain water when needed. Look for beavers, bald eagles, great blue herons, ospreys, and the ubiquitous Canada geese.

Continuing along the trail, cross several footbridges, one of which was built as an Eagle Scout project supported by local sponsors. Descend two sets of wooden-braced steps, and at a sign for Valley Trail to the left, stay right to continue on Cash Lake Trail toward the fishing pier. A steel bridge takes you over the drainage spillway, and a restroom is available on the pier. In season, anglers pull largemouth bass, bluegill, black crappie, the colorful pumpkinseed, chain pickerel, and even American eel from the waters. At this point, you can take the boardwalk along the fishing pier or cross the concrete berm. Whichever route you choose, the two merge beyond the end of the berm. At the end of the berm, follow the gravel path straight ahead (there's a service road to your left, also gravel) to regain Cash Lake Trail as it winds back into the forest.

After a short woodland walk, with many varieties of moss and lichen beckoning, a floating boardwalk takes you over calm, marshy waters onto a grassy meadow peninsula, edged by a wide variety of lush aquatic plants. Watch for beavers and turtles, listen for the bellowing of frogs, and be sure to have some sun protection handy. Follow the trail back into the woods and to the south shore viewing area, a favorite haunt for raptors. Rejoin the main trail after pausing at the viewing area to admire the scenery; it leads toward a floating bridge. Cross this and proceed along the shore through more woods.

When you reach the paved road, turn right; Lake Redington is on the left. To the right, a boardwalk wildlife lookout offers a good view of Cash Lake. Cross the road bridge over the south spillway and take the first paved path on the left to finish the hike at the visitor center. Check out the wild garden if you didn't stop earlier, or just rest your legs for a few moments, and savor your visit to one of the largest forested areas—more than 12,800 acres on North Tract and South Tract—remaining today in the Mid-Atlantic states.

MORE INFORMATION

Trails and grounds are open daily (except for holidays) from sunrise to sunset. The National Wildlife Visitor Center building is open Tuesday through Saturday, 9:30 a.m. to 4:30 p.m. Call 301-497-5760 for details about the refuge's many special-interest programs and tram tour availability. Visit fws.gov/refuge/patuxent for more information.

To preserve the refuge's trails and its habitats, bicycles and skis are not allowed. Dogs must be kept on leashes no longer than 10 feet. Very few rest stops or benches are available along the portions of the trail that run along Cash Lake. Fishing and hunting are allowed seasonally with a permit or license; call the refuge for details.

NEARBY

Just north of the refuge, near the intersection of Baltimore–Washington Parkway (MD 295) and MD Route 32, lies Fort George G. Meade, home of the National Security Agency (NSA). The NSA's public face is on display just outside the fort gates at the National Cryptological Museum, housing thousands of artifacts, including numerous working World War II German Enigma machines and a Navy Bombe used to break the German codes. Displays, with some artifacts dating back to pre–Revolutionary War times, cover the history, people, equipment, techniques, and locations of American cryptology. A research library, a small museum, and a gift shop are on-site. The outdoor Vigilance Park displays several reconnaissance aircraft, and visitors will also find a collection of military vehicles, such as Liberty and Sherman tanks, and a Nike Ajax missile.

SAVING A LIVING SYMBOL: THE BALD EAGLE

Not long ago, and not far from the nation's capital, the bald eagle bounced back from the brink of extinction. In 1969, staff at Patuxent Research Refuge, located between Washington, D.C., and Baltimore, Maryland, published data linking the pesticide DDT to thin eggshells among ducks living in the refuge. The research demonstrated that DDT was a major factor in population losses suffered by fish-eating birds, such as bald eagles. The majestic raptors' numbers had dropped to an estimated 487 breeding pairs nationwide in 1963. Thanks in part to Patuxent's work, the federal government banned DDT use in 1972.

Great harm had already been done, however, and human intervention was urgently required. Patuxent became involved in this phase, initiating a captive-breeding program to hatch each eagle pair's first clutch of eggs in an incubator. The parents usually produced a second clutch that they raised naturally in their nests. This approach worked so well—124 eaglets hatched at the refuge, earning it international attention—that Patuxent supplied eaglets to many states for their own recovery efforts.

States such as New York, using a technique called "hacking," placed incubator-hatched eaglets in elevated, isolated, human-made nests, where biologists fed them until they matured. Another conservation technique recognized that while eagles can hatch up to three eggs per nest, only two eaglets are likely to survive. Some of these "surplus" hatchlings were transferred to "foster parent" eagle pairs that readily adopted and raised them. Viability rates jumped for both eggs and live birds.

The Patuxent breeding program wound down in 1988, at which point eagle populations and eagle reproduction in the wild were clearly on the rebound. By 2006, breeding bald eagle pairs were present in all 48 contiguous states, and total breeding pairs had increased twentyfold, to more than 9,700 nationally. The Chesapeake Bay area, in particular, enjoyed great success: numbers increased from 32 pairs and 18 annual young in 1977 to 151 pairs and 172 eaglets in 1993. In 2007, the bald eagle was taken off the federal list of endangered and threatened wildlife—a major milestone.

Bald eagles have survived, with a little help from their friends, but vigilance is needed for their continued protection. Clean water, habitat preservation, and the enforcement of laws against toxins and other threats will always be vital to the support of this noble national bird.

12 LAKE ARTEMESIA AND NORTHEAST BRANCH TRAIL

This peaceful, mostly level hike meanders through hardwood forests, wetlands, and the domains of flyers both natural and human-made. A birding trail, fishing piers, and plenty of resting places at the lakeshore make this hike enjoyable for all ages.

Features 🚶🐕💧🚌🎣🚴

Location College Park and Berwyn Heights, MD

Rating Easy

Distance 3.5-mile loop

Elevation Gain 20 feet

Estimated Time 2 hours

Maps USGS Washington East

GPS Coordinates 38° 58.583′ N, 76° 55.393′ W

Contact Lake Artemesia Natural Area, pgparks.com/3244/Lake-Artemesia-Natural-Area, 301-699-7755

DIRECTIONS

From I-95/I-495 (Capital Beltway), take Exit 23 to MD 201 (Kenilworth Avenue) south. Drive 1.5 miles and then turn right onto Campus Drive. Free parking is available at the Ellen E. Linson Splash Park/Herbert W. Wells Ice Rink at 5211 Campus Drive, on your left past the bridge over the Northeast Branch of the Anacostia River.

By Metrorail, take the Green Line to the College Park–U of MD station and then follow the walking directions below.

TRAIL DESCRIPTION

The full Northeast Branch Trail is a 3-mile leg of the Anacostia Tributary Trails network, reaching through northern Prince George's County and eastern Montgomery County in Maryland. On this hike, you'll travel a section of the trail along Northeast Branch of the Anacostia River (Northeast Branch) and around the College Park Airport runway to its junction with the loop trail at Lake Artemesia. This hike is designed to be a Metro-friendly sojourn outside the boundaries of the city proper. If you drive to College Park, start the hike from the parking lot at the Ellen E. Linson Splash Park/Herbert W. Wells Ice Rink.

At the top of the steps coming up from the College Park–U of MD Metro station, head toward River Road. When you arrive at River Road, turn left and walk to its intersection with Campus Drive. Turn right on Campus Drive, passing the U.S. Food and Drug

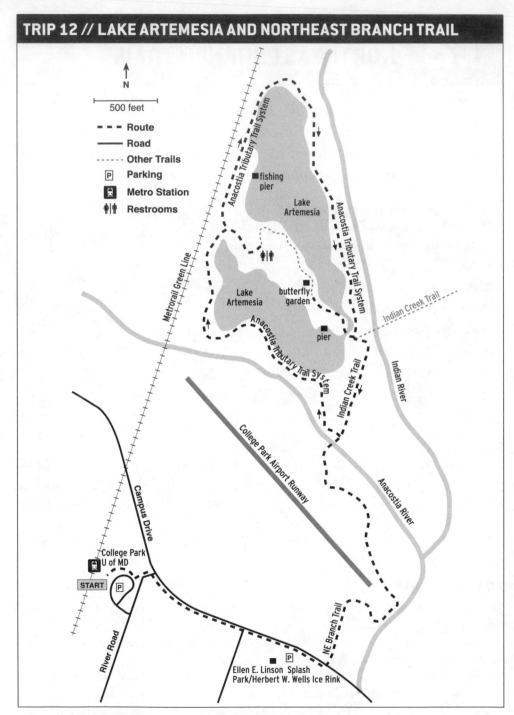

Administration building (5100 Campus Drive). Follow Campus Drive east for two blocks, to the parking lot at the Ellen E. Linson Splash Park/Herbert W. Wells Ice Rink.

Look for a paved connector trail from the parking lot that leads to unblazed Northeast Branch Trail. Turn left and follow Northeast Branch Trail as it goes under Campus Drive and toward a chain-link fence in the distance. Look for a couple of large, lovely American holly trees alongside the trail. The trail and fence will bend around the end of the College Park Airport runway. This is a perfect spot from which to watch a small craft landing on a pleasant day. (Bring a blanket if you plan to sit; no benches are provided.) Wilbur Wright trained the first military aviators at this airport, which celebrated its 100th anniversary in 2009 and was the site of the first controlled helicopter flight in 1924. Step up on the creek bank for a glimpse of the Northeast Branch running south to join the Anacostia River.

Continue along Northeast Branch Trail through the oak woods, past the Anacostia River Herring Restoration Area sign and over the wooden-decked steel bridge. By the far foot of the bridge, near Northeast Branch Trail's 0-mile marker, a sign points to the left for Lake Artemesia. Pass the black-painted chain-link fence and gate to enter Lake Artemesia Natural Area. Turn left on the lake's loop trail and follow it along the lake's southern shore. Watch for green herons and great blue herons, loons, and various ducks in the water. Check out the nesting boxes along the fence, home to swallows and eastern bluebirds year-round. Signs along the route describe local natural and human history.

The 38-acre lake was constructed in the 1980s, when the Washington Metropolitan Area Transit Authority needed sand and gravel to build up the nearby Green Line road-bed extension. In 1972, Artemesia N. Drefs, whose family had owned land in the vicinity since the 1890s, donated some acreage—where a small lake named Artemesia, for her mother and grandmother, already existed—to the county. The family had raised bass and

Alongside the trail bearing its name, the northeast branch of the Anacostia River runs with snowmelt on a spring-thaw day. Its bank is a good vantage point for spotting small aircraft traveling into and out of the nearby College Park Airport.

goldfish in these waters. Following Mrs. Drefs's wish for a lasting natural area on this spot, the Transit Authority struck a deal: it would use the fill soils it dredged out locally to build up the Green Line, thereby saving $10 million in material and transportation costs, and would spend $8 million turning the resulting excavation into a green haven for wildlife and humans.

Turn right onto the peninsula path if you're in need of a break; restrooms and a water fountain are available at the blue-roofed building. Then retrace your steps back to the lake loop trail and turn right to walk along the western shore. A floating fishing pier is on the right; local anglers say trout can be reeled in here. At the northern tip of the lake, a gazebo next to a copse of loblolly pines offers a good vantage point for watching gulls, ducks (ruddy and ring-necked), and grebes (pied-billed and horned) on the water and in the vegetation along the shoreline. Keep following the lake loop trail around to the eastern shore, watching for woodpeckers, cardinals, nuthatches, and other small birds in the forested area on the left.

Turn right to cross the steel bridge onto the peninsula again. You'll see the covered octagonal pier with plenty of benches on the left; the right-hand path leads to a butterfly and wildflower garden on the northern edge of the peninsula. Walk back across the bridge, take the right-center path, and then turn right to follow Indian Creek Trail back toward the sleepy Northeast Branch. You might see deer or rabbit tracks here or a black-crowned night heron near the water. After a short distance, Indian Creek Trail ends by the foot of the first steel bridge you crossed. Go straight over that bridge onto Northeast Branch Trail and back around the airport runway to the parking lot or Metro station.

MORE INFORMATION

Northeast Branch Trail and Lake Artemesia Natural Area are maintained by the Maryland-National Capital Park and Planning Commission's Department of Parks and Recreation, Prince George's County. The natural area and its trails are open daily, sunrise to sunset. These are multiuse trails, so be aware of bicyclists and other users. Bicycles may be rented at the Ellen E. Linson Splash Park/Herbert W. Wells Ice Rink. Leashed dogs are allowed. No alcoholic beverages are permitted. Fishing is allowed by permit; visit dnr.state.md.us/fisheries for details. For more information, visit pgparks.com/3244/Lake-Artemesia-Natural-Area or call 301-699-7755. In an emergency, call the park police at 301-459-3232.

Novice and expert bird-watchers will both enjoy Luther Goldman Birding Trail—a 2.2-mile trail with interpretive panels describing the types of birds that might be spotted along the way. The Prince George's Audubon Society also leads bird walks in the area. Learn more by visiting pgaudubon.org.

NEARBY

The College Park Aviation Museum is a small Smithsonian-affiliated venue on the grounds of College Park Airport and worth a visit. The museum's gallery displays historical and reproduction aircraft, many from the age of open-cockpit flight, and all associated with the history of the airfield, dating back to the Wright brothers. Hands-on activities and interpretive areas appeal to children of all ages. See collegeparkaviationmuseum.com for details.

13 MATTHEW HENSON TRAIL

This attractive and peaceful paved trail meanders along Turkey Branch through a state park and provides flora and fauna sightings uncommon in such a populated area.

Features 👟 🐕 ♿ 💧 ⛱

Location Veirs Mill and Colesville, MD

Rating Moderate

Distance 4.5 miles one way

Elevation Gain 235 feet

Estimated Time 2.5–3 hours

Maps USGS Kensington; online: montgomeryparks.org/parks-and-trails/matthew -henson-state-stream-valley-park/matthew-henson-trail

GPS Coordinates 39° 05.169′ N, 77° 02.053′ W

Contact Maryland-National Capital Park and Planning Commission's Montgomery Parks division, montgomeryparks.org/parks-and-trails/matthew -henson-state-stream-valley-park/matthew-henson-trail, 301-670-8080

DIRECTIONS

From I-495 (Capital Beltway), take Exit 33 for MD 185 (Connecticut Avenue). Drive about 3 miles and bear left onto Veirs Mill Road. Go about a half-mile and turn left at the light onto Randolph Road. Take the third right (at a traffic light) onto Dewey Road. Drive approximately four blocks until you see Winding Creek Local Park on the left (before Dewey Road makes a sharp curve right), and park in the lot here.

Leaving a second vehicle at the trail's end is highly recommended; see the last paragraph of the trail description. To do so, park on Alderton Road—this is a residential area, so make sure to follow signs for where to park.

TRAIL DESCRIPTION

Well maintained, peaceful, wonderfully quiet, and pleasantly hidden, Matthew Henson Trail, which opened in 2009, remains a largely undiscovered gem, particularly along its northern reaches. Deer, cottontail rabbits, mallard ducks, cardinals and finches, and butterflies are plentiful along the path, keeping you company and providing enjoyment on your walk. The trail and the state park surrounding it are named in honor of the Maryland native Matthew Henson, an explorer who was the first human being to reach the North Pole. (See "Matthew Henson and the Race to the North Pole," on page 57.)

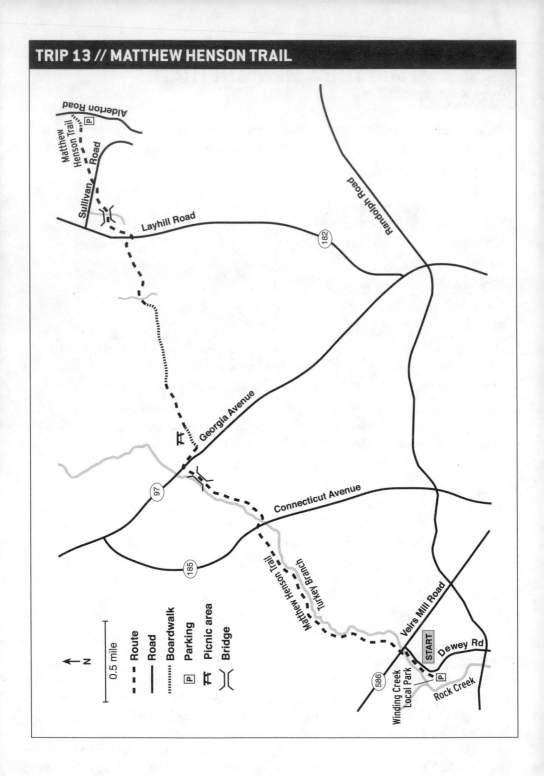

Legend:
- Route (dashed)
- Road (solid)
- Boardwalk (dotted)
- P Parking
- ⵠ Picnic area
-)(Bridge

0.5 mile

N ←

Alderton Road
Matthew Henson Trail
Sullivan Road
Layhill Road
182
Randolph Road
Georgia Avenue
97
Connecticut Avenue
185
Matthew Henson Trail
Turkey Branch
Veirs Mill Road
START
Dewey Rd
586
Winding Creek Local Park
Rock Creek

Lush ferns border the longest of Matthew Henson Trail's boardwalks as it runs downhill into a cool, shady marsh.

Begin at the parking lot of Winding Creek Local Park by looking for the white signs with green lettering pointing toward the trail. Head northeast along paved Matthew Henson Trail, following the extension of Dewey Road, and catch your first glimpse of babbling Turkey Branch. At the Veirs Mill Road crossing, the trail jogs left across an access road and then makes a quick right turn to cross the six-lane Veirs Mill Road. Watch for the black barred fences. Traffic sometimes travels at high speeds here; use caution.

Honeysuckle spills over the fence just across Veirs Mill Road, and the easy-to-follow paved trail continues parallel to residential Turkey Branch Parkway on the left and along a forest renewal area to the right. Wild grapevines and bamboo can be seen along this segment of the hike. The parks commission is working to remove invasive plant species here and to restore a natural habitat for plants and animals. Pass Grenoble Drive on the left and look for a grove of sycamores on the slope. Note the "10 mile" post. This and other markers indicate mileage for Matthew Henson Trail and connecting Rock Creek Trail. Subtract 9 miles from each for an accurate guideline—this is the 1-mile point on Matthew Henson Trail.

Near the rows of planted American hollies is the first of several benches along the trail. Just past it is a large hemlock tree with honeysuckle vines entwined in its branches, reaching 20 feet in the air. At mile 1.3 is an emergency call box (call boxes are also at mile 1.8 and mile 3.1). Approach the Connecticut Avenue overpass; connector trails lead up to this main road. Follow the main trail below the overpass, around to a curving boardwalk, and over a steel bridge. As the path meanders, look for a big, old, leaning willow tree to the right. Another steel bridge leads to the Georgia Avenue crossing, about 2.1 miles into the hike. Follow the painted crosswalk to cross the road.

The trail turns to the right, winds around a church, and begins to climb until about mile 2.8, where it descends to a long, wooden boardwalk through wetlands. Pause for a break or a picnic at the benches behind the church, or travel a little farther to a shade pavilion and picnic tables. Moving on, come to a downslope and the start of the 0.6-mile boardwalk, which passes through a cattail marsh and crosses a couple of small streams. A horse farm is to the right. At mile 3.7, cross Layhill Road, near another church. A crosswalk, push button, and walk signal make this an easy crossing.

The last leg of the trail bears left into an open meadow area where white-tailed deer are often seen. Flowering crabapple trees make a pretty picture in early spring. Cross the steel bridge and walk up a slope into a wide meadow, also frequented by deer. The final crosswalk of this hike takes you over the country-like, two-lane Sullivan Road and past the ball fields of Layhill Village Local Park. A last downslope leads to one more boardwalk, and soon the trail ends at the intersection with Alderton Road.

(*Note*: This is a one-way trail ending in a neighborhood. It's a good idea to leave a second car on Alderton Road, where street parking should not be a problem, or at Layhill Village Local Park if you're up for backtracking a bit.)

MORE INFORMATION

Matthew Henson Trail is maintained by the Maryland-National Capital Park and Planning Commission's Montgomery Parks division. To report trail problems or suggest repairs, call 301-670-8080. The only restroom available along this trail is a portable toilet at the starting point in Winding Creek Local Park. No trash receptacles are provided on the trail. The hard-surface trail has 0.6 mile of boardwalk. Wheelchair access is not available from the Layhill Village Local Park parking area but is available from the other two parking lots. For more information, visit montgomeryparks.org/parks-and-trails/matthew-henson-state-stream-valley-park/matthew-henson-trail.

NEARBY

A short distance north along Georgia Avenue (MD 97) is Olney Manor Recreational Park, which has 61 acres of play space, including ball fields (one lighted); basketball, handball, and lighted tennis courts; a playground; a skate park for skateboarding and inline skating; an indoor swim center; and a fenced 1-acre dog park. For more information, see montgomeryparks.org/parks-and-trails/olney-manor-recreational-park.

For the artistically inclined, the Mansion and Music Center at Strathmore, a few miles to the west in north Bethesda, is a set of venues showcasing performing and visual arts on a scenic 16-acre campus, with a café and dining hall on-site. An afternoon tea is offered several times a month. Visit strathmore.org for information, schedules, and ticketing.

MATTHEW HENSON AND THE RACE TO THE NORTH POLE

"The lure of the Arctic is tugging at my heart. To me the trail is calling! The old trail. The trail that is always new."

Matthew Henson was born in 1866 on a farm in southern Maryland. His parents, share-croppers, were born free Black Americans before the Civil War. Soon after his birth, they moved to Washington, D.C., in hopes of better opportunities. Orphaned by age 12, Matthew Henson sought adventure as a cabin boy on a merchant ship, sailing the world and learning about mathematics, navigation, and cultures. When his captain and mentor died, Henson returned to Washington, D.C., and found work in an outfitter shop. There he met the naval officer Robert Peary, who was determined to reach the North Pole but had military orders to lead a surveying expedition to Nicaragua. Peary hired Henson as his assistant and, impressed by the young man's abilities, later took him on an 1891 expedition to Greenland, seeking paths to the Pole. When Peary warned him of Arctic hardships, Henson responded, "I'll go north with you, sir, and I think I'll stand it as well as any man."

And he did. Peary insisted Henson join him on every attempt to reach the Pole. It would take eight brutal and deadly treks across the crevasses of the Arctic ice pack. The explorers befriended and learned from the Inuit natives. Some, including Henson and Peary, fathered children with Inuit women. But only Henson learned the Inuit language, and he was known as *Maripahluk*, or "Matthew, the Kind One."

Peary chose Henson as the only non-Inuit to accompany him on his final push to the Pole, in April 1909. A weakened Peary rode in a dogsled while Henson, nearly losing his life in a crevasse, forged ahead to plant the U.S. flag at the top of the world.

Explorer Matthew Henson wearing his fur suit. *Photo courtesy of the Library of Congress.*

Upon their return to the United States, tension arose in their relationship. Peary was lauded for the achievement while Henson received little recognition. Peary and Frederick Cook (a physician on the 1891 Greenland expedition who claimed to have reached the Pole a year earlier than Peary) were showered with glory, medals, and cash. Meanwhile, Henson began work as a federal clerk in New York and spent the next several years in obscurity.

It wasn't until 1937, when Henson was 70, that his contributions began to be recognized, and he was accepted as an honorary member to the exclusive Explorers Club. A few years later, in 1944, he received a Congressional Medal similar to the one awarded to Peary. In 1954, he was invited to the White House by the president, Dwight Eisenhower. Henson died a year later and was buried in New York. His remains were moved in 1987 to Arlington National Cemetery. His grave, marked by a memorial plaque, now rests adjacent to Peary's.

14 CALVERT CLIFFS STATE PARK

Calvert Cliffs State Park offers a perfect circuit hike, with a halfway point at a stretch of Miocene-epoch cliffs rich in sharks' teeth and other fossils.

Features 👫 🐕 💧 🅰 💲

Location Lusby, MD

Rating Moderate

Distance 4.8-mile loop

Elevation Gain 330 feet

Estimated Time 2–2.5 hours

Maps USGS Cove Point; online: dnr.maryland.gov/publiclands/documents /calvertcliffs_map.pdf

GPS Coordinates 38° 23.741'N, 76° 26.200' W

Contact Calvert Cliffs State Park, Maryland Department of Natural Resources, dnr.maryland.gov/publiclands/Pages/southern/calvertcliffs.aspx, 443-975-4360

DIRECTIONS

Calvert Cliffs State Park is on the western shore of Chesapeake Bay, near the mouth of the Patuxent River. From I-95/I-495 (Capital Beltway), take Exit 11 to MD 4 east (Pennsylvania Avenue) in the direction of Upper Marlboro. After approximately 36 miles, during which MD 4 becomes MD 4/MD 2, turn left onto MD 765, approximately 14 miles south of the town of Prince Frederick. Follow MD 765 a short distance to the park. Parking is available around the central picnic area (25 spaces) or at a side lot (40 spaces).

TRAIL DESCRIPTION

Calvert Cliffs State Park encompasses 1,079 acres and has 13 miles of hiking trails. It is a uniquely Chesapeake Bay treasure, containing 100-foot cliffs formed 10 to 20 million years ago during the Miocene epoch, when a warm, shallow sea covered southern Maryland. As the sea receded, the exposed cliffs began to erode. More than 600 species of fossils have been identified from the sands of Calvert Cliffs, including whale ear bones and skulls; crocodile snouts; the dental plate of a ray; and teeth from mako, snaggletooth, requiem, sand, tiger, and cow sharks, as well as the extinct megalodon. Remnants of these prehistoric creatures still frequently turn up today, and collecting fossils from the beach is allowed. In 1612, Captain John Smith noted these cliffs on a map, naming them Rickard's Cliffes in honor of his mother's family.

Begin the hike on Red Trail (also known as Cliff Trail and marked with red blazes), to the right of a pond adjacent to the picnic area. This trail runs 1.8 miles to the cliffs on

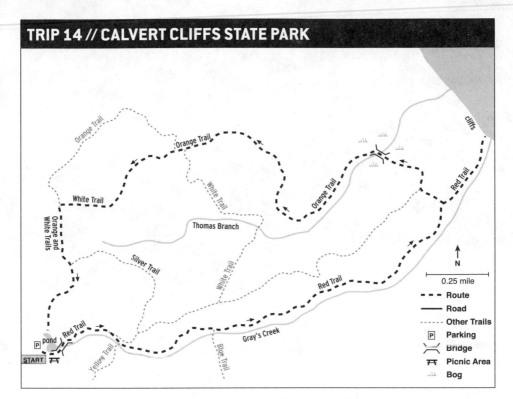

Chesapeake Bay. (Access to the clifftops is closed due to landslides.) Cross a bridge over the edge of the pond near the picnic area and follow the trail left to cross Gray's Creek. White oaks and chestnut oaks rise overhead. Holly bushes and mountain laurels spread out at eye level, and beach sand dusts the trail underfoot. Turn right onto a gravel service road, walk 50 yards, and turn right again to continue on Red Trail. Follow the small rapids of Gray's Creek as the water carves its way between ridges. Pass intersections with Yellow Trail at 0.2 mile and Blue Trail at 0.6 mile.

At 1.1 miles, the creek reaches an open tidal marsh replete with sunflowers, broad-leaf arrowhead (a variety of edible tuber), swamp mallow, invasive arrow arum, spatterdock, and white waterlilies. At 1.3 miles, a platform leads out over the marsh to a panoramic and aromatic viewpoint and, farther along, fecund pools of more broad-leaf arrowhead and waterlilies. After taking in the scenery, resume walking on Red Trail and arrive at Chesapeake Bay and the stunning Calvert Cliffs at 1.8 miles.

The cliffs are the park's most rewarding sight and most powerful attraction. More than 100 feet high, Calvert Cliffs contain the highest concentration of Miocene fossils on the East Coast. Scientists, rock hounds, and children are equally drawn to the cliffs to look for these ancient traces of life dating from millions of years ago. Don't be surprised to find people searching with the serious-minded fervor of prospectors!

Please keep in mind that the cliffs are fragile, eroding at a rate of 3 feet per year. The area directly beneath the cliffs is closed due to the potential for injury from landslides, and it is illegal to climb or hike onto the cliffs, or to collect fossils beneath them. Fossil hunting can be done along the open beach area. Swimming is not allowed.

Warm-season visitors enjoy the sandy Chesapeake Bay beach at Calvert Cliffs State Park, where ancient fossils and shark teeth have been found. *Photo by Alliecat1881, Creative Commons on Flickr.*

Return via Red Trail and turn right onto an access trail that leads to the service road and the intersection with Orange Trail. Bear to the right to start following orange-blazed Orange Trail, which plunges down the other side of the hill to a 150-foot-long bridge over Thomas Creek Bog, constructed in 1999 as part of an Eagle Scout project. The bridge affords access to the heart of the freshwater marsh, where sweet gum trees filter prismatic sun rays onto a surface dappled with waterlilies, arrowheads, and swarms of swift-moving dragonflies in summer.

After crossing the bridge, travel through a pine grove, following the edge of the bog as it narrows to a creek bed. Pass a connector trail that comes in from the left and, just after it, begin a steep, 80-foot scramble to the top of a ridge. Turn left along the top of the ridge and walk past sweet gums and top-heavy pawpaw trees before Orange Trail links up with White Trail at 3.6 miles, at which point the route is blazed in both colors. Arrive at an intersection—Orange Trail departs to the right—and proceed straight ahead to follow White Trail. After a short distance, begin a roller-coaster ride of a hike over folded terrain.

Climb the side of a ridge, tracing the hill's contours, and soon enter a grove of monumental yellow poplars and more leafy pawpaw trees. At 4.3 miles, reach a clearing with cornfields. White and Orange trails will intersect again here. Turn left to follow the trails, which run together for the rest of the hike. At 4.6 miles, after passing an intersection with Silver Trail and a large fire-warning siren, watch for large-leafed paulownia and black locust trees on the left—species not found anywhere else in the park. Finally, pass a gate leading to the service road, and bear right to stay on the combined trails for the remaining 0.1 mile back to the parking lot.

MORE INFORMATION

The park entrance is at 10540 H. G. Trueman Road in Lusby, Maryland. Entry to the park is $5 per vehicle; out-of-state visitors pay an additional $2 per vehicle (cash is preferred, but credit cards are accepted). Weather-resistant trail maps are available for sale at the gate. Leashed dogs are allowed. A recycled-tire playground provides the ultimate stop for children visiting the park. Portions of Calvert Cliffs State Park are open to hunting, including areas crossed by Orange Trail, so be alert and wear bright colors during fall deer season and spring turkey season.

One of Maryland's most popular parks, Calvert Cliffs receives large numbers of visitors on summer weekends and holidays. The park closes when it reaches capacity, and traffic is turned away from the entrance. If you are traveling with a group during summer or on a holiday, plan to carpool together or at least arrive at the same time. For more information, visit dnr.maryland.gov/publiclands/Pages/southern/calvertcliffs.aspx or call 443-975-4360.

NEARBY

Middleham Chapel, an Episcopal church constructed in 1748, is just north of the park entrance on MD 765. Also nearby are Flag Ponds Park (farther north on MD 2) and Battle Creek Cypress Swamp Sanctuary, a 100-acre site that is one of the northernmost habitats of bald cypress trees. A few miles north on MD 2 in Solomons, the Calvert Marine Museum (admission fee) is a popular family-friendly attraction, featuring tours of Drum Point Lighthouse and charming exhibits centering on maritime history, paleontology, and estuarine biology of the Chesapeake Bay region. A marsh walk leads to a river otter habitat.

15 JUG BAY WETLANDS SANCTUARY

A hidden treasure along the tidal Patuxent River in southern Maryland, this pristine wildlife sanctuary offers a peaceful ramble with stunning views of the wetlands from its boardwalks and many opportunities for glimpsing birds and other wildlife.

Features 🚶 💧 ⛰ $

Location Lothian, MD

Rating Easy to Moderate

Distance 5.3-mile loop

Elevation Gain 208 feet

Estimated Time 3 hours

Maps USGS Bristol; map available at the McCann Wetlands Study Center; online: jugbay.org/visit-us

GPS Coordinates 38° 47.082′ N, 76° 42.100′ W

Contact Jug Bay Wetlands Sanctuary, jugbay.org, 410-222-8006

DIRECTIONS
From I-495 (Capital Beltway), take Exit 11A for MD 4 South/Pennsylvania Avenue toward Upper Marlboro. Continue along MD 4 south for 10.5 miles. Turn right onto Plummer Lane, drive 0.5 mile, and turn right onto Wrighton Road. After 0.6 mile, turn left onto the Jug Bay entrance road. Continue to the parking lot by the McCann Wetlands Study Center.

TRAIL DESCRIPTION
Jug Bay Wetlands Sanctuary is made up of 1,700 acres of tidal freshwater marshes, forested wetlands, upland forests, riparian (riverbank) forests, fields, and open water. Please note that the sanctuary is not open every day; visitors are welcome from 9 A.M. to 5 P.M. on Wednesday, Friday, Saturday, and Sunday from March through November. From December through February, the sanctuary is also closed on Sundays.

Check in and pay to park at the McCann Wetlands Study Center. Parking is $6 per vehicle by cash or check only. The small museum is worth a pause to flip through the informative binders, previewing some of the sanctuary's plants and wildlife. Make sure to pick up a copy of the detailed map.

From the study center, walk through a small field toward the sign for Otter Point Trail. A broad observation deck on the right offers a sweeping view of the wetlands and gives you the opportunity to spot ospreys and eagles. In summer, look below to see the water

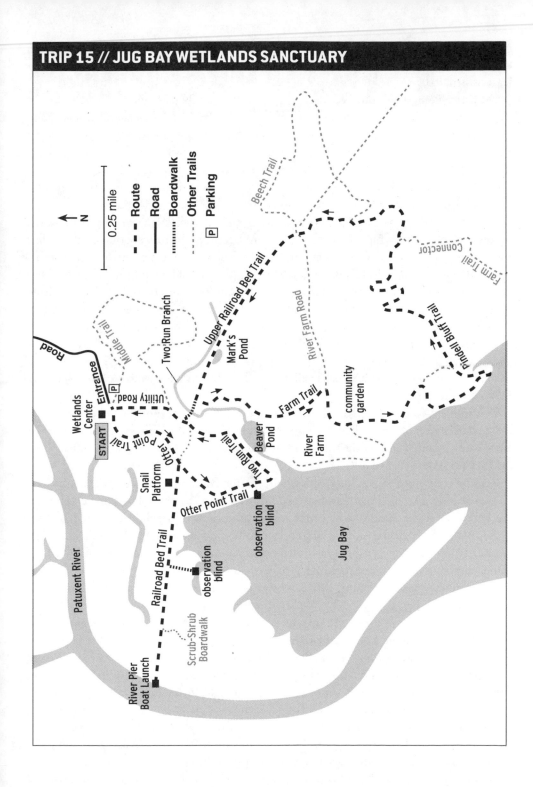

crowded with spatterdock, also known as cow lilies, with their heart-shaped leaves. In fall, ducks often congregate here. The scene is even more beautiful in winter, when visibility is least obstructed.

On Otter Point Trail, proceed along the wide, flat, sandy path through shady woods. Turn right at the sign for Railroad Bed Trail. This out-and-back diversion from the loop goes past two of the sanctuary's most impressive observation areas. Along this gravelly, elevated spur, look to either side to see water nearby, almost level with the trail at high tide. The Snail Platform, a wooden dock with a bench overlooking a peaceful marshy area, is on the right; watch for *Oxyloma* snails clinging to the cattails and arrow arum stalks. You also may see ospreys flying overhead and swallowtail butterflies passing through.

Continue on Railroad Bed Trail as it becomes grassier and mossier. On quiet days, watch for the flick of a deer's white tail on the path. Turn left onto a boardwalk that leads 250 feet into the wetlands to the observation blind, an enclosed viewing area with windows surrounded by open porches. Wildlife is less likely to be startled by your presence when you observe from a blind. Peer among the vegetation for muskrats, otters, and turtles, and listen for the clicking *kid-dik* call of the rail and the *ho-ho-ho* of the least bittern.

Retrace your steps on the boardwalk and turn left where the boardwalk joins the path to continue on Railroad Bed Trail. Pass the marked turnoff to the Scrub-Shrub boardwalk, which leads to a bench in the midst of shrub wetlands. In summer, an overgrowth of wild rice often renders this boardwalk impassable, but in winter it is a pleasant, peaceful spot for observation.

Continue on Railroad Bed Trail, and pass the Bill Steiner Canoe Shelter on your left. Immediately after, Railroad Bed Trail turns to boardwalk and terminates at the River Pier Boat Launch with a vista of the water and the Mount Calvert Historical and Archaeological Park across the Patuxent River.

Retrace your steps to the intersection with Otter Point Trail; turn right to continue along the loop. Dappled sun falls between tall trees and shorter holly plants on this flat section of the route. A sign and a bench mark the turnoff to the right to a small swamp blind. Walk along the narrow, curving connector boardwalk through the freshwater tidal swamp—populated with ash trees—to the viewing shed. (Watch out for wasps, which sometimes nest within the structure.) When you're ready, return to Otter Point Trail; it soon terminates at Otter Point, with a picnic table and a view of Jug Bay, perfect for a snack or a lunch break.

Go left from Otter Point to pick up white-blazed Two Run Trail, which traces the bluff above Two Run Branch. Look to the right to see peaceful, algae-covered Beaver Pond with its viewing platform; you may spot a heron. Two Run Trail gently climbs a root-covered slope through the forest and curves around the hilltop to the left, offering another view of the north end of Beaver Pond. At the intersection of Railroad Bed Trail and Two Run Trail, turn right to continue down a set of wooden stairs on Two Run Trail. Turn right on the boardwalk, crossing a shallow stream. Tiny lizards, such as race runners and skinks, tend to congregate here. You may see them darting ahead of you and zigzagging up trees. At the boardwalk's end, climb a staircase with rope railings.

Look for the sign for Upper Railroad Bed Trail. Follow this trail a short distance and then turn right onto white-blazed Farm Trail and climb another set of stairs. Farm Trail

Whether inside or outside the blind, the views at Jug Bay delight.

widens into a sunny clearing. On the right is a view down to a stream, and you can see a red farm building in the distance between the trees. The widened trail then forms a T intersection with a sandy road. Head right on Pindell Bluff Trail toward the farm and a picnic area. This section of road is shared with vehicles but quickly opens onto the farm property. Stay to the left, between the South County Community Garden and the River Farm building, and continue through the grassy lawn, keeping to the left of the Pindell Bluff Trail sign and the community garden.

At the edge of the mowed field, another sign marks where blue-blazed Pindell Bluff Trail reenters the trees as a shady forest path. This well-marked segment winds through the trees and is bordered on both sides with beds of young pines. Listen for the sounds of mourning doves and woodpeckers. At the next intersection, continue right on Pindell Bluff Trail and soon emerge to see Jug Bay. Its muddy waters may appear almost white in sunlight. Turn left to follow a slightly elevated rise that hugs the water. Here, the forest is less dense; look for a fern grove through the trees on the left. Circle right, around the edge of the ridge, and descend to overgrown Pindell Point.

Here, the trail hairpins. Take the lower trail to the left, doubling back below the same ridge you just descended. At the next intersection, turn right to continue on Pindell Bluff Trail on a narrow bog bridge, which may be slippery. Proceed up a brief but very steep incline to crest the ridge. The trail flits back and forth, with views of the Pindell Branch of the Patuxent River on the right through the trees. The route is not always distinct, but look for the blue blazes to stay on track. Watch for eastern box turtles, which often pass through these woods. The trail rejoins the river briefly and then climbs gently into a grassy section of forest, where the beds of young pines give way to dense fern groves.

Pass the intersection with Farm Connector Trail. At a signed intersection with Beech Trail (the sign may be a little hard to spot), bear left to stay on Pindell Bluff Trail. Emerge on River Farm Road; cross the road and follow the sign to Upper Railroad Bed Trail. This grassy, mossy trail is flanked by tall trees. It remains very flat and straight as the forest rises and a lush bed of ferns encroaches onto the path.

At the next intersection, stay left on Upper Railroad Bed Trail. The trail, knotted with roots, narrows as it sinks between two small swells, and then rises again before passing the intersection of a staff-only trail on the right. Soon you see water on two sides: Two Run Branch on the right, a little way down a slope, and small Mark's Pond on the left.

At the intersection with Farm Trail, stay straight. Retrace your steps down the stairs and along the boardwalk over the shallow stream; at the intersection with Two Run Trail, turn right onto the north section, which climbs steep wooden stairs before turning into a wide dirt path, winding past the fences that mark the edges of deer enclosures.

Climb gently to the intersection of Middle Trail, Two Run Trail, and Utility Road. Turn left to take Utility Road uphill to the McCann Wetlands Study Center through a section of mockernut hickory trees. Look for lovely, thin-leafed willow oaks and black walnuts on the short walk back to the McCann Wetlands Study Center and parking area.

MORE INFORMATION
Dogs, horses, fishing, and biking are not permitted at Jug Bay Wetlands Sanctuary, but picnicking is allowed. The minimal elevation change and the many opportunities to observe wildlife, in combination with the thoughtfully curated museum at the McCann Wetlands Study Center, make this an ideal hike for children and families. For more information, visit jugbay.org or call 410-222-8006.

Look for QR codes on blinds and other points of interest throughout the hike. These codes link to videos that provide more details about those particular locations.

NEARBY
If you haven't had your fill, Glendening Nature Preserve, the northern part of Jug Bay Wetlands Sanctuary, offers more miles of hiking trails. Beaver Rock Trail and Red Oak Trail offer opportunities for butterfly sightings, as the winged insects pass through forests and a cultivated cactus garden. Parking is free at the preserve.

16 WATKINS REGIONAL PARK

Peacocks and pollywogs, a Wizard of Oz*–themed playground, gentle hiking, and family fun await you in this pleasant park. In summer, an antique carousel, miniature golf, and a small-scale train ride add festivity to your visit.*

Features 🧑‍🦯 🐕 ♿ ⛺ ⛺ ⛺

Location Largo, MD

Rating Easy

Distance 2.2 miles round-trip

Elevation Gain 45 feet

Estimated Time 2.5–3 hours (including Watkins Nature Center and Old Maryland Farm)

Maps USGS Lanham; online: mncppc.org/DocumentCenter/View/8717/watkins -regional-park-map

GPS Coordinates 38° 53.292′ N, 76° 47.035′ W

Contact Watkins Regional Park, mncppc.org/3204/Watkins-Regional-Park, 301-218-6702

DIRECTIONS

From I-95/I-495 (Capital Beltway), take Exit 15A for MD 214 (Central Avenue) east. Drive approximately 3 miles and turn right onto MD 193 (Watkins Park Drive). The park entrance is about 1 mile ahead on the right. Follow the park road toward the Nature Center, past parking lots for the playground and farm. The parking lot for the Nature Center is on the left.

If using public transportation, take Metrorail's Blue Line to the Largo Town Center station. Catch the C26 bus, which brings you within 0.25 mile of the park entrance. Exit at the intersection of Watkins Park Drive and Keverton Drive. From there, look for signs to follow either Loop Trail or Spicebush Trail to the Nature Center. Check wmata.com for up-to-date information on schedules and routes.

TRAIL DESCRIPTION

Watkins Regional Park has lots going on: history, live animals (wild and domesticated, from bullfrogs to peacocks), camping, picnic shelters, ball fields, woods and wetlands, miniature golf, a restored carousel, a Nature Center, lovely nature trails, and even a miniature train ride in season. A colorful playground with a *Wizard of Oz* theme (ruby-slipper slides and a yellow "brick" road) recently replaced an older play area. With its appealing

TRIP 16 // WATKINS REGIONAL PARK

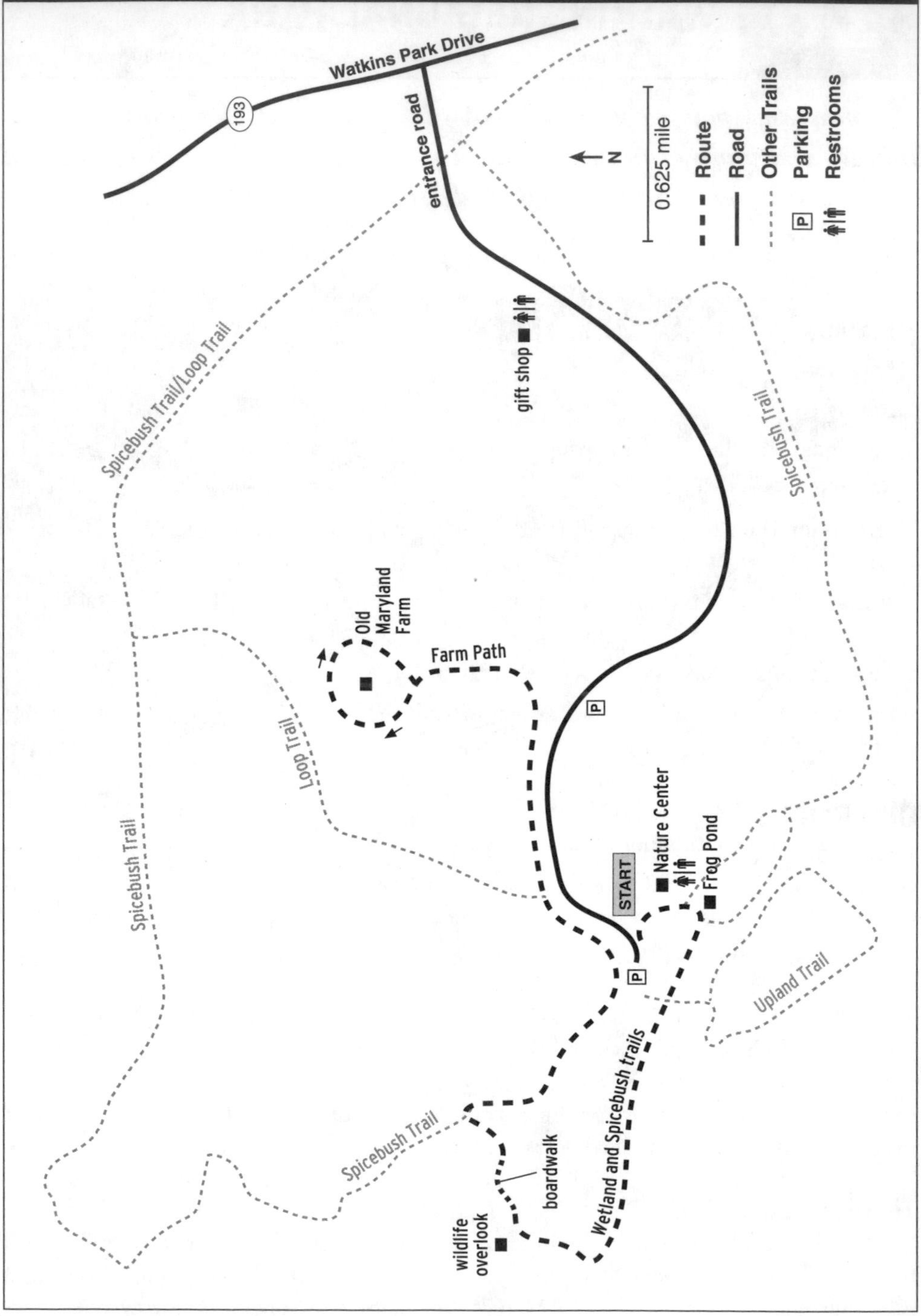

Watkins Park Drive
193
entrance road
gift shop
Spicebush Trail/Loop Trail
Spicebush Trail
Old Maryland Farm
Farm Path
Loop Trail
START
Nature Center
Frog Pond
Upland Trail
Wetland and Spicebush trails
boardwalk
wildlife overlook
N
0.625 mile
Route
Road
Other Trails
Parking
Restrooms

spectrum of offerings, you could easily spend an entire day at Watkins Regional Park—and you might decide to do just that once you arrive. Created in 1964, the park is named in honor of Robert M. Watkins, a chairman of the Maryland-National Capital Park and Planning Commission who led efforts to establish open recreational space in Prince George's County.

Walk from the parking lot across the bridge into the Nature Center, where several creatures are usually in residence, including owls, turtles, and snakes. Baby carriers and kid-friendly trail activity packs are available to borrow from the Nature Center (return them when you depart), as well as brochures on wildflowers and wildlife. The park offers programs throughout the week and hosts the First Friday Campfire on the first Friday of each month.

Exit through the rear doors and cross Frog Pond to the trailhead kiosk. At the kiosk, turn right and follow the yellow and blue trail markings for Wetland Trail and Spicebush Trail, which run together for a while. Pass a rustic amphitheater on the right and cross a small footbridge. Pass an intersection with green-blazed Upland Trail and then follow yellow-blazed Wetland Trail as it curves to the right and climbs a slope. Halfway up the slope, the trail veers left. Now you're on your way into the wetlands. Be prepared for mud if it has rained recently, even though trail maintainers have added gravel in some spots to assist with drainage and traction. Short boardwalk sections also help preserve the path.

Take time to search for turtles and tadpoles, as well as wildflowers of all kinds that thrive here. In spring, look for violets (blue, cream, and yellow), wild ginger, and jack-in-the-pulpits. Summer brings hyssop and strawberry-like cinquefoil; in late summer and early fall, find white boneset, mistflower, and Saint-John's-wort.

Cross the curving boardwalk of the wildlife lookout over the marsh, keeping an eye out for ospreys and eagles, as well as water critters. Beavers have been known to slap their flat tails for curious hikers. Among the ups and downs of this leg of the trail, look for the large 125-year-old tulip poplars. Also watch for a split: When blue-blazed Spicebush Trail veers left, turn right to continue on yellow-blazed Wetland Trail. The trail's terminus is at the western end of the Nature Center parking lot.

To continue your journey, walk along the length of the parking area and, at the eastern end, look for the paved path to the left that runs along the entrance road to a crosswalk. Take the path across the park road and turn right at the "Trail to Park Facilities" sign. This paved path, the park's Loop Trail, makes for pleasant walking under a canopy of trees. A stop sign marks a maintenance driveway—cross the driveway and then pass the seasonal snack bar and a miniature golf course.

Arrive at an intersection with a series of paved paths. Look to the left to spot the sign for Old Maryland Farm and follow that path (Farm Path), which curves around to the right (east) of the miniature golf course. As you follow Farm Path, you'll get a closer look at the big antique Chesapeake Carousel—believed to date from the turn of the twentieth century and attributed to respected carousel builder and carver Gustav Dentzel—as well as the small-scale train ride.

The carousel is considered a local gem, brought here and lovingly restored in the 1970s from the nearby bayside town of Chesapeake Beach, a popular summer resort destination in the early 1900s.

A curving boardwalk along Watkins Regional Park's Wetland Trail provides an inviting vantage point for observing beavers, waterfowl, and bald eagles.

If you hear piercing, agonized-sounding cries as you move along Farm Path into the woods, fear not! Those are the calls of Old Maryland Farm's resident peacocks strutting their stuff. Flocks of turkeys and chickens also are vocal at times. In addition to fowl, the farm features horses, sheep, goats, pigs, cows, display gardens, agricultural exhibits and demonstrations, and the Barn Cat Gift Shop.

When you've finished exploring the farm, retrace your steps back to the Nature Center parking lot.

The latter segment of the trail, from the Nature Center to Old Maryland Farm and back, is an easy-to-follow, paved asphalt path. If you are visiting with children young enough to be in a stroller or are looking for an accessible outing, consider the Nature Center building and the out-and-back Farm Path, which is about 1 mile. The park's Loop Trail is also paved, if you want to travel a bit more.

MORE INFORMATION

Restrooms are in the Nature Center. Both the Nature Center and Old Maryland Farm are open 10 A.M. to 5 P.M. Tuesday through Saturday, and 11 A.M. to 4 P.M. on Sunday. They are closed on Mondays. Attractions are open in season, roughly Memorial Day to Labor Day, plus weekends in September; call ahead to make sure.

NEARBY

Six Flags America, a short distance away, is a family-friendly draw for theme park enthusiasts, with nine major roller coasters and plenty of other thrill rides, plus old-school amusements and a water park to boot. See sixflags.com/America for details. A few miles to the south in Upper Marlboro, the Show Place Arena at Prince George's Equestrian Center offers year-round exhibits, shows, and events, from jumping competitions to rodeo. Visit showplacearena.com for the latest information.

HERE ALL THE WHILE: THE PISCATAWAY PEOPLE

The Piscataway have no land reservations, no large numbers or renown, and no federal tribal recognition. Until recently, they had no state tribal recognition. But hundreds of years ago, the Piscataway had power and population. They welcomed strangers to their native place. Today, they have a story to tell of a proud people long ignored, marginalized, and mistreated.

When Captain John Smith arrived in Virginia in 1607, the great chiefdoms of the Piscataway and Powhatan—weakened by recent tribal wars but holding firmly to their lands—stewarded Chesapeake Bay's western shores. The Piscataway, whose name is said to mean "where the waters meet," were mainly found north of the Potomac River in present-day Washington, D.C., and central Maryland, while the Powhatan lived to the south in Virginia's tidewater region. Smith referred to the northern group by the name they gave their hereditary high chief's house: *Moyaons*. The high chief (*tayac*) was advised by local chiefs (*werowances*), wise elders, and shamans and could demand tribute from villages or send their warriors into battle.

The Piscataway, descended from Algonkian peoples probably driven south by earlier periods of cooler climate, were cousins to the nearby Nacotchtank (Anacostans), Tauxenent (Dogue), Mattawoman, Nanjemoy, and Portobaco, all of whose names also still appear throughout the region. In their villages, the Piscataway built longhouses shaped like loaves of bread, with sapling frames and bark or mat coverings. The villages were protected by log palisades. Inhabitants cultivated the so-called three sisters (squash, maize, and beans), and they hunted, fished, and gathered. But they lacked immunity against unfamiliar European diseases, such as smallpox, cholera, and measles.

The Piscataway first worked with the British Catholic colonizers of Maryland, who arrived in 1634. The *tayac* Kittamaquund—who, with his wife, converted to Catholicism—offered the colonizers land to found St. Mary's City. The Piscataway hoped to benefit by using the settlers as a buffer against other tribes. But as the British population grew, relations between the colonists and the native peoples deteriorated. By 1668, the Piscataway were confined to two small reservations. In 1675, Colonial leaders forced the Piscataway to permit the rival Susquehannock, defeated in war by the Five Nations Iroquois (Haudenosaunee), to settle on these reservations as well. Conflict ensued. The Susquehannock headed north again and joined with the Iroquois against the Piscataway, making repeated incursions southward. The British offered no help. They, too, coveted the lands that remained to the Piscataway.

In 1697, the Piscataway relocated across the Potomac to Fauquier County, but Virginia colonists sought to send them back. In 1699, they moved again, to an island in the Potomac near Point of Rocks. By 1700, a chiefdom that likely had boasted 8,500 individuals a century earlier had dwindled—through war, disease, and loss of land and sustenance—to about 300. Some of the remaining tribal members moved north into Iroquois territory and eventually into New France (Quebec) and Ontario. Some may have gone south, joining the Meherrin. Evidence indicates that many Piscataway stayed on or returned to their ancestral lands.

In the 1800s and early 1900s, the Piscataway were also subjected to widespread discrimination under Jim Crow–style laws. Their identity as a native tribal people was ignored, leaving them void of Native American treaty protection. The Catholic Church, however, maintained records that more accurately described Piscataway families as native people. Anthropologists in the late 1800s also interviewed Piscataway people who claimed descent from the chiefdom.

Philip Sheridan Proctor began a Piscataway revival in the early twentieth century, claiming through his family lineage the title of Chief Turkey Tayac. In 1944, he invited Smithsonian scientists to examine an ancient carving of his people's revered forest guardian spirit above Piscataway Creek in Maryland. But in attempting to remove the stone for further study, researchers shattered the precious artifact.

After Turkey Tayac's death in 1978, the Piscataway fractured into three distinct communities: the Piscataway Indian Nation and Tayac Territory, the Piscataway Conoy Confederacy and subtribes, and the Cedarville Band of Piscataway Indians. In the 1990s, a Maryland panel acknowledged the validity of Piscataway descent claims, but the state did not officially recognize the groups—some 4,100 people—as a native tribe until 2012, under Governor Martin O'Malley.

"We were an unrecognized people," Natalie Standingontherock Proctor, a Piscataway leader, said in a 2013 Smithsonian blog interview. "But we were here all the while." Piscataway-hosted gatherings, such as the annual spring powwow and the Awakening of Mother Earth ceremony, are helping to bring about the cultural revival Turkey Tayac sought.

Accokeek Foundation's trails in Piscataway Park traverse a riverside forest and the National Colonial Farm, offering views of Mount Vernon.

Features 👥 🐕 💧 🏕 ⛪

Location Accokeek, MD

Rating Easy

Distance 4-mile loop

Elevation Gain Minimal

Estimated Time 2 hours

Maps USGS Upper Marlboro; National Park Service map on-site; online: nps.gov/pisc/planyourvisit/maps.htm; accokeekfoundation.org/trails

GPS Coordinates 38° 41.635′ N, 77° 03.946′ W

Contact Piscataway Park, National Park Service, nps.gov/pisc/index.htm, 301-763-4600; Accokeek Foundation, accokeekfoundation.org, 301-283-2113

DIRECTIONS

From the I-95/I-495 (Capital Beltway) outer loop, take Exit 2A (from the inner loop, take Exit 3) onto MD 210 (Indian Head Highway). Travel about 9 miles. After you pass Farmington Road, take the next right onto Livingston Road. Drive one block and turn right onto Biddle Road. At the stop sign, turn left onto Bryan Point Road. Follow it 3.5 miles and turn right into the Accokeek Foundation parking lot.

TRAIL DESCRIPTION

Piscataway Park, located within the traditional ancestral homelands of the Piscataway people both past and present, is in Prince George's County, Maryland, directly across the Potomac River from Mount Vernon. Congress created the 5,000-acre park to preserve the view from that historic icon exactly as it had been in George Washington's time, when the first president boasted, "No estate in United America is more pleasantly situated than this." Piscataway Park stretches for 6.0 miles along the Potomac, from Piscataway Creek in the west to historic Marshall Hall in the east, but the entire park is not connected by a trail system. The Accokeek Foundation manages 200 acres jointly with the National Park Service, and the hike described here covers this complete area, which includes a historical farm, a native tree arboretum, and fine views of Mount Vernon, Fort Washington, and the Potomac River.

Begin the hike at the visitor center just north of the parking lot. Behind the center is a gravel path that splits north and east. Follow the north fork and turn left to see a popular

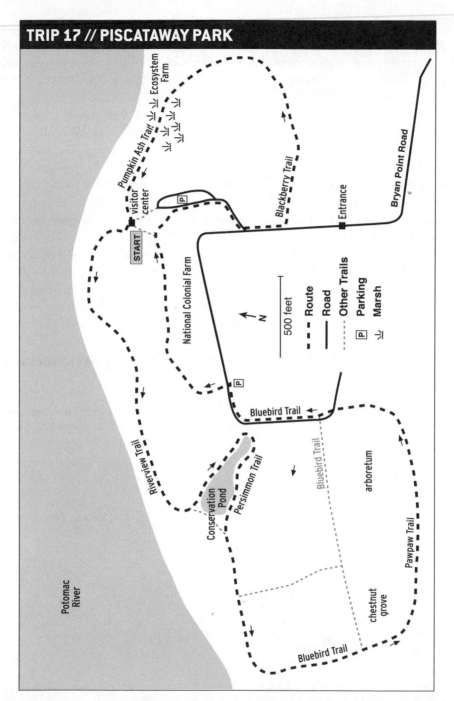

Ecosystem Farm

Pumpkin Ash Trail

Blackberry Trail

Bryan Point Road

visitor center

START

Entrance

National Colonial Farm

500 feet

- - - Route
—— Road
····· Other Trails
P Parking
🌲 Marsh

N

Riverview Trail

Bluebird Trail

Conservation Pond

Persimmon Trail

Bluebird Trail

arboretum

Pawpaw Trail

chestnut grove

Bluebird Trail

Potomac River

fishing pier with a view of Mount Vernon—a pleasant bonus. Then return to the split and take the east fork this time. Just before a line of evergreen cedars, turn right onto 0.8-mile Riverview Trail (dark-blue blazes). Follow the mowed swath of grass to a forested area along the Potomac River and travel westward along the forest's edge. This 6-acre riparian zone was planted between 1999 and 2002 and includes 60 species of trees and shrubs that protect 3.0 miles of Potomac shoreline from pollution, erosion, and nutrient runoff. Pass a side path that leads to the boat dock. The Riverview trail is unmarked here, so walk to the gravel road on the northern boundary of the National Colonial Farm and turn right, passing in front of the caretaker's residence. A posted sign on the right points to where the trail returns to open fields.

After a short distance, turn left onto 0.4-mile orange-blazed Persimmon Trail, which encircles a small pond. After traveling the loop, turn left, back onto blue-blazed Riverview Trail, and enter a larger section of riparian forest. Cross a wooden bridge over a tributary and leave the trees. Arrive at the intersection with Bluebird Trail and stay straight to start following this route, marked with light-blue blazes. Bluebird nesting sites line the way; the little habitats have entrances too small for competitors, such as starlings and house sparrows. These maintained nesting zones are helping to increase once-declining bluebird populations in the eastern states.

Continue on Bluebird Trail, watching out for electrified fences on the left. On the right is a grove of chestnuts. Where Bluebird Trail forks left on a roadway, stay straight to start following 0.5-mile, white-blazed Pawpaw Trail, which winds uphill through the type of mature hardwood forest that dominated the Potomac watershed before the intensive introduction of European farming methods. Exiting the woods, the trail ends at the upper edge of the native tree arboretum, where it reconnects with Bluebird Trail. The arboretum houses a variety of tree species, all extant in the Chesapeake region in the eighteenth century.

Visitors of all ages enjoy taking in the historic barns at Piscataway Park, which also offers stunning views of the Potomac River and Mount Vernon, as well as a working organic farm. *Photo by Alliecat1881, Creative Commons on Flickr.*

Continue north on the gravel road toward the barnyard. Bluebird Trail officially ends near a barn that houses rare heritage breeds under conservation, such as American Milking Devon cattle, Ossabaw hogs, Hog Island sheep, Icelandic chickens, and Jersey Buff turkeys. Continue through the National Colonial Farm and pass a tobacco barn before coming to a historical farmhouse and a reproduction outkitchen and smokehouse. Guides in period garb often provide historical interpretation to visitors on weekends in spring, summer, and fall.

Exit the farm between two zigzag split-rail fences and head south past the parking area along the access road. Follow the road briefly back toward the entrance, but keep an eye out for the difficult-to-spot trail marker—turn left at the marker onto 0.8-mile, purple-blazed Blackberry Trail and follow it to the edge of the Robert Ware Straus Ecosystem Farm. Turn left along the fence line and continue until the fence ends. Turn left onto 0.5-mile, yellow-blazed Pumpkin Ash Trail and cross along the river's edge, traversing a wooden boardwalk over a freshwater tidal area. Continue through a quiet patch of woodland to a picnic area and the parking lot.

MORE INFORMATION

Piscataway Park is free to enter. The visitor center has free and paid self-guided education kits and birding kits (field guide, binoculars, spotting scope) on loan. The Accokeek Foundation offers seasonal farm tours—visit accokeekfoundation.org/farm-tours to see the schedule of upcoming programs. The park has a canoe and kayak launch point on the Potomac River, just east of the fishing pier, and is also a stop on the 27-mile Potomac Heritage Trail On-Road Bicycling Route.

NEARBY

Historic Marshall Hall sits to the west of the park. Built in the early 1700s, it was the centerpiece of the Washington, D.C., area's first amusement park in the early 1900s. Indian Head, to the south along MD 210 at the confluence of the Potomac River and Mattawoman Creek, beckons visitors to explore its waters by kayak or stand-up paddleboard, which you can rent in Accokeek. Indian Head Rail Trail, designed for walking and cycling, is a 13-mile paved trail 0.5 mile from the center of Accokeek.

18 CEDARVILLE STATE FOREST

Cedarville State Forest offers a refreshing escape with gentle trails and a chance to explore the headwater of Zekiah Swamp.

Features

Location Brandywine, MD

Rating Easy

Distance 4.1-mile loop

Elevation Gain 230 feet

Estimated Time 2–3 hours

Maps Online: dnr.maryland.gov/publiclands/Documents/Cedarville_TrailGuide .pdf

GPS Coordinates 38° 38.612′ N, 76° 49.063′ W

Contact Cedarville State Forest, Maryland Department of Natural Resources, dnr.maryland.gov/publiclands/Pages/southern/Cedarville.aspx, 301-888-1410

DIRECTIONS
From I-495 (Capital Beltway), take Exit 7A for MD 5 South/Branch Avenue toward Waldorf. Turn slightly right and follow MD 5/Branch Avenue for 11.0 miles. Then turn left onto Cedarville Road. After 0.3 mile, turn right to stay on Cedarville Road. Continue for 2.0 miles and then turn right onto Bee Oak Road to enter the state forest. Stop at the visitor center to pay entrance fees. After leaving the visitor center, bear left at the intersection to continue on Bee Oak Road. Turn right at the intersection with a forest road, and follow the gravel road for 0.2 mile to the Charcoal Kiln parking area.

TRAIL DESCRIPTION
Sitting close to Washington, D.C., and its surrounding suburbs, Cedarville State Forest provides an escape for those looking to take a woodland break. The forest encompasses more than 3,800 acres—3,700 of them with a mix of bottomland hardwood, loblolly pine, and Virginia pine—and its trails offer easy to moderate hikes, suitable for an excellent day outdoors.

The forest is also home to the headwater of Zekiah Swamp, which empties into the Wicomico River and provides a home for wildlife. The abundance of wildlife was one of the reasons the Piscataway people used this land in winter for hunting and gathering. Colonists were unsuccessful in their attempt to drain the swamp—drainage ditches can still be spotted today. The Maryland Department of Human Resources purchased the land in

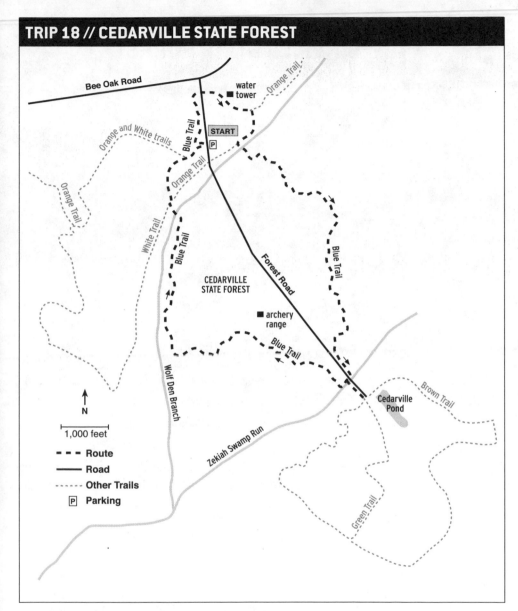

1930 for a forest demonstration area. In 1933, the Civilian Conservation Corps developed roads and trails.

Today, more than 19 miles of trails loop through the forest. Blue Trail offers an easy way to sample the park—hikers looking for an extended outing can add other trails.

The hike on Blue Trail starts at the Charcoal Kiln parking lot. The kiln here is the last of three that were operational in the park in the 1950s, producing charcoal that was used in other Maryland state parks for heat.

From the parking lot, follow the access trail past an informational sign and quickly arrive at an intersection. Turn right here to begin following conveniently blue-blazed Blue Trail. After a few minutes, the trail starts to bend to the right. Cross a forest road and pass a

The Zekiah Swamp Run feeds into the Zekiah Swamp, the largest hardwood swamp in Maryland.

picnic area to your left. With its wide treadway, the trail feels more like a forest road here. Pass a water tower before arriving at the intersection with Orange Trail. Continue straight to follow Blue Trail.

(*Note*: A portion of Blue Trail was closed at the time of publication due to an unsafe bridge. Should the closure still be in effect, follow the well-marked detour along Orange Trail to Forest Road. Turn left on Forest Road, cross the bridge, and then look for the detour signs to your left. Follow the detour, a service road, back into the woods and to Blue Trail. This adds 0.3 mile to the overall distance.)

The walk along Blue Trail is relatively easy as it meanders through the woods, crossing old forest roads. At 2.3 miles into the hike, the trail travels alongside Zekiah Swamp Run, offering pleasant views of this small stream. Then the trail intersects again with Forest Road. From here, it is worth turning left onto Forest Road for a short detour to Cedarville Pond. This 3-acre pond is stocked with bluegill, catfish, and bass and has numerous benches to allow for a relaxing stop. (Hikers seeking to tack on more miles could opt to take the Brown or Green loop trails around the pond. Doing so would add 2.0 to 2.5 miles to the route.)

To continue the route, follow Forest Road back to the intersection and turn left onto Blue Trail, which briefly follows Zekiah Swamp Run again before bending back into the forest. Here, the trail takes an interesting turn as it passes through an archery range. The 28-target range is certified by the Maryland Archery Association and the National Field Archery Association as a pro-am field and hunter competition course.

The trail leaves the archery range and crosses another forest road. While the walking is still easy, the trail begins to climb and fall more than in the beginning. It swings to the right and parallels Wolf Den Branch, which can be seen to the left. Cross Wolf Den Branch and arrive at a three-way intersection where Blue, Orange, and White trails meet. Proceed straight through the intersection to start following the now blue-orange-white-blazed trail. After a short distance, Orange Trail peels off to the left. Stay on the combined Blue and White trails straight through the intersection. The trails climb briefly before arriving back at the trailhead.

MORE INFORMATION

Cedarville State Forest's address is 10201 Bee Oak Road, Brandywine, MD 20613. Day-use fees are $3 per vehicle for Maryland residents and $5 per vehicle for out-of-state visitors. For those wanting to do more than hike, Cedarville State Forest offers numerous outdoors activities, including camping and hunting. Camping is available from April to October, and reservations can be made anytime online (parkreservations.maryland.gov) or from Monday to Friday, 9 A.M. to 5 P.M., by calling 888-432-2267. During hunting season, visitors using trails in hunting areas should wear blaze orange.

NEARBY

The town of Waldorf, a few miles south, offers restaurants and shopping opportunities. Hikers interested in exploring more of this region can also check out Piscataway Park (Trip 17).

19 BLOCKHOUSE POINT CONSERVATION PARK

This rewarding hike offers Potomac River views and a stroll through history.

Features 🚶🐕💧🌿

Location Potomac, MD

Rating Easy

Distance 2.7 miles round-trip

Elevation Gain 330 feet

Estimated Time 1–1.5 hours

Maps Online: montgomeryparks.org/wp-content/uploads/2016/08/BlockhousePoint_a11y.pdf

GPS Coordinates 39° 04.240′ N, 77° 18.550′ W

Contact Blockhouse Point Conservation Park, montgomeryparks.org/parks-and-trails/blockhouse-point-conservation-park-trails, 301-495-2595

DIRECTIONS

From I-495 (Capital Beltway), take Exit 39 to River Road/MD 190 W. Drive 10.0 miles on River Road. Pass the first parking lot on the left, and park at the second smaller lot across from Petit Way.

TRAIL DESCRIPTION

Blockhouse Point Conservation Park offers views of the Potomac River and the Chesapeake & Ohio Canal along trails that are part of a historical Civil War complex. The park consists of 630 acres, and trails pass through mature upland forests.

The park is named after one of the blockhouses that was associated with the Muddy Branch camps established by the Union army during the Civil War to guard against raids into Washington, D.C., from the Potomac River. Blockhouses were small fortifications built with loopholes to allow for firing in various directions. The blockhouse here was burned in 1864—Union troops had left the building to aid in the defense of Washington, D.C., against an attack by the Confederate general Jubal Early. The structure was never rebuilt.

Today, the trails navigate the routes taken by troops to get to the blockhouse and nearby camps—these routes are more than 140 years old. From the parking area, follow Blockhouse Trail, which slowly descends as it passes intersections with Fawn Trail and Turkey Fan Trail in quick succession. Look for trees common to upland forests: chestnut, red and white oaks, tulip poplars, and hickories.

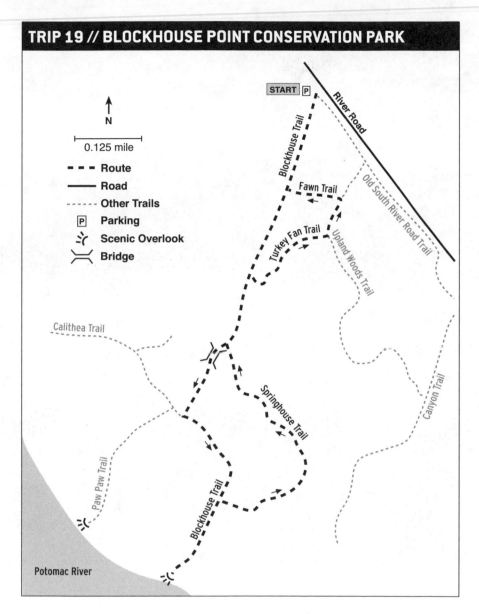

N

0.125 mile

- - - Route
——— Road
------ Other Trails
P Parking
Scenic Overlook
Bridge

START P

River Road

Blockhouse Trail

Fawn Trail

Old South River Road Trail

Turkey Fan Trail

Upland Woods Trail

Calithea Trail

Canyon Trail

Springhouse Trail

Paw Paw Trail

Blockhouse Trail

Potomac River

At an intersection with Springhouse Trail, follow Blockhouse Trail to the right and cross a wooden bridge. The trail climbs briefly and then reaches another intersection. Turn right here to stay on Blockhouse Trail. As the trail nears the river, it passes another intersection with Springhouse Trail and then starts to sharply descend before arriving at the overlook at 1.1 miles into the hike.

It is no wonder that sentries used this vantage point to guard the river. The site provides a stunning view of the Potomac. (The Maryland-National Capital Park and Planning Commission's Montgomery Parks division helpfully installed a selfie stand to allow visitors to capture the moment. These stands have been placed at particularly scenic sites in several parks throughout Montgomery County.)

Views from the overlook demonstrate the strategic importance of this site.

From here, follow Blockhouse Trail back uphill to the signed intersection with Spring-house Trail. Turn right onto Springhouse Trail, which slowly loops to the left and then descends to meet a small stream. The springs here were used as a water source for the troops stationed at the blockhouse.

The trail meets back up with Blockhouse Trail near the bridge you crossed earlier. Turn right onto Blockhouse Trail, which slowly makes its way uphill. At 2.0 miles into the hike, turn right at the signed intersection to follow Turkey Fan Trail. The climb gets a little steeper and then levels out. At the signed intersection with Upland Woods Trail, turn left to walk this trail briefly. Turn left at the next intersection onto Fawn Trail, which dips slightly and then meets up with Blockhouse Trail. Turn right to rejoin Blockhouse Trail for the last 0.2 mile back to the parking lot.

MORE INFORMATION

Blockhouse Point Conservation Park is open sunrise to sunset.

NEARBY

More hiking opportunities can be found along Muddy Branch Greenway Trail. This 9-mile natural-surface trail runs from the larger parking lot at Blockhouse Point Conservation Park to Darnestown Road in Gaithersburg, Maryland. The trail mostly follows the Muddy Branch stream, which empties into the Potomac. If the selfie stand whetted your appetite to be Instagram famous, the sunflower fields at nearby McKee-Beshers Wildlife Management Area await. Consider rounding out the day with a stop at Rocklands Farm Winery, which offers food trucks from local vendors on weekends and wine tastings for those looking to relax and refuel.

PEACE AND LONG LIFE: SPIRIT WITHIN A TREE

They live quiet, highly restricted, sometimes very long lives—often outlasting their care-takers—in cramped quarters. Grown usually from standard-sized stock or seed, they are kept artificially small, their appendages bound by fired clay, rope, and wire. They undergo frequent pruning and root reductions, performed with reverence and patience by skilled masters using the tools of an ancient art. Perhaps surprisingly, they thrive under such con-ditions and tend to live longer than their wild counterparts.

In the Japanese tradition, these tiny plants, often trees, are known as bonsai ("tree in pot") and grown in shallow, plain ceramic trays that showcase their beauty. Chinese growers call them *penjing* ("scene in pot") and cultivate them in deeper, more decorative containers, sometimes adding whimsical animal and human figurines. For centuries, both cultures have honored these miniature giants, a captured landscape symbolizing the inner forest.

Maintained as a symbol of spiritual simplicity, tranquility, and depth—allowed to grow and flower according to their natures, yet deliberately refined to a standard of minimalis-tic, truth-enhancing beauty—the plants are a sort of Buddhist "middle path" in high horticultural art. Western interest in bonsai blossomed in the 1950s and 1960s, when the Allies occupied Japan. Asian thought in general came into vogue in the United States at that time, thanks partly to the literary Beat movement. Sadly, by that time, many centu-ries-old bonsai in the ancient and renowned Japanese imperial collection and elsewhere had been destroyed by World War II bombs.

"Further limitations release deeper powers," wrote the poet May Sarton. She could have been speaking of one bonsai in particular in the National Arboretum's National Bonsai & Penjing Museum: a prized Japanese white pine about 3½ feet tall and 4 feet wide. When the United States dropped the atomic bomb on Hiroshima on August 6, 1945, this bonsai at the Yamaki Bonsai Nursery, just 2 miles away, survived. Concrete walls surrounding the nursery saved this bonsai and others from devastation.

A bicentennial gift to the United States from Japan, this nearly 400-year-old white pine bonsai survived the 1945 atomic blast at Hiroshima.

The tiny tree was donated to the United States in 1976 as part of a bicentennial peace-and-reconciliation gift by the bon-sai master Masaru Yamaki, a descendant of the grower who had begun training the little evergreen nearly 400 years ago, in 1625. Generations of the Yamaki family had cared for it ever since; the Yamaki family also survived the 1945 blast. This lush, healthy, venerable old tree's branches form successively rising, soft green arms steps—as if the plant itself is happily beckoning visitors to keep growing, to flourish, to overcome, and to seek peace in simplicity.

20 CAPITAL CRESCENT TRAIL

Popular with local commuters, this shady, gently descending paved rail-trail travels through historical areas in Maryland and Washington, D.C., offering views of the Chesapeake & Ohio Canal, the Potomac River, and several attractive old railway crossings.

Features 👥 🐕 💧 🏕 🚌 🚴

Location Bethesda, MD, and Georgetown, Washington, D.C.

Rating Moderate

Distance 7.8 miles one way

Elevation Gain −310 feet downslope

Estimated Time 3 hours

Maps USGS Washington West; online: cctrail.org/map

GPS Coordinates 38° 58.846′ N, 77° 05.655′ W

Contact Coalition for the Capital Crescent Trail, cctrail.org

DIRECTIONS

From I-495 (Capital Beltway), take Exit 34 (Wisconsin Avenue/Bethesda/Rockville) and follow MD 355 (Rockville Pike/Wisconsin Avenue) south 2.8 miles. Turn right onto Bethesda Avenue. Make a tight left onto Woodmont Avenue—the Capital Crescent Public Parking lot is on the left. When you leave the parking garage, be sure to note the exit, as the garage has several. Once at street level, head to the corner of Woodmont and Bethesda avenues. Next to Ourisman Honda, look for a paved path. A digital sign marks the start of Capital Crescent Trail and displays a daily tally of visitors to the trail. (Note that this trip is a one-way hike, so plan on taking public transportation to return to your car.)

If using public transportation, take Metrorail's Red Line to the Bethesda station. Exit the station through the bus transportation hub, heading west to Woodmont Avenue. Turn left onto Woodmont Avenue and continue south until it intersects with Bethesda Avenue. Capital Crescent Trail is on the right, next to Ourisman Honda—look for the digital sign indicating the trail's start. For information on Metrorail schedules, routes, and fares, visit wmata.com.

TRAIL DESCRIPTION

Capital Crescent Trail is a local rails-to-trails creation that follows the roadbed of the Baltimore & Ohio (B&O) Railroad's old Georgetown Branch line. This line began in the 1880s when the B&O's competitor, the Pennsylvania Railroad, refused to allow other rail

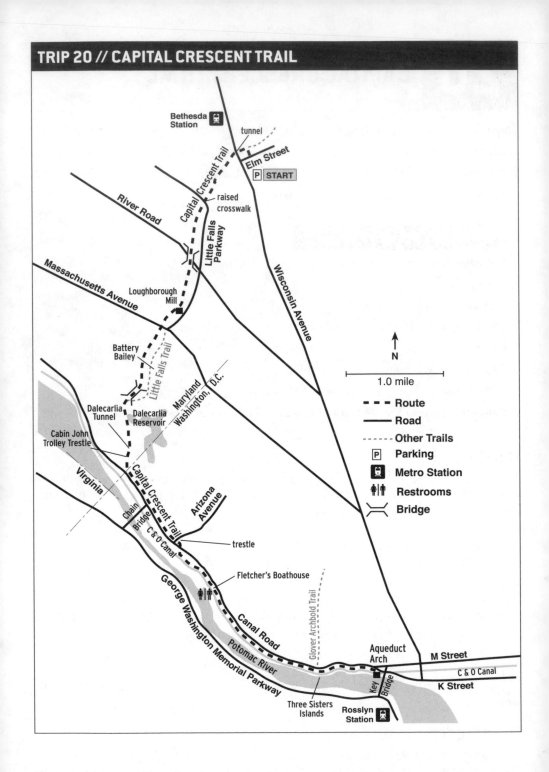

companies access to its Potomac River bridges in and around Washington, D.C. The B&O planned to build a new river crossing near present-day Chain Bridge, connecting Baltimore and Washington with cities in the South. By the early 1900s, rail companies were working more cooperatively, however, and the B&O's trans-Potomac connection north of Washington, D.C., was never built. (The Georgetown Branch line did operate from Georgetown to Silver Spring, mainly as a freight route, until 1985.) Local efforts created the present-day trail, which is popular with commuters, athletes, and leisure seekers.

Construction for the Metro's Purple Line has affected the northernmost portion of this trail, with the area east of Bethesda closed to accommodate the building of the new line.

Start the hike at the digital sign near Ourisman Honda, and turn onto the paved path. A little farther on, a water fountain and benches are available by a wayside sign about trail history. Many hikers may not notice that the trail slopes gently downhill. The first road crossing comes just before the 1-mile point: take the raised crosswalk over Little Falls Parkway. A quarter-mile farther, past a small park on the right with lovely white pines, cross Dorset Avenue, a more residential road. Pass milepost 4.5—no, the hike hasn't gone by this quickly! The mile count begins at the Lyttonsville–Silver Spring end. This is 1.3 miles for the hike—subtract roughly 3 miles from each milepost to estimate your progress. Here, find another rest and water stop by the inclined bridge over busy River Road.

Arrive at the marker for Loughborough Mill, built around 1830 by the local businessman and federal office seeker Nathan Loughborough. The mill closed in the early 1860s when the Loughborough family, Virginians by birth, moved south to support the Confederacy.

At milepost 5.5 (2.3) is a brief reference to and glimpse of Battery Bailey, a nearby Civil War fortification built to protect the Washington, D.C., water reservoir from Confederate attack. In another 0.4 mile, look for a majestic old oak tree on the right.

Cross what locals call the "bridge over nothing" at Little Falls Trail, which once protected the water conduits below from the railway's weight and vibrations. Those conduits allow water to flow from the Potomac River into the Dalecarlia Reservoir, now visible on the left. Just ahead is the brick Dalecarlia Tunnel, built in 1910—one of the trail's jewels. Walking through the cool, dim 341-foot-long passage, note the arched "step-backs" or "duck-ins" intended to protect track workers from passing trains.

At milepost 6.5 (3.4) is another rest and water stop, just before the Cabin John Trolley Trestle, which passes over an old streetcar route that was once popular with summer visitors traveling to the Glen Echo amusement park. In spring, look right to see crabapple trees blooming. Look left to see the Washington Aqueduct water tower, established in 1853. Now cross the boundary into the District of Columbia. (*Note*: Except at Fletcher's Cove and Boathouse, no resting places exist along the Washington, D.C., leg of the trail.)

The Chesapeake & Ohio (C&O) Canal is just below the trail at this point, and the Potomac River and many elegant cliffside homes are visible. Look above to get a sense of the Potomac's erosive power over time. The landscape is wilder here, and invasive kudzu spills over the branches of large trees. Wild strawberries and blackberries appear at the trail's edge in late spring and summer. In 0.5 mile, if the flora isn't too overgrown, it might be possible to spot historical Chain Bridge at river level. Vines also grow up and over the Arizona Avenue Trestle, another trail showpiece 0.5 mile ahead, built around 1910 with pieces salvaged from other structures.

Capital Crescent Trail's Arizona Avenue trestle was built around 1910 of metal salvaged from three older bridges. Decking for bicycles was added in the 1990s.

From here, the trail parallels the C&O Canal and its towpath. A half-mile more brings you to Fletcher's Cove and Boathouse at your mile 5.6. Portable toilets, a seasonal snack bar and boathouse, picnic tables, and water fountains are available in a shady riverside park. Pale-yellow columbines grow here as well. At your mile 6.7, the stone wall of the canal berm is exposed near some rough steps leading up to the towpath.

This leg of the trail has some spectacular vistas over the Potomac River. One, in particular, looks out on Three Sisters Islands, which mark the northernmost navigable point on the river for large craft. The water can smell brackish because the Potomac is a tidal river all the way up to Great Falls. At your mile 7.5, in the woods, is a stone-and-concrete bridge connecting the trail to Foxhall Road and Glover-Archbold Trail. Pass the green-painted Washington Canoe Club before reaching the stone Aqueduct Arch. The arch is actually an old abutment from a highly advanced canal bridge, built in 1843, that carried canal barges and mules across the Potomac River to connect with the Alexandria Canal. After the Civil War, the bridge was revamped with two decks to carry both water and road traffic.

At this point, climb the steps on the left up to the towpath, turn right, and cross beneath one overpass to the steps leading up to M Street NW. To return to Bethesda via public transportation, walk across Francis Scott Key Bridge into Virginia and proceed about four blocks to the Rosslyn station (Blue, Orange, and Silver lines). Farther away is the Foggy Bottom station (Blue, Orange, and Silver lines) at 23rd and I ("Eye") streets NW—aim for this station if you want to explore more of Georgetown.

MORE INFORMATION

The Coalition for the Capital Crescent Trail is an all-volunteer network that supports and promotes the trail, which is maintained by a public-private partnership between the Maryland-National Capital Park and Planning Commission's Montgomery Parks division and the National Park Service.

The Georgetown Branch portion of the Capital Crescent Trail, between Bethesda and Lyttonsville–Silver Spring, is closed due to construction for the Metro's Purple Line and likely will not reopen until late 2026 at the earliest. The Coalition for the Capital Crescent Trail maintains a Google Maps–based electronic map on its website. Visit the coalition's website (cctrail.org) for ongoing updates.

NEARBY

Restaurants and taxis are plentiful along M Street. The famous iron stairs from the film *The Exorcist* lead up toward the Georgetown University campus on the western side of the Car Barn, an old trolley storage and repair facility with a clock tower. (The film's screenplay was written by a Georgetown alumnus.) Just east of Francis Scott Key Bridge is a park dedicated to Key, the Georgetown resident and lawyer best known for penning "The Star-Spangled Banner."

CENTURIES OF PERSEVERANCE: THE CHESAPEAKE & OHIO CANAL

The dream of a transportation route to the Ohio River began in Colonial days. George Washington's numerous trips west to his headquarters in Cumberland, Maryland, both during the French and Indian War (Seven Years' War) and the Whiskey Rebellion, led to his long fascination with the river as a navigational route. He and Thomas Jefferson corresponded about this idea. Jefferson also was an advocate for development of waterways to the West. After the Revolutionary War, George Washington, envisioning a growing nation, selected sites for the new capital and a federal armory along the Potomac River. The Patowmack Company, organized by Washington himself in 1785, dredged shallows near Washington, D.C., and blasted locks around Great Falls. But progress seemed elusive; flooding damaged bypasses and sluices, stalling any forward movement and contributing to skyrocketing maintenance costs.

Ownership transferred to the Chesapeake & Ohio (C&O) Company—with the Erie Canal's former chief engineer onboard. The C&O pushed westward from D.C. in 1828 through the Potomac Valley's rugged terrain. By the numbers, the canal rises and falls more than 605 feet and requires 74 lift locks, 7 dams, 11 stone aqueducts and 1 wooden aqueduct to cross major streams, more than 240 culverts to cross smaller ones, and one 0.6-mile tunnel.

Just steps from Georgetown's bustling streets, the C&O Canal Towpath offers a serene footpath and glimpses of this historic route.

But by the time the canal reached Cumberland, Maryland—184.5 miles upstream—in 1850, the upstart Baltimore & Ohio (B&O) Railroad had beaten it there by eight years (and gone beyond). This complication limited the canal mainly to local traffic—coal for Georgetown's foundries and breweries, produce for city markets. By 1860, decades of legal battles and loan interest left the canal company facing massive deficits. The C&O would never come within 100 miles of the Ohio River.

Postbellum growth put investors into the black at last. But in 1889, with railroads enjoying ever-greater transportation dominance, a hurricane in the Washington, D.C., area caused flooding that shoved barges and lockhouses into the nearby Potomac. Repairs were prohibitively expensive, so the B&O Railroad took over the beleaguered waterway in 1890 and kept it going. By 1924, when another major flood hit, canal operations were halted. (Nature's bad moods likewise stumped later New Deal efforts to reinvent the canal as a recreation area.)

Following World War II, the U.S. Army Corps of Engineers proposed a plan to build several dams on the Potomac that would result in flooding some areas—including the historic downtown of Harpers Ferry. Plans were also floated to turn the canal into a parkway—an idea that the *Washington Post* favored. Outdoor enthusiast and Supreme Court justice William O. Douglas frequently hiked along the towpath and believed the canal was worth saving. In a letter to the *Washington Post*, he wrote "[t]he stretch of 185 miles of country from Washington, D.C. to Cumberland, MD is one of the most fascinating and picturesque in the Nation" and challenged the editors to hike the entire 184.5-mile C&O towpath with him. With widespread media coverage, this hike, which started on March 20, 1954 from Cumberland, fascinated the nation. Support grew in favor of preserving the canal—and the *Post* even adjusted its stance. In 1971, the C&O was designated a National Historic Park at last.

The canal was the 11th-most visited national park in the nation in 2021, with hikers and bikers exploring the towpath and the more than 1,300 historical structures that lie within the park's boundaries.

21 BILLY GOAT TRAIL AT GREAT FALLS

Billy Goat Trail at Great Falls is one of the metro region's most popular—and most spectacular—hikes, tracing the top of the 50-foot Mather Gorge above the Potomac River.

Features 🥾 ♿ 💧 🌸 ⬆️ 💲

Location Great Falls, MD

Rating Strenuous

Distance 5.2-mile loop

Elevation Gain 435 feet

Estimated Time 4–4.5 hours

Maps USGS Falls Church; Potomac Appalachian Trail Club Map D: Potomac Gorge Area; free National Park Service map of Chesapeake & Ohio Canal at visitor center; online: nps.gov/choh/planyourvisit/maps.htm

GPS Coordinates 39° 0.149' N, 77° 14.809' W

Contact Chesapeake & Ohio Canal National Historical Park, National Park Service, nps.gov/choh/planyourvisit/billy-goat-trail.htm, 301-739-4200

DIRECTIONS
From I-495 (Capital Beltway) near the American Legion Bridge, take Exit 41 (Carderock/Glen Echo) onto Clara Barton Parkway. Turn left onto MacArthur Boulevard. Go 2.5 miles to the intersection with Falls Road. Turn left into the Chesapeake & Ohio Canal National Historical Park entrance.

TRAIL DESCRIPTION
Billy Goat Trail is actually three separate trails, all linked by the Chesapeake & Ohio (C&O) Canal towpath on the Maryland side of the beautiful Potomac River's Great Falls. (For good hiking on the Virginia side of Great Falls, see Trip 45: Riverbend Park and Great Falls Park.) This hike proceeds downriver on section A—a difficult rock scramble—and returns via less-used forest trails. The C&O Canal towpath offers flat ground between the challenging sections. The land here falls within the Potomac Gorge, a biologically diverse 15-mile stretch located at the fall line. Surprisingly for a metropolitan region, this is one of the continent's most intact fall lines, unaffected by dams and riverfront development. At Great Falls, the river drops 60 feet in less than 1 mile. Rare plant species (Indian grass, rough rush grass, and bluestem—the latter more common to Midwest prairies) survive here, deposited during periods of intense flood scouring. Threatening these species are

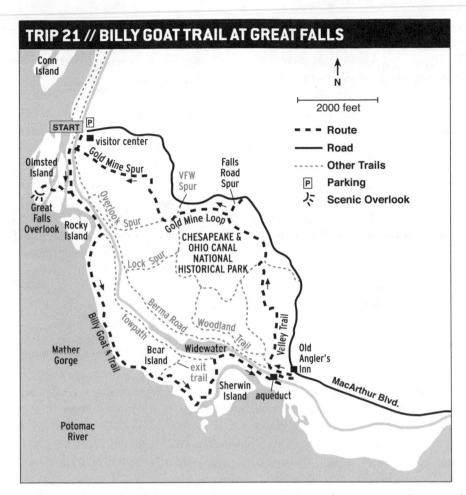

Conn Island

N

2000 feet

- - - Route
—— Road
----- Other Trails
P Parking
Scenic Overlook

START   P
visitor center
Gold Mine Spur
Olmsted Island
Great Falls Overlook   Rocky Island
Overlook Spur
VFW Spur
Falls Road Spur
Gold Mine Loop
CHESAPEAKE & OHIO CANAL NATIONAL HISTORICAL PARK
Lock Spur
Berma Road
Woodland Trail
Valley Trail
Billy Goat Trail
towpath
Mather Gorge
Bear Island
Widewater
exit trail
Old Angler's Inn
MacArthur Blvd.
Sherwin Island   aqueduct
Potomac River

humans (stay on the blazed trails) and nonnative species, such as Japanese honeysuckle, kudzu, and garlic mustard.

From the large parking lot, pass the circa-1850s Washington Aqueduct gatehouse and enter the Great Falls Tavern Visitor Center, which has in-depth exhibits on the ill-fated C&O Canal. The canal took decades to build and was quickly usurped as a transportation corridor by the B&O Railroad (see "Centuries of Perseverance: The Chesapeake & Ohio Canal," on page 92). The visitor center building was constructed in 1828 as a lockhouse, and in 1831 the lockkeeper added a three-story north wing as a hotel and tavern for weary barge workers. From the visitor center, cross the canal on the footbridge at lock 20 and turn left (downstream) on the towpath past locks 19 and 18. Turn right just before lock 17 for a 0.1-mile side trip over the pedestrian bridge to Great Falls Overlook on Olmsted Island. The overlook offers a tremendous view of Great Falls. The island landscape here, a jumble of flat boulders crisscrossed by deep crevices, was once the Potomac riverbed. Swirling, sediment-filled river eddies carved out the crevices and potholes over time. (See "Far Away in Time: The Geology of Great Falls," on page 220.) An ecologically unique bedrock-terrace forest, featuring white oak, northern red oak, hickory, Virginia pine, and federally endangered wildflower species, such as wispy yellow nailwort and hardy rock skullcap, thrives here and on Bear Island to the south.

Return to the towpath and pass lock 17. At 0.8 mile, 30 yards before a footbridge and a stop lock (the point where the canal enters Widewater, a natural channel left dry when the river shifted course), turn right onto blue-blazed Billy Goat Trail A. The 1.7-mile section follows the eastern edge of Bear Island, another ancient riverbed, atop Mather Gorge. Overuse is threatening the more than 50 rare plant and animal species on the island, so please do not stray from the path. American hornbeam has been replanted in several damaged areas.

Given the hike's popularity, this route is now a one-way trail, which helps protect the landscape and avoid "traffic jams" at some of the more challenging spots.

Start on rocky Billy Goat Trail A through the woods, arriving at a shelf of boulders over the gorge. To the right, level rocks at the cliff's edge make a nice picnic spot. Carefully scramble atop the narrow-edged boulders, following the blue blazes forward, before swinging behind an escarpment at the edge of the gorge and gradually descending toward the river. The rock hopping becomes slightly intense as the trail moves along. A challenging 50-foot traverse along a sloping cliff face is perhaps the most difficult portion of the hike for many visitors. Climb slowly, using your hands and feet to maintain contact.

(After the traverse, an "emergency exit" trail exists for those who'd prefer to leave the rocky trail. This exit leads back to the towpath—to continue with the hike from there, turn right on the towpath and follow it to where Billy Goat Trail intersects at the end.)

After the traverse, the trail snakes along the edge of the gorge, passing several ponds and rocky hills. Descend to a point of rocks above a large channel of the Potomac River. A seashell-filled landing, shaded by sycamores, is reachable at low water. The hill just to the left is Sherwin Island. Beyond it, on the opposite heights, is the conspicuous brick auditorium of The Madeira School, an all-girls private boarding school. The trail curves back toward the canal at the end of Bear Island, following a large channel on the right. Traverse several rocky hills cut by streams and then head left, away from the channel, to the C&O Canal towpath at the end of Widewater, at 2.5 miles.

Turn right onto the towpath and follow it to a bridge that leads to Old Angler's Inn; a sign marks the intersection. Cross the bridge and head up the wooden steps. At the top of the steps, turn left onto a broad path, Berma Road, that runs atop the Washington Aqueduct on the east side of Widewater. Just before a small fenced area, turn right onto a white-blazed connector trail. Rather quickly, the trail will split—keep right to start following blue-blazed Valley Trail.

Valley Trail soon splits—stay to the right and follow the fork through the woods. Pass a spur path on the right that leads to the Rockwood School. Arrive at the intersection with blue-blazed Gold Mine Loop and turn right to start following this trail. When the trail arrives at the intersection with Falls Road Spur, turn right onto the spur for a quick side trip to see the remains of the Maryland Mine.

Gold fever began at Great Falls when a Union soldier discovered specks of gold while washing skillets in a stream. Following the Civil War, investors swarmed the area and built several 100-foot-deep mine shafts. Profits were minimal, however, and pits, shafts, trenches, and tunnels came and went. The rusty ruins here were part of the Maryland Mine, which

Hikers make their way up the Billy Goat Trail's traverse, the most challenging part of the hike. *Photo by Sandra Shaklan.*

even in its heyday was a rickety contraption of sheds and shanties stuck together on stilts at different levels.

Return to Gold Mine Loop and turn right to continue the hike. Arrive at a four-way intersection where the loop trail "closes" and VFW Spur comes in—go straight here to follow white-blazed Gold Mine Spur Trail. At this point, there's a little less than a mile left on the hike. Pass an intersection with Overlook Trail, staying on Gold Mine Spur Trail until it arrives at an intersection with an unmarked trail to the right—double blazes signal the intersection. Turn left here. (If sections of Gold Mine Spur Trail feel almost road-like, it's not your imagination—the Washington and Great Falls Railroad once ran trolleys to the area.)

After 200 yards, arrive at a somewhat confusing turn—look for the wooden steps to the right to signal where to go. Just past the bottom of the steps, a spur path to lock 19 joins from the left. Go to the right to stay on the spur path as it descends to the trailhead near the visitor center.

MORE INFORMATION

Six-day park passes for C&O Canal National Historical Park are $20 per vehicle. The passes are valid for the Great Falls area on the Maryland side of the Potomac River and the Great Falls area on the Virginia side. Canal boat rides are offered seasonally, and tickets are available on a first-come, first-served basis. The National Park Service also offers ranger-guided hiking tours of Great Falls and biking tours on the C&O Canal. It's possible to book overnight stays (by advance reservation) at one of the lockhouses along the path—learn more by visiting the C&O Canal Trust's website (canaltrust.org/programs/canal-quarters/canal-quarters-lockhouses-overview).

Dogs are prohibited on Olmsted Island and Billy Goat Trail A. Swimming at Great Falls is prohibited due to dangerous underwater currents. To learn more about human pressures on the Potomac Gorge and what can be done to lessen them, consult The Nature Conservancy's *Good Neighbor Handbook: Tips and Tools for River-Friendly Living in the Middle Potomac Region* (2005).

For those seeking an accessible option, the towpath leads to the Great Falls Overlook from the Great Falls Tavern Visitor Center. The towpath is 0.5 mile from the visitor center. It is a graded gravel path, but it can get muddy and uneven after significant rain events. The bridges to the overlook are accessible ramps of wood and cement. Videos in the visitor center are closed-captioned, and exhibits are audio-described. American Sign Language interpretation services for ranger-led programs are available—email at least three weeks in advance to make arrangements.

NEARBY

Glen Echo Park (the site of a restored amusement park that once attracted crowds of Washingtonians), the Clara Barton House, and Cabin John Trail are all worthwhile visits on the Maryland side of the Potomac Gorge. And with the park pass valid for both sides of Great Falls, it's definitely worth taking advantage of the opportunity to explore both parks. (See Trip 45: Riverbend Park and Great Falls Park.)

Many of us who have come to D.C. from else-where—as visitors or for a longer stay—are surprised to learn how many green spaces the city offers, where people can escape the stress of the nation's power centers and enjoy the solace of woods, rivers, canals, and creeks. These retreats include large, forested areas, such as 1,754-acre Rock Creek Park (more than twice the size of Central Park in New York City), Kenilworth Park and Aquatic Gardens, and Theodore Roosevelt Island; they also include narrower strips of buffer land tucked between neighborhood streets and the

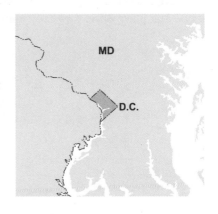

city's embassies, monuments, museums, bridges, and historical structures. Washington, D.C.'s long-standing moratorium on building any downtown structure reaching higher than the dome of the U.S. Capitol (enacted after the Washington Monument had been built) has created a sprawling skyline that encourages distinctive enclaves: the National Mall; neighborhoods such as Georgetown, Adams Morgan, Dupont Circle, Columbia Heights, Anacostia, and Brookland; and green spaces that draw hikers, cyclists, ballplayers, horseback riders, and inline skaters.

Rock Creek Park occupies a significant portion of Northwest Washington, D.C., and contains Civil War–era fortifications, historical structures, horse stables, and even a planetarium. Rock Creek Trail follows its namesake creek through the park and beyond, from the Potomac River at Foggy Bottom in the south to Lake Needwood, near Rockville, Maryland, in the north. East–west trails etch their way through the park's river valleys and rolling hills, offering creative hiking combinations, ranging from rugged treks, such as Pulpit Rock and Boulder Bridge (Trip 23), to connecting leafy corridors (Trip 24: Around Georgetown) to the Chesapeake & Ohio (C&O) Canal Trail, which parallels the Potomac on the Georgetown waterfront as it begins its journey to Cumberland, Maryland, 184.5 miles northwest.

Complementing the relative wilds of Rock Creek Park are the meticulously planned and engineered yet lovely green spaces of the U.S. National Arboretum (Trip 28) and Kenilworth Park and Aquatic Gardens (Trip 29). The arboretum is a haven for tree lovers, featuring rare dwarf conifers, ancient bonsai, and dawn redwoods, which were once thought extinct. Kenilworth Aquatic Gardens is fragrant with brilliant-flowered lotuses and waterlilies sustained within a marsh habitat. Both of these nature reservations straddle the Anacostia River, attracting ospreys, great blue herons, egrets, bald eagles, and a host of migratory songbirds. Take in more of the Anacostia River by exploring the Riverwalk (Trip 31) or Kingman and Heritage Islands (Trip 30); both trips are new additions to this book.

Two islands, the natural Theodore Roosevelt Island (Trip 27) and the human-made East Potomac Park and Monuments (Trip 26), offer secluded walks, thought-provoking memorials, and alluring flora (such as cherry blossoms in season) within the busy borders of Washington, D.C. If you've lived here a while, be a tourist again—enjoy a walking tour of the ever-popular National Mall (Trip 25), sometimes called the nation's backyard, which, with its famous monuments, Smithsonian museums, and lesser-known garden spots, serves as a perfect playground for nearly limitless exploration and enjoyment.

Rock Creek Park is a natural oasis in the heart of the nation's capital: 1,754 hilly, wooded acres contain the surprisingly turbulent Rock Creek, historical sites, and miles of challenging trails.

Features

Location Northwest Washington, D.C.

Rating Moderate

Distance 6.1-mile loop

Elevation Gain 840 feet

Estimated Time 2.5–3 hours

Maps USGS Washington West; Potomac Appalachian Trail Club Map N: Trails in the Rock Creek Area, Washington, D.C.; National Park Service brochure map available at the nature center; online: nps.gov/rocr/planyourvisit/maps.htm

GPS Coordinates 38° 57.537′ N, 77° 3.080′ W

Contact Rock Creek Park, National Park Service, nps.gov/rocr/index.htm, 202-895-6000

DIRECTIONS

From downtown Washington, D.C., take Connecticut Avenue NW north to Nebraska Avenue NW. Turn right onto Nebraska Avenue for 0.4 mile. Turn right onto Military Road and drive east 0.7 mile. Then turn right onto Glover Road to enter Rock Creek Park, driving 0.4 mile and taking the first left into the parking lot for the Rock Creek Park Nature Center and Planetarium.

If using public transportation, from either the Friendship Heights Metro station (Red Line) or the Fort Totten station (Red, Yellow, and Green lines), take Metrobus E2 or E3 down Military Road. Exit at Oregon Avenue opposite Glover Road. From the southeast side of the intersection, walk uphill a short distance to the nature center. Visit wmata.com for the latest bus schedules.

TRAIL DESCRIPTION

Rock Creek Park is a national park that covers 1,754 acres—more than twice the area of Central Park in New York City—and reaches from the northern tip of Washington, D.C., all the way south to the Potomac River at Foggy Bottom and Georgetown. Rock Creek Park was established by an act of Congress that was signed into law by President Benjamin Harrison on September 27, 1890, the same year Yosemite became a national park. The

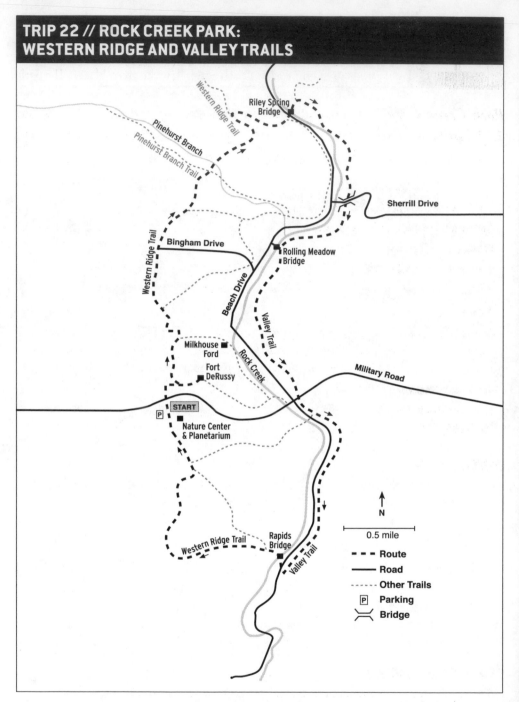

Riley Spring
Bridge

Western Ridge Trail

Pinehurst Branch

Pinehurst Branch Trail

Sherrill Drive

Western Ridge Trail

Bingham Drive

Rolling Meadow
Bridge

Beach Drive

Valley Trail

Milkhouse
Ford

Rock Creek

Fort
DeRussy

Military Road

P

START

Nature Center
& Planetarium

N

0.5 mile

Western Ridge Trail

Rapids
Bridge

Valley Trail

- - - Route
——— Road
········· Other Trails
P Parking
⋈ Bridge

park's two major trails are blue-blazed Valley Trail along the east side of the creek and green-blazed Western Ridge Trail along the park's western ridge. This hike centers on the northern half of the park and follows Western Ridge Trail north, cuts east across the wooded hills, and returns south on Valley Trail.

From the front door of the nature center, walk straight to blacktop Western Ridge Trail, which parallels Glover Road. Turn right, following signs to Fort DeRussy. Cross Military Road and proceed uphill. When you reach the National Park Service sign relating the history of Fort DeRussy, turn right onto the dirt path and follow the green blazes. The path splits, and the green-blazed fork goes to the left. Continue straight ahead to see the remains of Fort DeRussy. Look for a sign, a plaque, and a spur path on the left that leads around the structure's dirt-covered fortifications. Fort DeRussy was one of the forts surrounding Washington, D.C., during the Civil War. It was built in 1861 and placed on high ground to guard movement in the Rock Creek valley.

After visiting the fort, return to the intersection with green-blazed Western Ridge Trail and turn right onto that trail. Head downhill on a series of gradual, easy switchbacks. At 0.7 mile into the hike, where a sign points straight ahead for Milkhouse Ford, turn left and stay on Western Ridge Trail. Cross a small creek and turn right, traveling between the park police horse stables and garden plots. Turn left at a T intersection with a service road. Follow the service road briefly and then turn right to rejoin the green-blazed blacktop trail.

Cross Bingham Drive and turn right into the woods to follow the trail, now dirt. Ascend through thickets of viburnum shrubs rich with red berries through fall and cut to the left at a Y intersection to stay on the green-blazed trail. The trail goes down a hill and intersects with Pinehurst Branch Trail at the bottom. Stay on Western Ridge Trail as it bends to the right and then turns left. Cross the stream and head uphill through beeches and oaks. At the top of the hill, the trail passes through a narrow section. Stay on the green-blazed trail as it passes an intersection with an unnamed white-blazed trail before arriving at another intersection with an unblazed, unnamed path. Turn right onto this unmarked path as it makes its way downhill toward the Riley Spring Bridge. As the bridge comes into sight, bear to the left at the Y intersection to head toward Beach Drive and the bridge.

Cross the bridge over Rock Creek and turn right onto blue-blazed Valley Trail, where a sign indicates a distance of 1.6 miles to Military Road. Rock Creek is gentle and meandering here, and the trail travels alongside the creek, making for a pleasant walk. After a half-mile, the trail passes through an area of gnarled black birches and under Sherrill Drive Bridge before fording a small feeder stream and passing Rolling Meadow Bridge on the right. Cross a wooden walkway over another stream. Just after crossing the stream, the trail comes to a three-way split. The blue blazes can be hard to spot here, but aim for the trail in the middle, which climbs uphill and then drops back down to Beach Drive before crossing under Military Road.

Here, Valley Trail follows Beach Drive south to the park police station. Just after the station, look for the blue blazes, which lead back into the woods. The trail is a little rockier in this stretch with some steep pitches as it wends its way along the ridge to a wooden bridge spanning a small ravine. Turn right immediately after the bridge to stay on blue-blazed Valley Trail.

Go back downhill over more rocky terrain, following Rock Creek on the right. The Rapids Bridge soon comes into sight. To safely exit Valley Trail, proceed a few steps past the bridge to find a short access trail that brings to you to Rock Creek. Cross the creek on Rapids Bridge. This bridge offers perhaps the best view of Rock Creek in the entire park, with water slamming over, under, and around large boulders to the north and south. Turn left at the T intersection at the end of the bridge, walk approximately 75 yards, and turn right onto an unmarked trail. Go steeply uphill, staying to the left at a Y intersection to cross over Ross Drive. Cross Ridge Road at 5.7 miles. Green-blazed Western Ridge Trail lies straight ahead; turn right to start following this trail that will soon cross Grant Road. A picnic area will soon come into view. Cross Ridge and Glover roads in quick succession and stay on Western Ridge Trail as it climbs back to the nature center.

MORE INFORMATION

Be sure to pick up a park map and brochure at the nature center before you start your hike. The amenities at Rock Creek Park include 29 picnic areas, a large recreation field, 25 tennis courts, a public golf course, a 1.5-mile exercise course, bicycle routes, 13 miles of bridle trails, an equestrian field, and a horse center. For more information, visit nps.gov/rocr or call 202-895-6000.

Hikers looking for an accessible option can explore Edge of the Woods Trail, which begins near the front door of the nature center. This 0.25-mile paved path leads past oak, tulip, and chestnut trees.

Valley Trail runs alongside Rock Creek, giving hikers a chance to enjoy this easy stretch with water views.

NEARBY

After all this hiking, you'll likely have a good appetite. Head to the Adams Morgan neighborhood, centered at 18th Street and Columbia Road NW, to sample a wide array of restaurants featuring cuisines from across the world. See washington.org /dc-neighborhoods/adams-morgan for ideas.

If you are up for more walking, stroll to Meridian Hill Park, also known as Malcolm X Park, along 16th Street between W and Euclid streets NW, a noncontiguous section of Rock Creek Park. Here, you can enjoy an unusual cascading waterfall of 13 successive basins and see the statue of Joan of Arc, the only female equestrian statue in the city. If you visit on a Sunday, stop and join the regular Sunday afternoon drum circle and dancing—a tradition here since the 1950s. Work is currently under way (as of summer 2022) in the lower terrace of Meridian Hill Park, which will create an accessible route to the lower level at 16th Street NW, as well as other improvements to the park. Visit nps.gov/places/meridian-hill-park.htm to learn more.

RINGING AROUND THE CITY

From 1861 to 1864, Washington, D.C., was transformed into a heavily fortified city—perhaps the most fortified in the world at the time—with its "ring forts" known as the Civil War Defenses of Washington. Construction of these forts began partially in response to the Confederate victory at the First Battle of Manassas—leaders in the capital were concerned that the city was ill-equipped to adequately defend itself.

The U.S. Army's chief engineer, Major John G. Barnard, gathered resources and began the process of fortifying the capital city. By 1865, Washington, D.C., was circled by 68 enclosed forts and batteries, emplacements for 1,120 guns, 93 additional unarmed batteries with 401 emplacements for field guns, 20 miles of rifle trenches, and 800 cannons. The defenses were linked by 32 miles of military roads.

Today, remnants of these forts are managed by the National Park Service and can be visited. Rock Creek Park (Trip 22) houses the well-preserved earthworks of Fort DeRussy, among others. Fort Reno (previously known as Fort Pennsylvania) in Northwest Washington, sits at the city's highest elevation of 476 feet; it guarded the approach from what was then called Rockville Pike (now Wisconsin Avenue). Fort Mahan was constructed to guard Benning Bridge. Fort Dupont was shaped like a hexagon and protected by a moat. It had 2,000 square feet of barracks with a mess hall, plus officer's quarters.

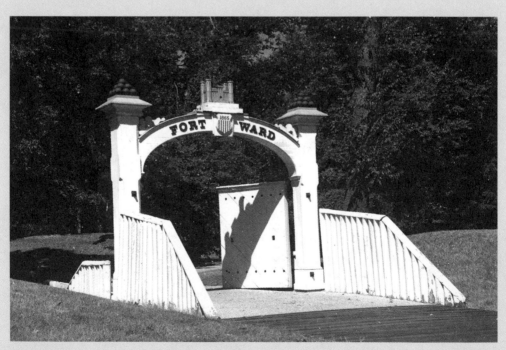

Fort Ward is one of the best-preserved forts, with 90 percent of its earthen walls intact. Visitors can explore the site to learn more about the fort itself and the post–Civil War community ("The Fort") that developed around it.

Fort Stevens, in Northwest Washington, was the site of a battle in 1864 as the Confederate lieutenant General Jubal Early approached the city. After two days of fighting, the battle ended with Early unable to advance. Most famously, U.S. president Abraham Lincoln observed the battle—this is considered to be the only time a U.S. president has been under enemy fire. A popular and well-repeated, although unconfirmed, anecdote is that someone shouted, "Get down, you fool!" at Lincoln as the fort came under fire while he was surveying its defenses.

Many of the forts are also linked to the development of African American communities surrounding them. Formerly enslaved people who had escaped from plantations in Maryland and Virginia came to the forts and eventually settled in the neighborhoods nearby. To document that history, the National Park Service is now working with American University to learn more about those neighborhoods with the African American Civil War Descendants Study. The study is initially looking at eight communities: Fort Davis, Fort Dupont, and Fort Mahan in Anacostia; Fort Bunker Hill in Northeast Washington; and Fort Reno, Fort Slocum, Fort Stevens, and Battery Kemble in Northwest Washington.

After the war, many of the forts and the areas around them were returned to the original landowners. The idea of connecting the forts came up several times, including in the McMillian Plan, the name given to the document issued by the Senate Park Commission in 1902. This report proposed creating a parkway system that would connect the forts and was one of the recommendations outlined by the commission to improve the appearance of Washington, D.C.

The parkway construction did not occur, but many of the forts are connected today by hiking and biking trails—and the defenses themselves are part of the Potomac Heritage Scenic Trail. The most well-known trail may be 7-mile Fort Circle Hiker-Biker Trail, mostly natural surface, which connects six forts as it weaves through Ward 7 and ends in Ward 8. The starting trailhead is within walking distance of the Minnesota Avenue Metro station. The trail passes Fort Mahan—it is possible to spot the Washington Monument from here—and then makes its way past Fort Chaplin before arriving at Fort Dupont. The route passes Fort Davis, Battery (Fort) Ricketts, and Fort Stanton. The nearby Anacostia Community Museum contains exhibits that provide more information about the history of the community.

23 ROCK CREEK PARK: PULPIT ROCK AND BOULDER BRIDGE

Encounter two highlights of the park during this short hike: the ascent of Pulpit Rock and views of the picturesque Boulder Bridge.

Features 🐕 💧 🅰

Location Northwest Washington, D.C.

Rating Moderate

Distance 1.5 miles round-trip

Elevation Gain 130 feet

Estimated Time 1 hour

Maps USGS Washington West; Potomac Appalachian Trail Club Map N: Trails in the Rock Creek Area, Washington, D.C.; online: nps.gov/rocr/planyourvisit/maps.htm

GPS Coordinates 38° 56.655′ N, 77° 03.017′ W

Contact Rock Creek Park, National Park Service, nps.gov/rocr/index.htm, 202-895-6000

DIRECTIONS

From downtown Washington, D.C., take Connecticut Avenue NW north to Calvert Street NW. Turn left onto Calvert Street NW, and then turn left onto the entrance to Rock Creek Parkway/Beach Drive NW. Turn left onto Beach Drive NW and follow it for 2.2 miles. Turn left onto Broad Branch Road NW and then immediately turn left to enter the Rock Creek Park parking lot.

TRAIL DESCRIPTION

Pulpit Rock offers a short and vigorous outing for hikers looking to squeeze in a quick adventure in Rock Creek Park. This trip adds Boulder Bridge, one of Rock Creek's many marvels, and returns with an easy stroll that takes advantage of the pedestrian-only section of Beach Drive. In a little less than 1.5 miles, hikers can sample all that Rock Creek Park has to offer.

From the parking lot, head toward the lot entrance and turn right. Go over the bridge and proceed toward the crosswalk where Beach Drive and Blagden Road NW intersect. Cross Beach Drive with caution—while there is a stop sign for drivers turning off Blagden Road, the traffic on Beach Drive does not have one.

Once across the road, look for a signpost on the left indicating the start of Theodore Roosevelt Trail. The yellow-blazed trail winds its way uphill. Tread carefully along this

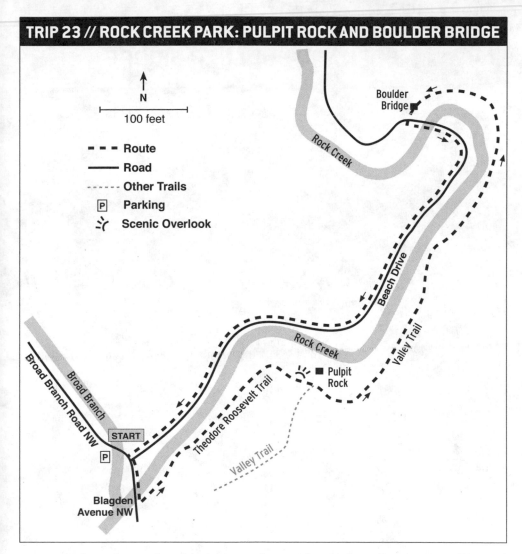

route, which is often rocky and rooty—and sometimes both at the same time. The trail quickly arrives at a split—bear right to keep following the yellow blazes uphill.

The trail parallels Rock Creek, offering excellent views of the water, before swinging to the right for the final push to Pulpit Rock. In just 0.2 mile from the start, arrive at the intersection with Valley Trail. Turn left onto the blue-blazed trail and in just a few steps arrive at the top of Pulpit Rock.

Pause a few minutes to enjoy the scenery and explore the top of the rocks. Pulpit Rock was a favorite spot of President Theodore Roosevelt, who was known to take members of his Cabinet and foreign dignitaries on energetic outings in Rock Creek Park.

When ready to resume the hike, continue along Valley Trail as it makes its way back down the hill and nears the creek again. After the rocky climb to Pulpit Rock, Valley Trail's wide path is a pleasant change. Near the bottom of the descent, proceed straight

Pulpit Rock was a favorite hike of President Theodore Roosevelt's.

through an intersection with an unmarked trail to stay on Valley Trail as it runs along the creek. The wide path eventually narrows again with a rocky stretch.

As the trail and the creek start to bend slightly to the left, Boulder Bridge comes into view. This stunning bridge, built in 1902, was designed by W. J. Douglas and is on the National Register of Historic Bridges.

Although hikers can retrace their steps back to the beginning, staying along Beach Drive offers the advantage of a car-free section and an easier path. (*Note*: At time of publication, the National Park Service was studying the feasibility of this road closure. Visit nps.gov /rocr for the latest information.) To return via Beach Drive, keep following the trail as it approaches the bridge. At the intersection, Valley Trail departs to the right—follow the side path forward to Beach Drive and turn left to cross Boulder Bridge.

From Beach Drive, hikers may be able to get a better view of Pulpit Rock—look for a weathered historical informational sign to the right to signal where to stop, and then look to the left across the creek to admire this rock formation.

The weathered sign marks where the Blagden and Argyle mills once stood. In the early 1800s, Rock Creek was the site of 26 mills. The Blagden Mill processed wheat, rye, and corn; Argyle Mill processed fertilizer. Beyond the sign is a faint trace of the old mill road and part of the millrace, which channeled the current of water that drove a mill wheel.

After taking in the sights, continue on Beach Drive to the gate that blocks Beach Drive from traffic. Use the crosswalk to cross Broad Branch Road NW and arrive back at the parking lot.

MORE INFORMATION

Rock Creek Park offers a wealth of amenities, including 29 picnic areas, a large recreation field, 25 tennis courts, a public golf course, a 1.5-mile exercise course, bicycle routes, 13 miles of bridle trails, an equestrian field, and a horse center. For more information, visit nps.gov/rocr or call 202-895-6000.

NEARBY

Take advantage of paved, multiuse Rock Creek Trail to walk a little farther south to Peirce Mill. Built in 1829 by Isaac Peirce, the mill was in operation through the 1890s. In the 1920s, it housed a tea room. It was transferred to the National Park Service in 1933 as part of New Deal legislation and was restored to its former layout in 1936. Today, the mill is available for park visitors to explore, with hours changing seasonally. Accessible parking is next to the mill, and the main and back doors are wheelchair accessible for visitors to see the first floor. Visit nps.gov/rocr/planyourvisit/peirce-mill-visitor-center.htm for the latest hours of operation.

24 AROUND GEORGETOWN

Follow woodsy avenues on each side of Georgetown for a secluded circuit hike around the leafy heart of Northwest Washington and through the southern section of Rock Creek Park.

Features

Location Northwest Washington, D.C.

Rating Moderate

Distance 6.9-mile loop

Elevation Gain 800 feet

Estimated Time 3.5 hours

Maps USGS Washington West; Potomac Appalachian Trail Club Map N

GPS Coordinates 38° 55.499′ N, 77° 03.141′ W

Contact Rock Creek Park, National Park Service, nps.gov/rocr/index.htm, 202-895-6000

DIRECTIONS

Public parking is very limited in availability and duration, so driving is not recommended for this hike. Using public transportation, take Metrorail's Red Line to the Woodley Park-Zoo/Adams Morgan station on Connecticut Avenue.

TRAIL DESCRIPTION

Rock Creek Park encompasses not only the wide swath of forest along the Rock Creek valley in Northwest Washington but also several narrow strips of parkland circling Georgetown: Montrose, Dumbarton Oaks, Whitehaven, and Glover-Archbold. This circuit hike takes advantage of these green avenues in the midst of an urban landscape. Sights include Connecticut Avenue Bridge, Holy Rood Cemetery, an abandoned railway to the former amusement park in Glen Echo Park, canal locks, Francis Scott Key Bridge, and Mount Zion Cemetery.

From the Woodley Park-Zoo/Adams Morgan Metro station, head downhill on 24th Street and cross Calvert Street. At the bottom of the hill, south of Connecticut Avenue Bridge and its famed Roland Hinton Perry lion sculptures, turn right onto paved Rock Creek Trail. Near the bridge across Rock Creek, turn right on gravel Parkway Trail (unmarked), which follows the west bank downstream. Take this leafy route past Norman-stone Trail on the right. Just before going under ivy-covered Massachusetts Avenue Bridge, look for the remains of a quarry on the right. Workers at this quarry mined norite stone, a

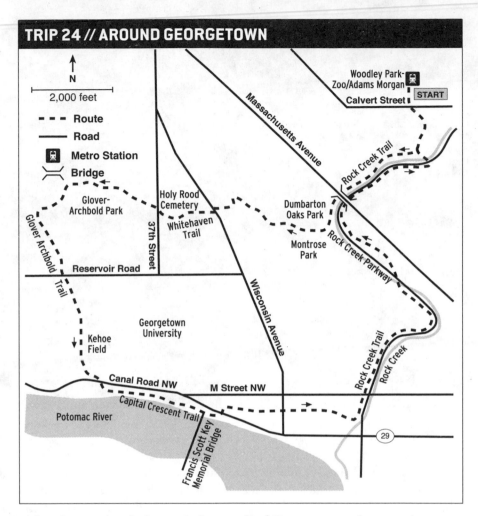

N

2,000 feet

- - - Route
— Road
Metro Station
Bridge

Woodley Park-
Zoo/Adams Morgan
Calvert Street
START

Rock Creek Trail

Glover-
Archbold Park

Holy Rood
Cemetery

Dumbarton
Oaks Park

Glover Archbold Trail

37th Street

Whitehaven
Trail

Montrose
Park

Rock Creek Parkway

Reservoir Road

Wisconsin Avenue

Georgetown
University

Kehoe
Field

Rock Creek Trail

Rock Creek

Canal Road NW

M Street NW

Capital Crescent Trail

Potomac River

Francis Scott Key
Memorial Bridge

29

type of sea-bottom basalt that underlies much of Georgetown and was used to construct the buildings at Dumbarton Oaks.

At 0.7 mile, cut away from Rock Creek and follow the dirt trail uphill along a rocky tributary, skirting the north end of Montrose Park and eventually reaching a T intersection with Lovers' Lane and the entrance to Dumbarton Oaks Park. The park was named for Dumbarton Oaks, the former private estate and gardens of Mildred and Robert Woods Bliss, and now houses a research library under the auspices of Harvard University. The institute's museum collections, gardens, and music room are open to the public most afternoons (admission fee). When the Blisses donated their estate to Harvard, they also turned over much of the land to the American people, and the National Park Service began to administer it as Dumbarton Oaks Park.

Enter the park, and proceed on a dirt trail along the left side of the creek. This "in-between" landscape—rich in sugar maples, American beeches, tulip trees, flowering dogwoods, oaks, and hickories—was originally part of the private estate, serving as a buffer between the formal gardens and the wilds of Rock Creek Park.

A busy thoroughfare from a quiet spot: the Francis Scott Key Bridge connects Rosslyn, Virginia, as seen from the C&O Canal towpath in Washington, D.C. *Photo by Stephen Mauro.*

Hike past a stone bridge and crumbling stone chimney, with hornbeams and dogwoods arching overhead, and then head uphill. Enter a small, bowl-shaped field with wildflowers, pass through wild shrubbery and a swampy section, and then climb a dirt switchback on the far side of the bowl. Upon reaching Whitehaven Street NW, turn left toward Wisconsin Avenue.

Cross Wisconsin Avenue, turn right, and walk a block for a short detour to Holy Rood Cemetery, one of the highest points in the District of Columbia. This cemetery was established in 1832 by Georgetown's Holy Trinity Catholic Church, which sits about a mile to the south. (John F. Kennedy attended this church when he lived in Georgetown during his Senate years and when he lived in the White House as president.) The cemetery has gravestones in various states of disrepair, is near the arterial bustle of Wisconsin Avenue, and offers a tree-framed view of the Washington Monument—these elements together create a uniquely Washington, D.C., atmosphere.

After strolling around the cemetery, return south down Wisconsin Avenue and turn right onto 35th Street. Just before Whitehaven Parkway, turn right onto yellow-blazed Whitehaven Trail and ascend the wooden steps up the ridge. Level off and descend the steps to 37th Street. Cross the street and enter Whitehaven Park, following a line of maple trees and passing a dog park. Return to the brush and follow the yellow blazes past a community garden on the left and a rope climb on the right to reach a T intersection at a row of townhomes. Turn right, still following the yellow blazes. At a Y intersection, take the left-hand path through hornbeams and beeches. Upon reaching another T intersection, turn left onto the yellow-blazed Glover-Archbold Trail.

Heading south toward the water, cross Foundry Branch and hike uphill through a maple-rich forest. Cross Reservoir Road, turn left past a bus stop, and turn right downhill on a barely discernible dirt trail. Walk beneath several large tulip trees and past black walnuts to the right. Continue straight to reenter the woods, passing a trail that comes in from the right. Go under an abandoned, rusted railroad bridge (the remains of a trolley line that once took people to an amusement park at what is now Glen Echo Park) and come to Foxhall Road. Turn left onto Foxhall Road and then turn left onto a path going downhill to reach a pedestrian tunnel beneath the Chesapeake & Ohio (C&O) Canal. Go through the tunnel and come out onto Capital Crescent Trail. Take the signed side path to the left to immediately connect with the gravel/clay towpath in C&O Canal National Historical Park.

Continue east on the towpath. Just after you pass arched Francis Scott Key Bridge, cross to the north side of the canal. Continue east through Georgetown. The path becomes brick, passing a series of lift locks, the National Park Service visitor center, and a bust of the Supreme Court justice William O. Douglas (see "Centuries of Perseverance: The Chesapeake & Ohio Canal," on page 92) before reaching Rock Creek Trail. Follow the trail as it bends left and then parallels busy Rock Creek Parkway. The trail turns left into the woods and crosses the bridge over Rock Creek, with Mount Zion Cemetery on the left and a clearing on the right, where old Lyons Mill once stood.

Proceed beneath Massachusetts Avenue Bridge, on the opposite bank from the first section of the hike. Follow the trail as it meanders along the creek for nearly a half-mile, cross a footbridge, and return to the exercise area just before Connecticut Avenue Bridge. Turn left uphill along Shoreham Drive, cross Calvert Street, and return to the Woodley Park-Zoo/Adams Morgan Metro station.

MORE INFORMATION
This hike has no fee, and dogs are permitted.

NEARBY
Well worth a visit, Dumbarton Oaks' pre–Columbian and Byzantine collections and its gardens are open to the public most afternoons. Visit doaks.org for details and fees.

FOR THE LOVE OF CHERRY TREES

Eliza Scidmore, an American travel writer and photographer and the National Geographic Society's first female trustee, made her initial tour of Japan in 1885 with her brother George, a U.S. diplomat who lived in Japan at the time. She was enchanted by the beauty of the flowering cherry trees (sakura)—a poignant, centuries-old symbol of ephemeral life, love, and springtime in Japanese culture. Upon returning to Washington, D.C., she approached the superintendent of public buildings and grounds to propose that such trees be planted along the Potomac's riverbanks, which were then being reclaimed from swampland. The superintendent—and his successors for the next 20-plus years—refused or ignored her requests.

Meanwhile, another world traveler, David Fairchild, a botanist with the Department of Agriculture, also had taken a fancy to the fragile, delicately rosy, fleeting sakura. He made a test planting of 100 trees on his suburban Maryland estate and found them well suited to the local climate. For Arbor Day 1908, Fairchild presented cherry saplings to children from each Washington, D.C., school to be planted in their schoolyards, based on a common tradition in Japan. Fairchild also suggested transforming the road that is now Independence Avenue SW into a "field of cherries." Scidmore, in attendance, finally saw her efforts begin to take off.

Scidmore then decided to plant sakura in the nation's capital even if she had to raise the funds herself. In early 1909, she wrote to First Lady Helen "Nellie" Taft. Helen Taft had traveled in Japan en route to Manila in 1900, when her husband, William Howard Taft, had been appointed commissioner of the Philippines. Later, as the U.S. secretary of war in 1905, William Howard Taft had helped negotiate the treaty that ended the Russo-Japanese War and had been warmly welcomed in Japan. Helen Taft was strongly interested in beautifying D.C. and embraced the cherry tree idea.

Suddenly sakura were all the rage. While visiting Washington, D.C., in April 1909, Jokichi Takamine, a Japanese chemist and discoverer of adrenaline, heard of the plan and asked a friend, the Japanese diplomat Kokichi Midzuno, if the First Lady would accept a donation of 2,000 cherry trees. Midzuno encouraged the gift and suggested making it in the name of the city of Tokyo. The First Lady gladly accepted. A few days later, the superintendent of public buildings and grounds, Colonel Spencer Cosby, ordered the purchase of 90 Fugenzo cherries, which were planted south of today's Lincoln Memorial. (They have since disappeared.)

In January 1910, Tokyo's gift of 2,000 trees landed in Washington, D.C.—infested with invasive insects. President Taft ordered them burned, with the exception of a dozen or so that were planted experimentally in East Potomac Park. The destruction of the trees nearly set off an international incident. Letters of explanation and deep regret flew east and west between Secretary of State Philander Knox, the Japanese ambassador Viscount Chinda, Colonel Cosby, and Tokyo mayor Yukio Ozaki.

Diplomacy saved the situation. Mayor Ozaki, wishing to show his gratitude to President Taft for the 1905 treaty, was gracious and undaunted. With Takamine's financial help,

Tokyo generously gifted a second shipment of 3,020 trees—comprising 12 varieties, including 1,800 Yoshino cherry trees, with their famous single white-pink blossoms—that arrived in March 1912. On March 27, Helen Taft and Viscountess Chinda, the Japanese ambassador's wife, planted D.C.'s first two Yoshino cherry trees along the Tidal Basin's northern bank.

Cherry blossoms—and the annual festival that began in 1935—quickly became a powerful tourist attraction, drawing humans and many other visitors. The small, bitter fruits serve as important food for birds, and in 1982, beavers were first spotted cruising the Tidal Basin for a potential home. When three beavers were humanely trapped in 1999 after getting their teeth into at least eight trees, their release location was kept top-secret due to heated controversy and a local desire for revenge against the vandals.

The National Park Service continues to propagate and plant cherry tree grafts along the Tidal Basin, preserving the genetic line and incomparable loveliness. When postwar Japan asked for help in replacing trees damaged by World War II bombings, Washington, D.C., repaid Tokyo's gift with cuttings from the Tidal Basin Yoshino trees in 1952 and again in 1982.

The expected life span of a Yoshino cherry tree is 45 years. Yet a century later, some 60 of the original trees sent in 1912, and possibly even a handful of the diseased 1910 shipment, survive as a blooming testament to life and springtime—perhaps even to love.

25 NATIONAL MALL

This hike explores the natural beauty found in many peaceful urban nooks and landscaped gardens along the National Mall—plus a few well-known monuments.

Features

Location Southeast, Southwest, Northwest Washington, D.C.

Rating Easy to Moderate

Distance 3.8 miles one way

Elevation Gain –70 feet downslope

Estimated Time 3 hours

Maps USGS Washington East, USGS Washington West; online: nps.gov/nama/planyourvisit/maps.htm

GPS Coordinates 38° 53.143′ N, 77° 00.360′ W

Contact National Mall and Memorial Parks, National Park Service, nps.gov/nama/index.htm, 202-426-6841

DIRECTIONS

Public parking in the city's tourist areas is very limited in availability and duration, so driving is discouraged for this hike. Using public transportation, take Metrorail's Blue, Silver, or Orange Line to the Capitol South station. Exit at 355 1st Street SE, just south of the southwest corner of First and C streets SE.

TRAIL DESCRIPTION

This urban walk takes you along a route ideal for appreciating the forethought of city planner Pierre L'Enfant (1754–1825), the classically trained French architect-engineer who enlisted with the Americans during the Revolutionary War. Following the war, in 1791, L'Enfant was appointed by President George Washington to devise a fitting layout for the capital city of a brand-new nation. This hike also features museums, memorials, and a plethora of natural retreats tucked amid the eager scrum of tourists from around the world.

Exit the Capitol South station and walk left to the corner of First and C streets SE. Continue uphill one block along 1st Street SE and cross Independence Avenue. Stay on 1st Street to get a good view of the U.S. Capitol's dome. The Capitol grounds, considered a jewel of landscape architecture, were designed by Frederick Law Olmsted, whose other credits include New York City's Central Park and Boston's "Emerald Necklace." Note how Olmsted's ironwork viewing shelter is placed perfectly for appreciating Freedom Triumphant (or

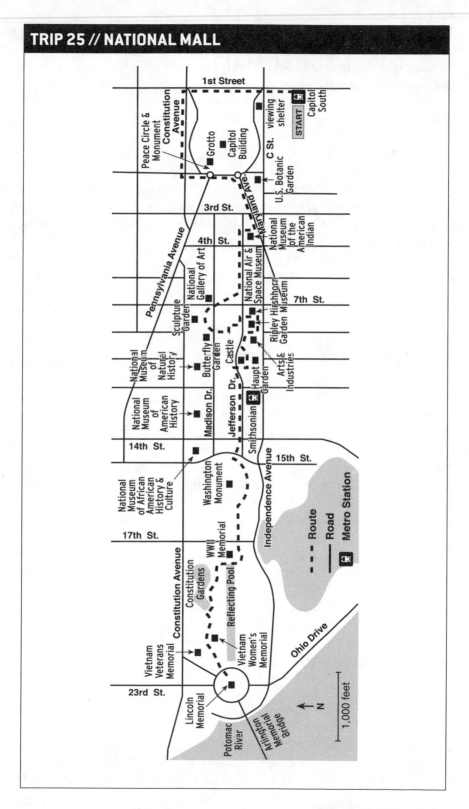

simply Freedom), the 19½-foot bronze statue crowning the Capitol's cast-iron dome. Also notice the dozens of trees planted on the Capitol grounds. Many are the official trees of various states; others are dedicated to historical figures and events. Unfortunately, some have succumbed to storms or to the construction of the Capitol's visitor center.

This area is known today as Capitol Hill; early Americans called it Jenkins Hill, and L'Enfant termed it "a pedestal awaiting a monument." On this height, L'Enfant decided, would sit the "Congress House," honoring the American people, whose representatives would meet in the edifice. To the right is Pennsylvania Avenue, which leads to the "President's Palace"—now known as the White House. L'Enfant's street plan included wide avenues named for each of the then-existing states, running diagonally across a grid of numbered and lettered streets. L'Enfant planned a long, open "grand avenue" running westward from the Capitol. Over time, this became the National Mall (yet to come into view on this hike).

Turn left at the intersection with Constitution Avenue NE, which quickly changes to Constitution Avenue NW, and follow it past the Capitol building. Turn left onto 1st Street NW and arrive at Peace Circle, named for Franklin Simmons's Peace Monument, which depicts Grief sobbing on the shoulder of History in memory of sailors lost during the Civil War. The monument's Carrara marble has suffered serious degradation from acid rain and weathering; restoration efforts are under way to prolong the statue's life. Cross the circle toward the Capitol Reflecting Pool and turn back to see the West Front, where presidential swearing-in ceremonies have taken place since Ronald Reagan's first inauguration in 1981.

Facing the Mall again, walk south, to your left, toward the conservatory of the United States Botanic Garden. Inside, visitors can enjoy rooms of cacti, orchids, and desert and tropical plants. Outside, visitors find inviting open-air plots, including the quilt-inspired First Ladies Water Garden and a pesticide-free butterfly garden.

Follow Maryland Avenue SW away from the Capitol, toward the yellow-beige National Museum of the American Indian. This building's flowing forms were designed based on consultation with American Indian communities and individuals, with an east-facing entrance and the building itself bearing similarity to a wind-sculpted rock formation. Cross 3rd Street into the museum's entrance courtyard, looking along Maryland Avenue to see Nora Naranjo-Morse's organic sculpture *Always Becoming*, and then walk around the building to enjoy the water feature, the fire pit, and the landscaping that echoes the connections to the land as it once was.

Cross 4th Street and continue along Jefferson Drive's southern sidewalk, observing a to-scale representation of the sun and the first planets of the solar system that stretches for blocks past the National Air and Space Museum. Cross Jefferson Drive and walk diagonally across the grassy Mall toward the corner of 7th Street and Madison Drive NW. Just across 7th Street is the southeast gate of the National Gallery of Art's whimsical Sculpture Garden. Enjoy splashing fountains in a large pool that becomes an outdoor ice-skating rink in winter. Many trees thrive here, including magnolias, cedars of Lebanon, and Kentucky coffee trees. Walk out to Madison Drive through the garden's southwest gate. Quickly turn right into the Butterfly Habitat Garden, where four different landscapes attract many of the 80 or so butterfly species seen in Washington, D.C. Return to Madison Drive and cross the grass back to the southern side of the Mall.

The classic spire of the Washington Monument (as seen from the Lincoln Memorial, terminus of this hike along the National Mall) provides a classic vista of Washington, D.C., looking east past the Reflecting Pool toward Pierre L'Enfant's 2-mile-long grand avenue of green space. *Photo by Brian Holland, Creative Commons on Flickr.*

Head toward a doughnut-shaped concrete building, the Hirshhorn Museum and Sculpture Garden, and pause in its sunken sculpture garden on the north side of Jefferson Drive. Among 60 other works is a piece by Auguste Rodin titled *Crouching Woman*. Cross Jefferson Drive and the Hirshhorn's fountain courtyard, turn right onto Independence Avenue SW, and turn quickly right into the Mary Livingston Ripley Garden. Ripley, an avid gardener and the wife of a former Smithsonian Institution secretary, planned a Victorian-style fragrant garden on this spot, which had been slated to become a parking lot. The Smithsonian Women's Committee, founded by Ripley, supported the idea and named the garden after her. The garden path leads back to Jefferson Drive. Turn left, pass the Arts and Industries Building, and enjoy the Kathrine Dulin Folger Rose Garden's scented splendor.

Follow the path to the left (south side) of the red Maryland sandstone Smithsonian Castle visitor center into the Enid A. Haupt Garden, with its old-fashioned, formal, clipped-shrubbery parterre beds. Note the entrances to two underground museums, the African Art Museum and the Sackler Gallery, as well as the Asian-inspired, compass-pointed, granite-and-water Moongate Garden. Walk around the Castle's west end and turn left to follow Jefferson Drive west across 14th and 15th streets SW. Look across the Mall to your right to see the National Museum of American History and the newest Smithsonian Institution museum, the National Museum of African American History & Culture, with its three tapered levels inspired by the three-tiered crowns found in art from Yoruba. The bronze-colored metal lattice enwrapping the building is a tribute to ironwork crafted by African Americans who were enslaved in the South.

Head toward the Washington Monument and climb toward its base. At the top of the slope, look straight up at the monument. An odd trick of perspective makes it seem like the obelisk is tipping over on top of you. Now turn around and take some time to enjoy the panorama—north to the White House, east to the Capitol, south toward the Thomas Jefferson Memorial, west to the Lincoln Memorial and Reflecting Pool—and then walk west downhill toward 17th Street NW.

Cross 17th Street NW and proceed down the wide entrance avenue of the World War II Memorial. The green wall bears 4,048 golden stars, one for every 100 Americans who died in the war. Walk up the curving ramp to the left (past the Delaware column), through the Pacific arch, and around to the back of the wall. Look for a gate, inside which is one of two "Kilroy Was Here" inscriptions featured in the memorial. The long-nosed, mischievous Kilroy character boosted morale during the war years, as soldiers cheerfully vied to see who could doodle him in the most unexpected places.

Proceed across the eastern end of the Lincoln Memorial Reflecting Pool, and turn left onto the second path, which emerges at the edge of the Constitution Gardens pond, opened in 1976 for the national bicentennial. Its central island, dedicated to the signers of the Declaration of Independence and reached by a pedestrian bridge, is a haven for ducks and geese. Algae overgrowth has caused serious fish die-offs here; the National Park Service and the U.S. Fine Arts Commission are developing plans to deepen the pond and to improve the habitat. When the path splits near a hexagonal snack bar, keep left, proceeding toward the Vietnam Veterans Memorial. Pass the Vietnam Women's Memorial statue, created by Glenna Goodacre: three nurses and a wounded soldier. To your right, you have a full view of the polished black wall of the Vietnam Veterans Memorial, designed by

Maya Lin. Continue west along this walkway toward the hike's terminus, the massive marble Lincoln Memorial.

Myths surrounding this memorial and fascinating coincidences in the president's life abound. Despite rumors to the contrary, the structure does not have one step for each year of Lincoln's life, although a similar memorial at his Kentucky birthplace does. Nor does this marble Lincoln turn its back on the South, although Robert E. Lee lived for many years just across the Potomac at Arlington Plantation, now Arlington National Cemetery. (See Trip 50: Arlington National Cemetery and Marine Corps War [Iwo Jima] Memorial.) Lincoln's statue actually faces east. Take time to ponder the president's own words from his Gettysburg Address and his second inaugural address that are engraved on the memorial's interior walls—familiar yet poignantly powerful in their fuller context. Look down one of the step landings for the plaque marking the spot where Martin Luther King Jr. stood as he delivered his "I Have a Dream" speech in 1963.

From here, the walk to the Foggy Bottom station (Blue, Silver, Orange lines) is about eight blocks north, at 23rd and I ("Eye") streets NW, or retrace the path back to the National Mall to get to the Smithsonian station (Blue, Silver, Orange lines).

MORE INFORMATION

For Metrorail information, visit wmata.com to see the latest schedules and fare information. Leashed dogs are permitted outdoors on the National Mall but dogs are not allowed on Metrorail or in the museums. For current information and updates on tourism and special events in Washington, D.C., and on the National Mall, visit washington.org.

NEARBY

It's easy to make a full day of this hike by exploring any of the museums that surround the National Mall—Dorothy's ruby slippers, Harriet Tubman's hymnal, and the jaws of an ancient Megalodon are just a sample of what lies within these buildings. Entrance is free, but some museums require timed-entry passes. Visit si.edu/museums for more details. Hardy explorers up for more monuments can add East Potomac Park and Monuments (Trip 26).

26 EAST POTOMAC PARK AND MONUMENTS

Filled with architectural and natural beauty, this scenic, mostly level loop route features four memorials to revered Americans, four bodies of water, and dozens of cherry trees.

Features

Location Southwest Washington, D.C.

Rating Easy to Moderate

Distance 6.6 miles round-trip

Elevation Gain 30 feet

Estimated Time 3–4 hours

Maps USGS Alexandria; online: nps.gov/nama/planyourvisit/maps.htm

GPS Coordinates 38° 52.645′ N, 77° 02.198′ W (Parking Lot C)

Contact National Mall and Memorial Parks, National Park Service, nps.gov/nama/index.htm, 202-426-6841

DIRECTIONS

This hike is designed to be a Metrorail-friendly sojourn within the city. Using public transportation, take the Blue, Silver, or Orange line to the Smithsonian station and use the Independence Avenue exit.

If you drive, begin your hike at a different point along the route (see Trail Description). Be advised that parking can be hard to find and traffic is often at a near-standstill during cherry blossom season in early spring. From downtown Washington, D.C., take Constitution Avenue (US 50) west. Turn left at 15th Street SW (becomes Raoul Wallenberg Place at Independence Avenue SW). Turn left at Maine Avenue SW and immediately turn right onto East Basin Drive SW. Turn left onto Ohio Drive SW. Continue past the park police headquarters to the stop sign at Buckeye Drive SW and turn right. Go to the next stop sign, at Ohio Drive SW, and turn right. Drive under the railroad bridge; three free parking lots (C, B, and A) are available on your right for the founders' memorials. Park here and begin your hike as indicated later in the Trail Description.

TRAIL DESCRIPTION

East Potomac Park is one of Washington, D.C.'s larger and better-known green spaces, but even in the busy spring tourist season, visitors have room to stretch out and recreate. The park offers multiple leisure facilities and impressive groves of ornamental cherry trees that put their energy into flowering rather than fruiting. East Potomac Park is a perennial

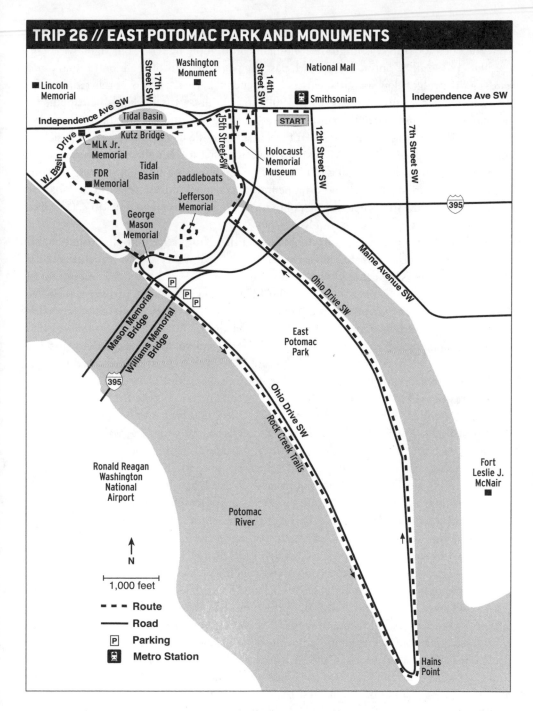

favorite for enjoying the beauty of several varieties of cherry blossoms in season, usually late March to late April.

From the Independence Avenue SW exit of the Smithsonian Metrorail station, turn left (west) on Independence Avenue SW, crossing 14th Street SW and 15th Street (Raoul

Wallenberg Place) SW and passing the brick U.S. Forest Service headquarters. Pause to view the obelisk of the Washington Monument through the trees on your right. (See Trip 25: National Mall.) Continue westward, past the planting beds of the Floral Library and across Kutz Bridge, a low span that carries Independence Avenue SW over the Tidal Basin. The basin was constructed in the early 1900s to help drain the lowlands hereabouts by taking in the overflow when the Potomac's water levels rise with the Chesapeake Bay tides. Despite this effort, many structures near the Tidal Basin "float" upon mucky soil—including the round-topped Jefferson Memorial across the water to your left, which was recently renovated to improve its seawall and pilings. Proceed along the sidewalk, noting on your left the satiny bark of the Yoshino ornamental cherry trees and the small stone Japanese lantern marking the spot where the first of these iconic trees was planted in 1912. (See "For the Love of Cherry Trees," on page 116.)

Turn left onto the path leading to the Martin Luther King Jr. Memorial. This much-anticipated outdoor plaza was dedicated in 2011 to the civil rights leader. Its centerpiece, a standing statue of King carved upon a "stone of hope" liberated from the "mountain of despair," was inspired by lines from his 1963 "I Have a Dream" speech (delivered from the Lincoln Memorial steps, where Trip 25 concludes). Note that the memorial sits along a line between the Jefferson Memorial and the Lincoln Memorial.

Proceed along the Martin Luther King Jr. Memorial wall to West Basin Drive. Turn left and then left again to enter the Franklin Delano Roosevelt Memorial, dedicated in 1997. In the plaza, observe the life-sized bronze sculpture of Franklin Delano Roosevelt (commonly known as FDR) sitting in a wheelchair—a testament to his life after polio struck in his 20s. Because FDR was elected four times to the presidency, and because those years were eventful for Americans, this memorial was designed with four open-air "rooms" representing each four-year term. The quotations, sculptural works, and waterfalls in each room symbolize the mood of that term. In the first room, for instance, look for inspiring speech excerpts such as "The only thing we have to fear is fear itself." In the second room, note the sculptures representing hardships of the Great Depression era.

In the third room is a larger statue of the president, wearing his signature Inverness cape and sitting in a straight-backed chair with casters visible at a close look. The lack of an obvious wheelchair in this statue, even though FDR himself avoided drawing attention to his disability, was at the center of a controversy that led to the creation of the smaller statue in the entrance plaza. Next to FDR sits his beloved Scottish terrier, Fala. As you move into the "world stage" of the fourth and final room, take in the statue honoring FDR's wife, Eleanor, who was a U.S. delegate to the United Nations following World War II.

Two paths lead out of the memorial to the Tidal Basin; take either one as both lead to the Thomas Jefferson Memorial, this hike's next landmark. Watch out for low-hanging tree limbs, standing water, and buckled pavement on the walkways. Cross the low stone bridge at Ohio Drive SW and take the nearest path along the water's edge to your left, following it until you emerge onto the plaza beneath the domed marble edifice. Look up at the north façade of this beautiful neoclassical structure, reminiscent of the third president's own designs for Monticello, his residence, and the University of Virginia rotunda. Notice the frieze above the columns. Young Jefferson, 33, stands before the other members of the committee assigned to draft the Declaration of Independence: John Adams and Benjamin

East Potomac Park offers views of several of D.C.'s famous monuments, including the Washington Monument.

Franklin, most notably. Climb the steps, if you like; be sure to turn around at the top and enjoy the view across the water to the White House, a mile away. The memorial's interior is both inspiring and cool on a warm day.

Walk back to Ohio Drive/East Basin Drive along the large square lawn, turning right just past the hexagonal snack bar. Proceed to the stop sign near the stone bridge and then cross to your left to enter the George Mason Memorial, a circular garden. Mason's beliefs strongly influenced both Jefferson's draft of the Declaration of Independence and James Madison's draft of the Bill of Rights, which spelled out clear constitutional limits on the new federal government's power over individuals and states. In spring, the garden blooms with daffodils and flowering shrubs. Turn left when leaving, proceed around a curve, and walk under the bridges toward the memorial parking lots.

If arriving by car, start your hike here. Cross Ohio Drive SW and turn left to begin your walk. (*Note*: Some of the concrete path close to the water may be closed for repairs as the trail makes its way around the park.) In spring, look for flowering cherry trees with flexible branches resembling willows; this weeping Higan variety bears small pink-purple flowers, usually in early to middle April. Continue on a long straightaway, where locals like to fish along the riverbank. Look across the Potomac River to catch a glimpse of the limestone Pentagon—headquarters of the U.S. Department of Defense—and the three curving, soaring spires of the Air Force Memorial. Farther downriver are the towers of the Crystal

City neighborhood in Arlington, Virginia. Also notice the yellow arches on the terminal at Ronald Reagan Washington National Airport, designed by the architect Cesar Pelli. (The curving, northern aerial approach over the Potomac to the airport, known as the River Visual, is considered one of the more interesting and challenging for pilots nationwide.)

Walk past a playground and picnic area. As you approach Hains Point, East Potomac Park's southern tip, Old Town Alexandria and the Woodrow Wilson Memorial Bridge come into view several miles to the south. Major General Peter Conover Hains—a member of the U.S. Army Corps of Engineers and a veteran of the Civil War, the Spanish-American War, and World War I—designed the Tidal Basin. East Potomac Park was created largely from soil dredged by the Corps to create that artificial lake. Hains Point marks the confluence of the Anacostia and Potomac rivers.

As you round the point, watch for green-and-white helicopters. Anacostia Naval Air Station, the Washington, D.C., home to the presidential flight group known as Marine Helicopter Squadron One (or HMX-1 Nighthawks), isn't far away. Across the channel from you is Fort Lesley J. McNair, with its ornate National War College building and neat brick Generals' Row. The Washington Channel on the east side of the park provides a safe harbor for private watercraft, rescue squads, and fishing vessels.

To the left, past a stop sign, are the park's golf course, miniature golf range, and swimming pool. Continue past the tennis complex and then cross under the highway and railroad bridges on this leg of Ohio Drive. At the intersection, walk straight across the road (this is still Ohio Drive), turn right on the sidewalk, and quickly turn left onto a narrow path leading down to the water's edge.

If you arrived by public transportation, follow the sidewalk to your right to the traffic light at Maine Avenue SW. Cross the avenue and continue north on 15th Street (Raoul Wallenberg Place) SW, passing the Bureau of Engraving and Printing and the United States Holocaust Memorial Museum. At the corner of Independence Avenue, turn right at the red Forest Service building; retrace the two blocks to return to the Smithsonian Metro station.

If you came by car, this will be your first close-up look at the Tidal Basin, so follow the walkway along its edge, past the Maine Avenue parking area and paddleboat kiosk. If you visit in early spring while the famed Yoshino cherry trees are in bloom, it might look as though huge, pale pink snowballs are ringing the basin. (See "For the Love of Cherry Trees," on page 116.) Proceed along the water toward Independence Avenue. Turn left to cross Kutz Bridge and continue your hike from the beginning of this trail's description.

MORE INFORMATION

The National Park Service maintains and administers East Potomac Park and the memorials along the Tidal Basin. For more information, visit nps.gov/nama or call 202-426-6841. Restrooms and water fountains are available at the memorials and at several locations in East Potomac Park. Park roads are sometimes closed due to flooding, and parking anywhere nearby can be difficult in spring during cherry blossom time. For a classic D.C. experience, consider renting a Tidal Basin paddleboat (seasonal; fees apply) at the kiosk in the parking area along Maine Avenue SW. This hike is in the heart of Washington, D.C., with many museums and places of interest nearby.

NEARBY

Hungry—or thirsty—hikers can make their way to the Wharf neighborhood, a little less than 1 mile away, which is home to various restaurants and shops. Kayak and paddle-board rentals are also available here for those who'd like to take their explorations to the water. Those eager for more D.C. tourism can couple this hike with a visit to the National Mall (Trip 25).

27 THEODORE ROOSEVELT ISLAND

Theodore Roosevelt Island in the Potomac River offers a secluded, woodsy landmass to explore between the tall buildings of Arlington, Virginia, and the National Mall in Washington, D.C.

Features

Location Arlington, VA, and Washington, D.C.

Rating Easy

Distance 2.3-mile loop

Elevation Gain Minimal

Estimated Time 2–2.5 hours

Maps USGS Washington West; online: nps.gov/this/planyourvisit/maps.htm

GPS Coordinates 38° 53.745′ N, 77° 04.010′ W

Contact Theodore Roosevelt Island, National Park Service, nps.gov/this, 703-289-2500

DIRECTIONS

From downtown Washington, D.C., take Constitution Avenue (US 50) west. Continue as it becomes I-66, and cross Theodore Roosevelt Bridge, staying in the right lane. Take the first right exit and then turn right onto George Washington Memorial Parkway (GW Parkway) going north. (The island is reached only from the northbound lanes of the parkway.) Take the first right turn (after 300 yards) into the Theodore Roosevelt Island parking lot. To return to Washington, D.C., exit the parking area and drive 0.8 mile north on GW Parkway. Take the first left exit onto Spout Run Parkway, and then take the first left exit onto southbound GW Parkway.

If using public transportation, take the Blue, Orange, or Silver line to the Rosslyn station and walk 0.8 mile to the trailhead. Hike north downhill on North Moore Street, cross 19th Street, turn right onto Lee Highway, cross North Lynn Street, and turn left down North Lynn. At the far corner, turn right onto Mount Vernon Trail and follow it south to the trailhead.

TRAIL DESCRIPTION

In the early 1800s, the island later designated Theodore Roosevelt Island was the summer home of John Mason, son of the Virginia statesman George Mason. John Mason erected an elegant brick mansion on the highest point of land, providing views across the Potomac River to the White House and the U.S. Capitol. Georgetown's wealthy elite would gather for dinners and dances on the Masons' manicured lawn beneath stately oak and linden

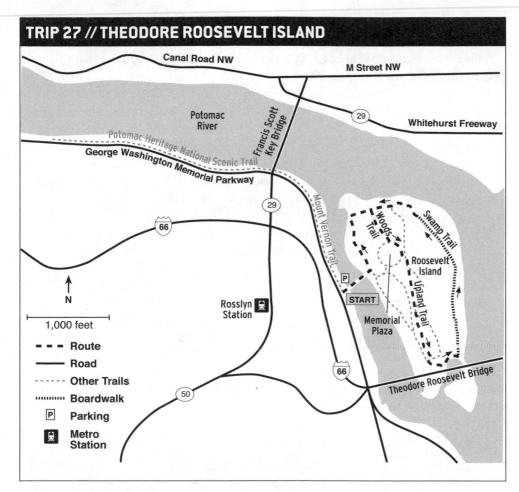

trees. In 1833, Mason was forced to relinquish his island as collateral for unpaid loans, but the family story held that the Masons moved because the mosquitoes had gotten too bad.

During the Civil War, the island was both a camp for refugees who had escaped slavery and an encampment for the First Regiment of United States Colored Troops.

In 1931, the Theodore Roosevelt Memorial Association purchased the 88.5-acre island and donated it to the federal government as a tribute to the former president. The Theodore Roosevelt Memorial, officially dedicated in 1967, stands upon this island, which was planned as a bird and wildlife sanctuary to honor the naturalist president. Nearly 200 species of birds pass through here in the course of a year.

This hike samples several well-maintained trails on Theodore Roosevelt Island. From the parking lot on the west bank of the Potomac River, head a short distance to the long, wide footbridge that crosses the Potomac, which is called Little River in this section. While crossing, look to your left to see Francis Scott Key Bridge (locally known as Key Bridge) and Georgetown, and south to Theodore Roosevelt Bridge. As you step onto the island, you'll see a kiosk displaying a trail map. Turn left onto Swamp Trail and follow the broad path along the western shore. Tree diversity here enriches the hike; expect to see sycamore, yellow poplar, beech, elm, holly, ash, hop hornbeam, black walnut, young maple, and large pin oak.

Arrive at an intersection marked by a sign that describes the causeway built in 1805 between the northern end of the island and Virginia. The former causeway was built for foot traffic and to serve as a dam to flush out the accumulated sediment on the north end of the island, allowing ships to reach Georgetown. The causeway was not completely removed until 1979.

Your route lies to the right, but take a few dozen steps straight ahead to enjoy the views of the Key Bridge and Georgetown. Also watch for a small, thorny deciduous tree that is rare for this area: the Osage orange, which flowers in June and bears distinctive fruit in fall. The softball-sized, yellow-green fruit has a bumpy surface and a milky juice that smells faintly of oranges, but it isn't generally considered edible for humans.

Retrace your steps and take Swamp Trail to the left, climbing the gentle ridge that runs the length of the island. At the next intersection, marked by a sign with information about Roosevelt's Rough Riders and a water fountain, turn right and walk down broad Woods Trail to arrive at the Theodore Roosevelt Memorial. You enter the memorial from the back, so make sure to proceed into the center to get the full experience. It is startling to find such an elaborate memorial in the middle of the woods. A moat flanked by large willow oaks encircles four 21-foot granite tablets and a 17-foot bronze statue of Roosevelt.

The conservationist and president Theodore Roosevelt's 17-foot-tall likeness greets visitors to his namesake Potomac River island, which is both a memorial and a bird sanctuary. *Photo by Ted, Creative Commons on Flickr.*

After exploring the memorial, return to its center. Facing the statue, turn to your right and exit across one of the stone bridges. Follow the path and arrive at the intersection with Upland Trail. Turn right onto Upland Trail, which is marked with periodic blue blazes. In winter, look through the trees to the left to see marshland below and the Watergate Hotel and the Kennedy Center across the water. Bear right when the trail forks and pass a sign with information about the Mason estate. Most of the trees on the island are younger than 100 years because much of the land was cleared for farming and gardens in the late 1800s, but in this area, the trees are older and larger. At an intersection, turn right to head downhill and then turn left to join Swamp Trail. Follow the path as it swings to the left, passing very close to Theodore Roosevelt Bridge.

Here, Swamp Trail becomes a wide, elevated boardwalk that runs 800 yards through the swampy portion of the island. Look for a short section of boardwalk that extends into the marsh to give you closer views.

Swamp Trail transitions back to a dirt path, heading slightly uphill, and passes the intersection with Upland Trail and Woods Trail that you encountered at the start of your journey. On this now-familiar ground, continue on Swamp Trail back to the footbridge.

MORE INFORMATION

The park is open daily from 6 A.M. to 10 P.M. Parking is free, but space is limited and the lot tends to fill on weekends. Restrooms on the island close in the colder months, typically October to April. A portable toilet is available in the parking lot during those months. Visit nps.gov/this to learn more.

NEARBY

An alternate circle around the island is available via boat; rent one at Thompson Boat Center or the former Jack's Boats (now Key Bridge Boathouse) underneath Key Bridge on the Georgetown bank. Also visit the nearby memorial to Theodore's fifth cousin, Franklin D. Roosevelt, along the Tidal Basin in Southwest Washington; you will also find a statue of Theodore's niece—and Franklin D. Roosevelt's wife—Eleanor Roosevelt. (See Trip 26: East Potomac Park and Monuments.)

WHAT'S IN A NAME: MR. SMITHSON'S LEGACY

Inside the ornate red sandstone Smithsonian Castle on the National Mall stands the crypt of James Smithson (circa 1765–1829), the English gentleman scientist whose large fortune founded the Smithsonian Institution. Smithson never visited the United States during his life, and his moldering bones, resting here now, can't tell us what manner of man bestowed such an amazing gift.

Recent scholarship, however, delves into the world of this previously shadowy historical figure. Born James (or Jacques) Louis Macie, he was the offspring of an illicit romance between the widowed aristocrat Elizabeth Macie and Hugh Smithson, the first Duke of Northumberland. Unacknowledged and unsupported by his father, James boldly took the family name Smithson in his 30s, after his parents' deaths.

He gained renown for his work in the exciting new fields of chemistry and mineralogy. Following his student prodigy career at the University of Oxford, Smithson was inducted into the exclusive, influential Royal Society at age 22—an honor for someone that young—and soon published the first of his many papers in its journal. On the strength of these accomplishments, plus his personal charm and exuberance, he embarked upon a grand tour of the European continent, seeking scientific insights, kindred minds, and mineralogical specimens for his growing collection. He carried a portable laboratory, experimented with the properties of minerals (even tasting and sniffing them), and made strides toward systems of classification. He became friends with many of the era's brightest scientists, witnessed events of the French Revolution, and became a prisoner of war during Europe's lengthy Napoleonic Wars. He knew aeronauts, aristocrats, politicians, and inventors. But he had neither a wife nor children.

In his will, he made an unusual request. His fortune was to be left to his nephew—but should the nephew die childless, the fortune would be donated "to the United

Inside the Smithsonian Castle's north portico is the crypt of James Smithson (a.k.a. James Macie), the English gentleman-scientist and mysterious benefactor of the vast museum complex that bears his chosen name. *Photo by Rain0975, Creative Commons on Flickr.*

States of America, to found at Washington, an establishment for the increase and diffusion of knowledge." It was to bear his chosen name and be known as the Smithsonian Institution. Smithson's nephew died in 1835, and the bequest was transferred to the United States. Astonished U.S. leaders wondered who Smithson was, what he intended, and why. Theories abound—he was an admirer of young America's Enlightenment-inspired ideals: a united country and open society, free from standing armies and the scourge of constant war. Another theory posits that Smithson bore a grudge against the aristocratic privilege ingrained in England. "My name will live on in the memory of men when the titles of [my ancestors] are extinct or forgotten," he once vowed.

His bequest certainly made his name famous around the globe, creating what is today the world's largest museum and research complex—holding upward of 154 million items across museums, libraries, research centers, and a zoo. But his motive might always remain a mystery.

28 U.S. NATIONAL ARBORETUM

The U.S. National Arboretum offers an ever-changing hike of rich discovery, thanks to its many special collections containing flora and fauna from around the world.

Features 👫 🐕 💧 🚌

Location Northeast Washington, D.C.

Rating Easy to Moderate

Distance 8.2-mile loop

Elevation Gain 800 feet

Estimated Time 4.5–5 hours

Maps USGS Washington East; map available free in arboretum brochure; online: usna.usda.gov/visit/map

GPS Coordinates 38° 54.388' N, 76° 58.141' W

Contact National Arboretum, usna.usda.gov, 202-245-2726

DIRECTIONS

From downtown Washington, D.C., take New York Avenue NW (US 50) east, which becomes NE at North Capitol Street. Pass the intersection with Bladensburg Road and drive 750 feet. Bear right to enter the access road running parallel to New York Avenue NE. Drive 0.25 mile to the arboretum gates and enter the park. Pass the first parking lot and follow Hickey Lane to the administration building. Park in the lot here.

If using public transportation, take Metrorail's Orange or Blue line to the Stadium-Armory station and transfer to northbound Metrobus B2. Exit the bus at Bladensburg Road and R Street NE and walk 0.2 mile east on R Street NE to the arboretum. Visit wmata.com for the latest bus and Metro schedules.

TRAIL DESCRIPTION

Founded in 1927, the U.S. National Arboretum in Northeast Washington, D.C., is a 446-acre living museum dedicated to plant research and education. The goal of this hike is to see the entire grounds with stops to study or admire the various collections. Driving and biking are speedier ways to visit the arboretum, but viewing its wonders on foot helps put each new collection into perspective and offers an intimate look at the diverse plant life.

From the parking lot, walk past the tram kiosk and proceed beyond the koi pond to the National Bonsai & Penjing Museum, a complex of structures reached through a Japanese garden. The museum houses trees maintained in miniature, and the Japanese Pavilion has a must-see white pine that survived the Hiroshima atomic blast in 1945 (see "Peace and

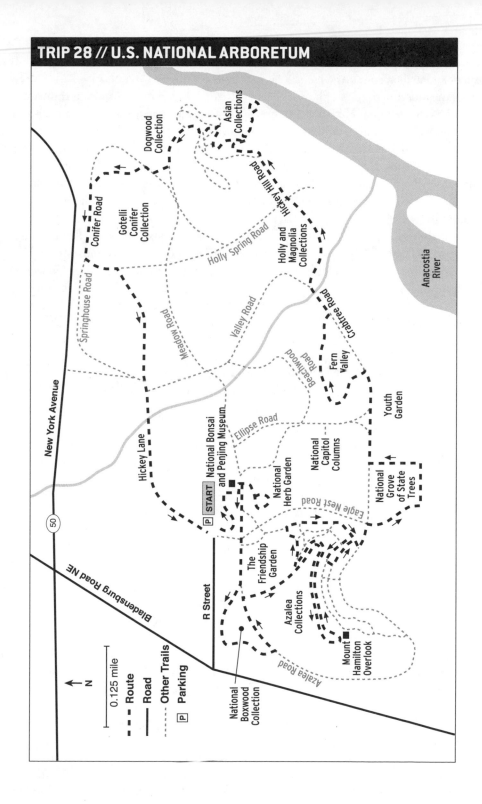

Long Life: Spirit within a Tree," on page 86) and was one of 53 bonsai given to the United States by the Japanese government to commemorate the 1976 U.S. bicentennial. The American Pavilion contains *Goshin*, a famous bonsai work by John Naka.

Exit the museum to the south onto Meadow Road, where a right turn leads immediately to the 2.5-acre National Herb Garden. Enter beneath a hanging garden, follow a cul-de-sac path lined with hundreds of herb species—more than 50 types of peppers alone—and proceed to a rose garden with historical varieties once widely cultivated across Europe. Return to Meadow Road, which becomes Azalea Road, and turn left. Continue past the intersection with Eagle Nest Road and turn right down the path that leads past the National Boxwood Collection and the beds of perennials that bloom from late February through July.

From Azalea Road, turn left and then take the first right just before the entrance to the Boxwood Collection. Walk past a parking area to a mulch path that ascends Mount Hamilton. This 40-acre section of high ground is adorned with the stunning Azalea Collections, which showcases its colors best in April and May. Proceed to the overlook by turning right at the first fork and traveling 0.25 mile to where the path ends in a cul-de-sac, affording fine views of the U.S. Capitol 2.0 miles to the southwest.

Returning from the overlook, turn right at the fork, stay left past a second fork, and then turn left at a third fork to loop around Lee Garden. As you go around the north side of the pond, turn right at the intersection to head south, and then turn left at the four-way intersection to arrive at a tended avenue known as Henry Mitchell Walk. At its end is Morrison Garden, a squared-off structure of bricks housing 15,000 Glenn Dale hybrid azaleas arranged in overlapping colors and bloom times.

Exit the garden at the south end and turn right onto the circle. Turn right and then immediately left to join a steep mulch path on the south side of Mount Hamilton. Travel this path for a short distance and take the first right, followed by another right. When you return to the circle, turn right to link up with paved Azalea Road.

Turn left onto Azalea Road. Walk 100 yards and turn right onto Eagle Nest Road, along the left side of the National Grove of State Trees. Follow Eagle Nest Road to the parking lot and turn left. Look to the left to locate a semicircular marble display etched with the leaf of each state's tree. Once ready to resume, continue toward the other end of the parking lot. Turn left here to follow a roadway lined with scarlet oaks (the official tree of Washington, D.C.), and then turn right back onto Crabtree Road.

Follow Crabtree Road to a left turn onto Ellipse Road, which leads to the National Capitol Columns. After viewing them, return south on Ellipse Road and turn right onto Crabtree Road, passing the Youth Garden on the right and two small side paths on the left before turning left into the main entrance to Fern Valley. This area is planted with ferns, wildflowers, shrubs, and trees native to the eastern United States and is a prime spot for bird-watching. At a central intersection near a shed, turn left and circle around to the north to proceed through Fern Valley, a microcosm of the natural ecology of eastern forests. Cross the stream and arrive back at Crabtree Road.

Turn left onto Crabtree Road and then quickly right onto Hickory Hill Road, passing the Holly and Magnolia Collections on the left. Continue past the intersection with Holly Spring Road and trek uphill to the Asian Collections. Take the first right and follow a

One of the National Arboretum's signature attractions is this forest of Corinthian columns that once graced the East Front of the U.S. Capitol, watching over presidential inauguration ceremonies from the 1820s to the 1950s. *Photo by Simon, Creative Commons on Flickr.*

sharp descent that wraps around China Valley. Return on the path and turn right, climbing steep stone steps to the pagoda. Turn left and then take the first right to skirt the edge of Asian Valley. Turn right at the T intersection and travel around a circle, turning right at its opposite end to dip down into the Japanese Woodland. Turn left at an alcove at the southern end, go straight past a three-way fork, and continue north to a parking area on Hickory Hill Road.

Hickory Hill Road makes a U-turn back to the west, passing the Dogwood Collection on the right. Take the first right past a stand of dawn redwoods onto Conifer Road. Beyond them, turn left into the maze of the 7-acre Gotelli Dwarf and Slow-Growing Conifer Collection, making your way generally north through 1,400 firs, cedars, pines, yews, and spruces. After navigating the trees, return to Conifer Road and turn left onto it. From here, return to the administration building parking lot via a 1.25-mile walk: first turn left onto Holly Spring Road and then quickly right onto Hickey Lane, which drops into the parking lot from the north.

MORE INFORMATION

The U.S. National Arboretum is open daily (except December 25) from 8 A.M. to 5 P.M. Admission is free. The National Bonsai & Penjing Museum is open 10 A.M. to 4 P.M. daily except for federal holidays from November through February. During times of high visitation, the arboretum may restrict traffic to facilitate parking. Tram tours run on weekend and holiday afternoons in season. Purchase tickets at the information desk in the administration building. Tram tours last 35 minutes and cost $4 for adults and $2 for children 4 to 6; tours are free for children younger than 4. Trams depart from the Arbor House gift shop near the Friendship Garden. For more information, visit usna.usda.gov or call 202-245-2726.

NEARBY

While in Northeast Washington, D.C., consider a visit to two other sites of great beauty and spiritual uplift. The Basilica of the National Shrine of the Immaculate Conception, on the campus of Catholic University, is one of the ten largest churches—and home to one of the most stunning displays of mosaic art—in the world. See nationalshrine.com for details and directions.

Just a few blocks away from the basilica, at the Franciscan Monastery of the Holy Land in America, the building and stunning grounds evoke Saint Francis of Assisi's deep love of birds, flowers, and all creatures. The site contains numerous holy shrines from around the world. Visit myfranciscan.org for more information.

29 KENILWORTH PARK AND AQUATIC GARDENS

This easy hike visits ponds teeming with summer-blooming waterlilies and lotuses, as well as the last remaining preserved tidal marshland on the Anacostia River.

Features 👥 🐕 💧 ⬆️ 🚌

Location Northeast Washington, D.C.

Rating Easy

Distance 2.5-mile loop

Elevation Gain Minimal

Estimated Time 1.5–2 hours

Maps USGS Washington East; map of the aquatic gardens available for free in the visitor center; online: nps.gov/keaq/planyourvisit/maps.htm; anacostiaws.org /images/Files/maps/2017_Update_ART_web.pdf (map with water trails)

GPS Coordinates 38° 54.778′ N, 76° 56.412′ W

Contact Kenilworth Park and Aquatic Gardens, nps.gov/keaq/index.htm, 202-692-6080

DIRECTIONS

From downtown Washington, D.C., take New York Avenue NW (US 50) east, which becomes NE at North Capitol Street. Use the right lane to take the Maryland 201 S/I-295/ Kenilworth ramp toward Alexandria. Merge onto Maryland 201, and then take the exit toward Eastern Avenue/Aquatic Gardens. Continue onto Kenilworth Avenue NE and then turn right onto Douglas Street NE. Turn right onto Anacostia Avenue NE. The park is on the left.

If using public transportation, take the Orange Line to the Deanwood station and then walk across the pedestrian overpass to Douglas Street. Walk north on Douglas to Anacostia Avenue and turn right into the park entrance (0.4-mile walk). Visit wmata.com for the latest Metro and bus schedules.

TRAIL DESCRIPTION

Kenilworth Aquatic Gardens, at the northern end of 11-mile-long Anacostia Park, on the east side of the Anacostia River 8.0 miles north of its confluence with the Potomac, protects the last remaining tidal marshland in the District of Columbia. It is on the ancestral homeland of the Nacotchtank people.

The location has a history rooted in the commercial production of waterlilies and lotuses. The W. B. Shaw Lily Pond was started by W. B. Shaw, who imported lilies and lotuses from

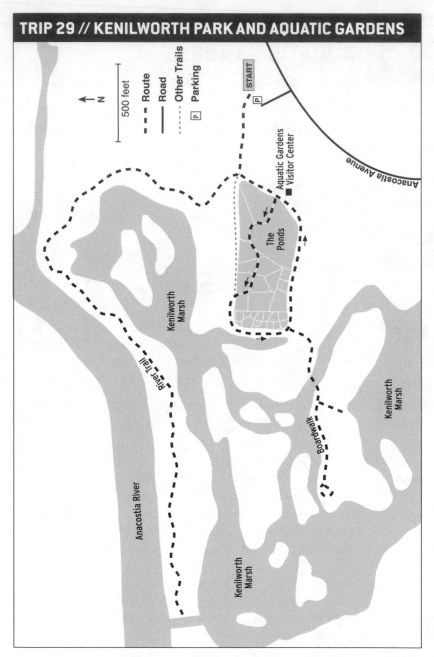

Asia, Egypt, and South America and built a greenhouse and sales office (today's visitor center). L. Helen Fowler, Shaw's daughter, grew the business and advocated for the protection of the marsh. The spot was a favorite of outdoorsy Washingtonians, including President Calvin Coolidge. In the 1930s, when a misguided U.S. Army Corps of Engineers project to fill in the wetlands threatened the aquatic gardens, the National Park Service (NPS) stepped in and purchased the land for $15,000, renaming the site Kenilworth for the nearby farm community.

Today, the site has 75 acres of freshwater tidal marsh and 45 ponds filled with tropical and hardy waterlilies, lotuses, and other aquatic species. The best time of year to see these blooming water plants begins in late May, peaks in July, and ends in mid-September. The best time of day to view the surreal spectacle of night bloomers closing and day bloomers opening is the early morning. Afternoon heat and sun cause the day bloomers to close. In general, the hardy lilies are in the central ponds, the tropical lilies (including the giant, platter-like *Victoria amazonica*) are in the western ponds farthest from the visitor center, and the lotuses are in the large pond in front of the visitor center and the southern ponds.

To begin the hike from the parking lot, follow the gravel path past the greenhouses to the left, go through a gate, and reach a sign marking points of interest. Take the second right to begin the 1.5-mile out-and-back trip on River Trail. This trail runs along an artificial spit and borders a marsh on the left that the NPS constructed in 1992. At 0.2 mile, at the concrete ruins of an old tower on the left, reach the Anacostia River and follow it to the left. Wintertime affords views of the river and the stone seawall (constructed by the Corps of Engineers) on the opposite shore. In spring and summer, blackjack and northern red oak, red and silver maple, willow, tupelo, sycamore, black locust, black birch, holly, black walnut, sweet gum, and yellow poplar make up the view to the right.

Hike 100 yards farther to a bench on the left with wide-open views of the wetlands: vibrant and almost tropical in summer, and peaceful in winter. At 0.75 mile, River Trail ends at a bench underneath a dual-trunked sycamore tree on the right. Take the path leading down to the riverbank and the inlet where tidal waters reach the marsh. A stone wall to the left ends abruptly in broken shards; the wall once blocked the very water that now feeds this natural ecosystem. Return to River Trail and retrace your steps to head back to the aquatic gardens.

Back at the entrance sign, continue along the southern edge of the ponds. Pass several distinctive trees (an American bald cypress, a large magnolia, a few hollies) and a wooden greenhouse (built in 1913) before reaching the visitor center. Stop in to pick up a hand-drawn map of the ponds and to see interesting relics, such as Helen Fowler's 1936 book on growing waterlilies, complete with her pastel drawings. The center also has information on particular plant species found at the gardens, including the pink-flowered East Indian lotus. Some of these lotuses, the offspring of 600-year-old seeds discovered in Manchuria and planted in 1951, thrive in the pond behind the center.

From the visitor center, step around back and look for the East Indian lotus if visiting in summer. Then head straight onto the dike between a giant pond of lotuses on the left and a pond of yellow-flowered spatterdock on the right. Continue to a pond ahead, turn left, and then take the first right and stay left at the fork, traveling through the heart of the winter-hardy waterlily collection. Head toward the tropical lilies by crossing a wooden walkway, turning right at the next T intersection, and going left around the outside edge of the *Victoria amazonica*. This tropical lily, native to the Amazon River basin, is the most dramatic in the park. Its leaves can grow 7 feet wide with the edges turning up to form a platter-like rim. The flowers open at dusk.

Continue south on the gravel road between the tropical lilies and the marsh, and turn right onto the boardwalk at the sign reading "Boardwalk Closed at 4 P.M." Walk onto the zigzag walkway past a few rare paperbark maple trees and continue straight to the far platform. Take in the ecological bounty of this midmarsh zone, including native cattails,

A pink East Indian lotus, India's national flower, blossoms in Kenilworth Aquatic Gardens, offering nectar to bees and other insects. *Photo by Stephen Mauro.*

buttonbush, wild rice, arrow arum, pickerelweed, and two wild varieties of a flowering aquatic plant: spatterdock and American lotus. Also look for great blue herons, great egrets, belted kingfishers, and raptors.

On the way back, detour to the right to visit a second platform; then return to the gardens and turn right, walking along the southern rim past more East Indian lotuses. Pass the front of the visitor center and turn right to get back to the parking lot.

MORE INFORMATION

Kenilworth Aquatic Gardens is open daily, 8 A.M. to 4 P.M., and is closed January 1, Thanksgiving Day, and December 25. The parking lot is locked at 4 P.M. Leashed dogs are allowed in the gardens. For more details, visit nps.gov/keaq or call 202-692-6080. The adjacent Kenilworth Park is open from 8 A.M. to dusk.

The Friends of Kenilworth Aquatic Gardens has more information about the gardens, including birding guides and a seasonal guide. Visit kenaqgardens.org to learn more and to see a list of upcoming events.

NEARBY

Directly across the Anacostia River from Kenilworth is the U.S. National Arboretum (Trip 28). The Anacostia Riverwalk (Trip 31) runs along the east and west banks of the river. Learn more about Anacostia's history by visiting the Frederick Douglass National Historic Site, the Anacostia Community Museum, and the Anacostia Historic District, all in southern Anacostia.

RECLAIMING GREEN SPACE

Washington, D.C., contains a plethora of green space—more than 9,500 acres of parks. Put another way, there are 16 acres of public parkland for every 1,000 residents, according to a report by the National Capital Planning Commission. While Rock Creek Park often dominates the conversation, parks abound in every ward of the city. Wards 7 and 8, the area east of the Anacostia River, contain a significant amount of green space, with 1,000 acres in Ward 7 and 650 acres in Ward 8. Fort Dupont Park, in Ward 7, is the second-largest park in Washington, D.C., with 376 acres.

What Wards 7 and 8 lack are trails. The Fort Circle Hiker-Biker Trail is the main trail in this vicinity, with 6 miles in Ward 7 and 1 mile in Ward 8. It connects several of the forts built to defend D.C. during the Civil War. (See "Ringing Around the City," on page 106.) The 0.4-mile George Washington Carver Trail, near the Smithsonian Anacostia Museum, provides an easy loop for hikers to explore. In contrast, Rock Creek Park boasts more than 36 miles of trails.

Groups like Ward 8 Woods Conservancy are working to develop opportunities for additional trails. The group aims to create a future where all residents in the District of Columbia have access to trails and green space.

One of the top challenges that conservancy volunteers are tackling is trash. Wards 7 and 8 have the lowest rates of recycling in the district, and trash collection issues hamper efforts to keep cans from overflowing. The conservancy leads monthly cleanup days to help remove trash from parks and has established an awareness campaign about how to prevent litter. It also set up an advocacy program to work with landlords to encourage them to take on timely trash removal. To engage more residents, the conservancy has created programs that allow people to adopt areas bordering parkland and work to keep those areas litter-free.

Invasive species removal is another priority—species such as English ivy, porcelain oak, and honeysuckle can crowd what trails are in place. The monthly cleanup days include removing these invasive plants. Nathan Harrington, head of Ward 8 Woods Conservancy, estimates they've cut back vines from more than 4,000 trees.

Lack of funding is also an issue—many of the parklands in this area have been neglected, leaving it up to groups such as Ward 8 Woods Conservancy to make them a priority. After challenges getting trash removed after cleanup events, the conservancy purchased its own truck. The group also hires local residents, some of whom have faced barriers to employment, to serve as park stewards. Park stewards help remove trash and invasive species from parks and share the conservancy's mission with other local residents. In this role, they receive training for future green jobs.

As Ward 8 Woods Conservancy works with residents to reclaim green space, it is also advocating for the creation of more trails in Wards 7 and 8. In 2021, the conservancy proposed a new hiking trail for Ward 8: Suitland Parkway Northside Trail. This 2.2-mile trail would explore rock outcroppings and ravines and would connect with the existing George Washington Carver Trail. The land is currently owned by the D.C. Department of Transportation, and plans to submit a formal proposal are under way—updates on this work can be seen on the group's website (ward8woods.org/proposed-suitland-parkway-northside-trail/). If successful, this would be the first new trail in Ward 8 in a generation.

The hyperlocal organizing, as Harrington explains it, falls under the idea of "clean it, claim it." Far too many people feel disconnected from the land, he notes, but forging these connections through cleanup days and advocating for the expansion of green space and trails is an act of empowerment.

Volunteering is one of the best ways to get involved, says Harrington. The Ward 8 Woods Conservancy hosts two cleanup events each month, one at Fort Stanton and the other near Shepherd Parkway, to remove invasive species and trash. These events attract anywhere from 5 to 50 people to assist with the day's goals. More than 100 school groups have attended the cleanup events.

30 KINGMAN AND HERITAGE ISLANDS

Kingman and Heritage Islands offer a quiet escape and wildlife viewing opportunities.

Features 👨‍🦯🐕💧⛺🚌🎣

Location Northeast and Southeast Washington, D.C.

Rating Easy

Distance 2.2-mile loop

Elevation Gain Minimal

Estimated Time 1–1.5 hours

Maps Online: kingmanisland.com

GPS Coordinates 38° 53.771′ N, 76° 58.083′ W

Contact Kingman and Heritage Islands, kingmanisland.com, 202-488-0627

DIRECTIONS

From I-295, take the exit toward Benning Road. (If driving north on I-295, the exit will be on the left.) Continue westbound on Benning Road NE. Turn left onto Oklahoma Avenue NE. Turn at the first driveway on the left into the main entrance for The Fields at RFK Campus (previously RFK Parking Lot 6). After parking, proceed into the main recreation area—access to Kingman and Heritage Islands is near Field 1.

If using public transportation, take the Blue or Orange line to the Stadium-Armory station. Exit the station in the direction of RFK Stadium and follow 19th Street SE north toward the stadium. Turn right onto C Street NE and then turn left onto 21st Street NE. Make a slight right onto Oklahoma Avenue NE. Enter The Fields at RFK Campus and proceed as noted above. The D6, 97, and B2 buses also stop at the Stadium-Armory station. Visit wmata.com for the latest schedules and fare information.

TRAIL DESCRIPTION

Kingman and Heritage Islands offer a short and pleasing hike with water views. Kingman Lake, a side channel of the Anacostia River, surrounds Heritage Island and borders the west side of Kingman Island. The main channel of the Anacostia River is to the west of Kingman Island. These human-made islands are the result of a project in the early part of the 1900s to dredge the Anacostia River (see Trip 31 for details).

Today, the islands host rare ecosystems—tidal swamp forests, wildflower meadows, and vernal pools. More than 100 species of wildlife also call these islands home. Portions of both islands are state conservation areas, and part of Kingman Island is designated a critical wildlife area. Much of the work to restore the islands and protect these ecosystems has

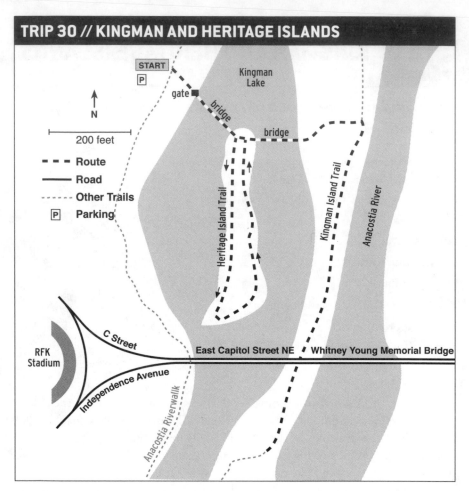

been performed during the past 20 years by students and scientists—and it continues today. Each year, thousands of students from Washington, D.C., schools visit the island to learn more about this environment and conservation efforts.

Finding the entrance might be the hardest part of the hike. Once in The Fields at RFK Campus, head to Field 1. Just past the field, look for the path that leads toward the river. Cross the Anacostia Riverwalk's West Bank Trail. A large gate and a wooden sign signal the entrance to the islands. Pass through the gate and walk across the wooden bridge to arrive first at Heritage Island. Turn right to follow the path as it begins its 0.4-mile loop around the island. RFK Stadium is in sight, but it's the magnificent water views from this path that grab attention. Reach the end of the island and follow the path as it bends to the left. Wooden boardwalks protect muddy and delicate areas.

Arrive back at the start of the loop and head to the right to cross the wooden bridges that lead to Kingman Island. Take a moment to look for turtles in the water below—also watch for egrets and great blue herons.

Once over the bridges, enter a meadow and look for an interpretive sign that provides information about the work to restore this native Mid-Atlantic meadow. Then follow the gravel path as it bends to the right. Arrive at an intersection with a dirt path and turn right to start following the trail on Kingman Island. It passes under Whitney Young Memorial Bridge at 1.1 miles into the hike—look for an installation that spells out "Trash Free D.C."

Walking on this wide, flat trail is peaceful and easy, with the river flowing to the left. At a picnic table, look for a short paved path to the right and follow it to enjoy views over Kingman Lake. Then turn around and retrace your steps back to the bridges and to the parking lot.

MORE INFORMATION

The islands are open from dawn to dusk. Fishing is allowed, and fishing licenses can be obtained from the D.C. Department of Energy and Environment (DOEE). The DOEE owns the islands, but they are managed by Living Classrooms of the National Capital Region, a nonprofit that provides educational, workforce development, and environmental programming. A floating dock with a kayak launch is available near the Benning Road entrance to the islands.

Visit kingmanisland.com for more information about the islands, including their history and a list of upcoming events.

NEARBY

The Fields at RFK Campus offers opportunities to extend a day outdoors with a picnic area and playground. The turf fields can be reserved for a wide array of sporting activities: kickball, baseball, softball, soccer, and lacrosse. The Celebration Pavilion can be reserved for events. Visit rfkfields.com to learn more.

The wooden bridges connecting the island are prime locations for spotting wildlife.

31 ANACOSTIA PARK AND RIVERWALK

Explore both sides of the Anacostia River during this ramble which delivers stunning water views.

Features

Location Southeast Washington, D.C.

Rating Easy

Distance 5.2-mile loop

Elevation Gain Minimal

Estimated Time 2–2.5 hours

Maps Online: nps.gov/anac/planyourvisit/maps.htm

GPS Coordinates 38° 52.505′ N, 76° 58.620′ W

Contact Anacostia Park, National Park Service, nps.gov/anac/index.htm, 202-472-3884

DIRECTIONS

From I-295 going north, take Exit 5C toward 11th Street SE/Martin Luther King Jr. Avenue SE. Turn right onto Martin Luther King Jr. Avenue SE, and then turn right on Good Hope Road SE to enter the park. In the park, turn right onto Anacostia Drive. Pass the swimming pool and park at the lot next to Pirate Ship Playground. Accessible parking spots are available here.

If using public transportation, take the Green Line to the Anacostia station. Exit the station toward the Metro parking lot (follow the signs). Turn right and walk alongside the unnamed road. Enter the park through the fence gate. The U2, V7, and V9 buses stop at the corner of Pennsylvania Avenue SE and Fairlawn Drive. From that corner, walk west on Fairlawn, turn right onto Nicholson Drive, and walk to Anacostia Drive. Visit wmata.com to view the latest schedules and fare information.

TRAIL DESCRIPTION

This hike starts in Anacostia Park on the east side of the river. The area making up the park has a vibrant history. It was originally home to the Nacotchtank people, who were the primary residents along the eastern shore of the Anacostia in the seventeenth century (Anacostia is the latinized form of the tribe's name). With the abundance of wildlife and the fertile land, the Nacotchtank were prosperous hunters, farmers, and gatherers. In 1608, John Smith explored the river, and English colonists soon arrived, displacing the Nacotchtank.

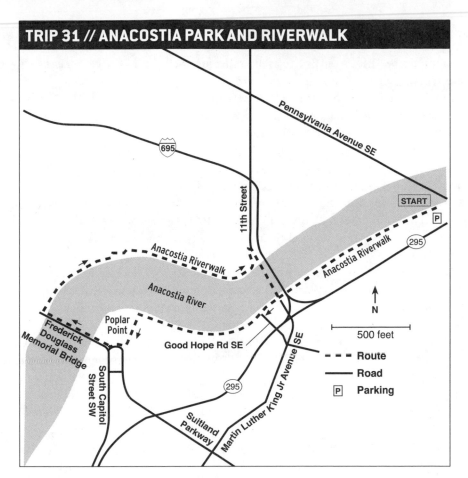

As plans for the new capital city of the young United States developed, the Anacostia River—known then as the Eastern Branch—was appealing for the creation of deep-water ports. The Washington Navy Yard was established on the west bank of the river, but American troops burned it down during the War of 1812 amid fears that the British would try to capture ships and ammunition.

Plans for the park did not get under way until 1901, when the McMillan Commission recommended that the area be transformed into green space, similar to what had been done with East Potomac Park and West Potomac Park. The Anacostia River and Flats Act, passed by Congress in 1914, set the stage for moving forward. The U.S. Army Corps of Engineers created a seawall, dredging the river and using the sediment to fill in the wetlands behind the wall. The National Park Service took over management of the park in 1933.

The Anacostia Riverwalk is a 20-mile trail that runs on both sides of the river. To start the hike, head toward the river from the parking lot and turn left onto the paved path. Interpretive signs are interspersed along the route, detailing history about the park and the surrounding areas.

Even while I-295 is in sight, it is easy to tune out the traffic by focusing on the magnificent river views to the right. It's possible to see planes landing at and taking off from

Washington National Airport; the dramatic new Frederick Douglass Memorial Bridge frames the views; and there may be cheers from the nearby baseball stadium.

Pass under the 11th Street Bridge at 0.8 mile into the hike. Near the intersection with Good Hope Road, reach a signpost with distances to historical Anacostia (to the left outside the park), including the Frederick Douglass House.

Continue along the Riverwalk. In just a tenth of a mile, arrive at a marker for the Bonus Army Wayside. The Bonus Army was the name given to World War I veterans who came to Washington, D.C., in 1932 to demand the payment of a promised wartime bonus. Many of them created a camp at what is now the park. (See "Franklin D. Roosevelt's Tree Army: The Civilian Conservation Corps," on page 175.)

At 1.6 miles, cross over and explore West Bank Trail. Turn to the left, just before Poplar Point, and follow the sidewalk toward Frederick Douglass Memorial Bridge. This bridge offers even more stunning views of the river, to the north and to the south. Take time to admire the scenery.

Once across the bridge, walk toward the water and then follow a wooden boardwalk that makes its way up the river. (*Note*: Road construction in this area may cause diversions for pedestrians. If this is the case, simply work your way around the construction and head back toward the boardwalk to resume the route.)

Compared with the initial segment, this stretch of the Riverwalk hums with activity as it passes through Yards Park. The Riverwalk runs alongside restaurants and boat rental businesses. Small parks dot the way, with benches providing ample opportunities to rest. At 3.2 miles, the boardwalk enters Navy Yard Waterfront Park. Bicycles and pets are not allowed here, but wheelchairs, strollers, and service animals are permitted. Trail signs point out interesting facts about the location. Look for one that marks the site where the remains of the Unknown Soldier, buried now in Arlington National Cemetery, arrived in November 1921.

At 3.6 miles, the Riverwalk exits Navy Yard Waterfront Park and approaches 11th Street Bridge—this is the return route to Anacostia Park. Turn left just before the bridge and follow the sidewalk up to 11th Street SE. Turn right to cross the bridge.

Using this bridge as a connector allows another opportunity to enjoy the sights along the river. Take advantage of one of the two overlooks on the south side of the bridge to see more panoramic views. Once across the bridge, look to the right for a path that leads downhill and into Anacostia Park. Follow this path, which connects with Good Hope Road SE, and then turn right to follow the Riverwalk for a little less than a mile back to the parking lot.

MORE INFORMATION

Anacostia Park is open daily from 6 A.M. to 10 P.M. The park has several picnicking and grilling areas; large groups require a permit. Fishing and boating are allowed—a fishing license is required. The park also boasts the only roller-skating rink in the National Park Service properties. This open-air rink operates from Memorial Day to Labor Day, 9 A.M. to 5 P.M. Skate rentals are available. Visit nps.gov/anac/index.htm for more information about Anacostia Park.

The Anacostia River hums with activity as boaters, hikers, runners, and bicyclists explore the path—by land or by water.

NEARBY

Frederick Douglass lived in the Anacostia area during his later years, from 1872 until his death in 1895. His home, Cedar Hill, is now the Frederick Douglass National Historic Site and preserves much of this historic residence. The library is filled with bookcases, and the National Park Service has a list of the books for those interested in seeing what Douglass liked to read. Visit nps.gov/frdo/index.htm to learn more.

Yards Park, which this hike passes through, is filled with restaurants and even has a winery, providing a multitude of options for snacking and relaxing.

Even with its ever-intensifying suburban development, northern Virginia remains geologically and ecologically diverse, containing (from west to east) the Blue Ridge Mountains, the verdant hills and stream valleys of Virginia's Piedmont region, and the tidal marshlands of the Atlantic coastal plain. An obvious choice for nature lovers is to go west, away from the suburban sprawl, to the farmlands and horse fields of Loudoun and Fauquier counties. Here, hikers can explore Virginia's Piedmont region at Virginia Outdoors Foundation's Preserve

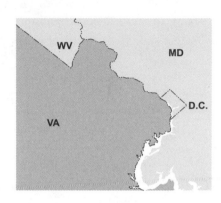

at Bull Run Mountains (Trip 41), Sky Meadows State Park (Trip 39), or G. Richard Thompson Wildlife Management Area (Trip 40). Farther to the west is Signal Knob (Trip 38) in the Massanutten area, offering hikers a challenging trek topped with scenic views. Look north for a gentler outing at Banshee Reeks Nature Preserve (Trip 43) near Leesburg, a well-kept secret that includes meadows, berry patches, and a scenic creek.

Closer to Washington, D.C., in busy Fairfax and Prince William counties, hikers can meander through the creased and folded landscape of Virginia's Piedmont region, following stream valleys where old mills and mines reflect the way people once lived. Northern Virginia has its fair share of long out-and-back trails, frequented by bicyclists and hikers, including Washington and Old Dominion Trail, Gerry Connolly Cross County Trail (Trip 34), with its historical Colvin Run Mill; and Bull Run Occoquan Trail (Trip 35), which in some spots feels remote enough to rival the Appalachian Trail.

Along the Potomac south of D.C., facing east toward southern Maryland, are Mason Neck State Park (Trip 36) and Gunston Hall: River Trail (Trip 37). Nesting in these tidal marshlands and delicate sandy cliffs are bald eagles, ospreys, and great blue herons. A bit inland is Prince William Forest Park (Trip 33), once the training ground for eagle-eyed secret agents. A little farther south—new to this edition—is the picturesque Crow's Nest Natural Area Preserve (Trip 32).

Meadowlark Botanical Gardens (Trip 44) is a human-crafted haven with wildflowers, water features, and even a Korean bell garden. Hikers can also enjoy the largely forested inland areas of Huntley Meadows Park (Trip 47) and Manassas National Battlefield

Facing page: By climbing the observation tower at Huntley Meadows in Alexandria, Virginia, you can gain a bird's-eye view of a classic Mid-Atlantic marsh.

Park-(Trip 42), where centuries-old hardwoods have survived the axes of settlers and the bulldozers of developers.

Upstream along the Potomac River, north of Washington, D.C., are the roiling waters of Great Falls Park (combined with Riverbend Park in Trip 45), Theodore Roosevelt's favorite spot to clear his head of the rigors of the presidency. In this same region is Scott's Run Nature Preserve (Trip 46). These hikes combine hilly climbs with walks along the Potomac River. Nestled alongside George Washington Memorial Parkway are two more hikes new to this edition—Turkey Run Park (Trip 48) and Potomac Overlook Regional Park (Trip 49)—which offer more Potomac views and nearby escapes for Washingtonians and others seeking an easy outdoor adventure.

32 CROW'S NEST NATURAL AREA PRESERVE

This preserve offers easy trails and diverse flora for hikers to enjoy.

Features

Location Stafford, VA

Rating Easy

Distance 5.8 miles round-trip

Elevation Gain 405 feet

Estimated Time 2.5–3 hours

Maps Online: dcr.virginia.gov/natural-heritage/document/cnnap-trailmap.pdf

GPS Coordinates 38° 21.720′ N, 77° 20.526′ W

Contact Crow's Nest Natural Area Preserve, dcr.virginia.gov/natural-heritage/natural-area-preserves/crowsnest, 540 658-8690

DIRECTIONS

From I-95 take Exit 140 (Stafford). Take Route 630 (Courthouse Road) 1.0 mile east to Stafford (intersection of Route 630 and US 1). Cross US 1 and continue east on Route 630 for about 2.5 miles. Turn right onto Route 629 (Andrew Chapel Road) and continue for 0.9 mile. Go under the railroad overpass at the community of Brooke and turn left onto Route 608 (Brooke Road). Continue for 1.4 miles, and then turn right onto gravel Route 609 (Raven Road). Cross the one-lane bridge over Accokeek Creek and continue for 0.2 mile. The Raven Road access gate for Crow's Nest Natural Area Preserve is on the left. Follow the gravel road for about 1.5 miles to the parking area.

TRAIL DESCRIPTION

Crow's Nest Natural Area Preserve is one of 66 natural area preserves in Virginia. The original 2,872 acres were purchased in 2008 and 2009. In 2018 and 2020, the Northern Virginia Conservation Trust dedicated two additional parcels of land, bringing Crow's Nest to 3,056 acres.

Crow's Nest mostly sits on a peninsula between Potomac and Accokeek creeks and is home to 60 percent of the marshland in Stafford County, providing nesting sites for bald eagles. Its tidal creeks also offer potential habitat for the shortnose sturgeon, an endangered species of fish. The preserve supports the globally rare coastal plain dry calcareous forest, with the chinquapin oak as a characteristic tree. Numerous large trees can be seen at Crow's Nest, including a variety of oak and hickory species as well as American beech and tulip poplar.

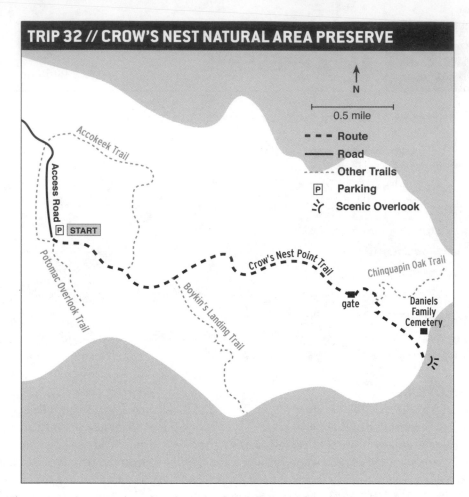

The preserve's 8.0 miles of trails make for pleasant walking, and it is easy to add more trails to further explore this unusual place.

Crow's Nest Point Trail is an excellent way to see the preserve, delivering on all accounts. This trail, clocking in at 5.5 miles for a round trip, wends its way through the woods and arrives at an overlook where Potomac and Accokeek creeks meet.

To start the hike, pass through the wooden gate near the informational sign to begin green-blazed Crow's Nest Point Trail. In 0.5 mile, pass the intersection with Accokeek Loop Trail. The walking here is very smooth, and in early spring, wildflowers dot both sides of the path—keen- eyed visitors will notice dutchman's breeches, Virginia saxifrage, and slender toothwort. In another few tenths of a mile, pass the intersection with Boykin's Landing Trail. Stay on Crow's Nest Point Trail, a wide path that gently rolls up and down, making for a pleasant hike.

Arrive at a gate and turn to the left to keep following the green-blazed trail, which narrows a bit and starts to descend with mild switchbacks. Pass the intersection with Chinquapin Oak Trail, and stay straight to keep following Crow's Nest Point Trail. Arrive at an intersection with a wide path—turn left here. In 2.5 miles from the start, arrive at a memorial marking the Daniels family cemetery. Stone plaques detail the family's history, which includes relatives of George Washington and James Madison.

The main attraction is just a short distance ahead. Arrive at the Crow's Nest Point overlook and sit on its perfectly situated bench to linger and enjoy the water views. Bird-watchers may be able to spot one of the 60 species of songbirds that call this area home. A sign cautions hikers not to approach the cliff's edge because the footing is unstable. Low wooden posts mark safe viewing spots. After taking in the sights, simply retrace the path back through the woods and to the parking lot.

More explorations are possible by tacking on some of the other trails. Incorporating either Potomac Overlook Trail or Chinquapin Oak Trail, the newest in the preserve, would add another mile to the journey. Accokeek Loop Trail would add 2.0 miles, and Boykin's Landing Trail would add 3.0 miles.

MORE INFORMATION

Crow's Nest Natural Area Preserve is open from March 15 to October 31, 8 A.M. to 8 P.M., and from November 1 to March 14, 8 A.M. to 5:30 P.M. The parking area off Raven Road offers space for 18 cars and is open Thursday through Sunday. Maps are at the trailhead. Hunting is available by a lottery system; visit the preserve's website at dcr.virginia.gov /natural-heritage/natural-area-preserves/crowsnest for more information.

The overlook at Crow's Nest can delight bird-watchers, whether expert or novice, as they try to spot one of the many species that call this area home.

NEARBY

The preserve can also be explored by water. The Brooke Road parking area is the trailhead for Crow's Nest Water Trail, an 8-mile paddling route. Paddlers can make their way around the peninsula and beach their boats by Boykin's Landing Trail should they wish to explore the trails both by land and by water. The Brooke Road parking area has an ADA-accessible canoe and kayak launch facility. For visitors wishing to add a short walk, the parking area also links up with a 0.5-mile trail that runs along Accokeek Creek and delivers up-close views of the tidal marsh.

33 PRINCE WILLIAM FOREST PARK

Prince William Forest Park is the largest forested region in the D.C. area. Its trails run along the north and south forks of Quantico Creek and span the hilly terrain in between.

Features

Location Triangle and Quantico, VA

Rating Moderate to Strenuous

Distance 7.9-mile loop

Elevation Gain 600 feet

Estimated Time 3 hours

Maps USGS Quantico and USGS Joplin; free National Park Service map at visitor center; online: nps.gov/prwi/planyourvisit/maps.htm

GPS Coordinates 38° 33.660' N, 77° 20.989' W

Contact Prince William Forest Park, nps.gov/prwi/index.htm, 703-221-7181

DIRECTIONS

From the Capital Beltway, take Exit 170 on the inner loop of I-95/I-495 (or take Exit 57 of the outer loop of I-495) and go south on I-95 for about 20 miles. Then take Exit 150B onto VA 619/Joplin Road. Go 0.4 mile and take the second right into the park on Park Entrance Road. Proceed about 0.5 mile to the visitor center and Pine Grove picnic area. Park at the far end of the parking lot.

TRAIL DESCRIPTION

Prince William Forest Park, a unit of the National Park Service, protects more than 15,000 acres in the middle of the busy I-95 corridor in Quantico, Virginia. The north and south forks of Quantico Creek flow through the park, and a large percentage of the 37 miles of hiking trails travel along them.

This 7.9-mile hike traces the natural and human history of the park. The hike starts northwest along the south fork of Quantico Creek, travels east over forested hills that were once farmland, and returns southeast along the north fork of Quantico Creek.

From the west end of the Pine Grove parking lot, cross an open field and start downhill on the western stretch of Laurel Trail Loop—this section is marked with yellow and green blazes.

The trees here are typical of the park's upland: flowering dogwoods and hollies below, beech limbs spreading horizontally, and yellow poplars towering above. In 0.3 mile, South Orenda Trail intersects—stay on Laurel Trail Loop and quickly arrive at a suspension

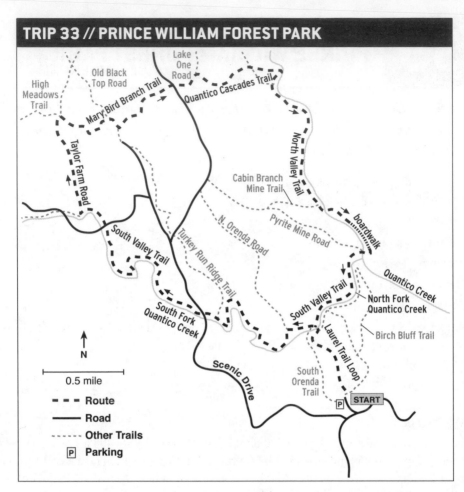

Map labels:
High Meadows Trail
Old Black Top Road
Lake One Road
Mary Bird Branch Trail
Quantico Cascades Trail
North Valley Trail
Taylor Farm Road
Cabin Branch Mine Trail
boardwalk
South Valley Trail
Turkey Run Ridge Trail
N. Orenda Road
Pyrite Mine Road
Quantico Creek
South Valley Trail
North Fork Quantico Creek
South Fork Quantico Creek
Birch Bluff Trail
Laurel Trail Loop
Scenic Drive
South Orenda Trail
N
0.5 mile
START

- - - Route
——— Road
········· Other Trails
P Parking

bridge with a sign marking that South Valley Trail lies that way. Cross the bridge, pausing for a moment to enjoy the views, and then turn left to start following white-blazed North Orenda Road. At 0.6 mile, at the next intersection, turn left onto narrow, white-blazed South Valley Trail, which curves back toward the creek.

Follow the creek along its lush bank, catching views of several picturesque waterfalls streaming from the cliffs on the opposite shore. At 1.1 miles, cross a small bridge over the Mary Bird Branch (named for an early homesteader) and immediately begin a steep climb up a ridge between the side and main streams, one of two big elevation gains on the south fork. Drop back down to a grove of sycamores, and at 1.4 miles, pass the intersection with Turkey Run Ridge Trail.

Go straight to stay on South Valley Trail. Cross Scenic Drive, a 12-mile paved road circling the center of the park. Come to an area rich with knotty black birches, pass a spur path that leads to parking lot B on Scenic Drive, and cross two small bridges over barely trickling side streams. This area is the fall line, where Quantico Creek plunges down erosion-resistant, gray-green boulders to the soft sedimentary rock of the coastal plain. Pass a spur to parking lot C, and soon after, at 2.2 miles, cross a bridge over another side stream. Immediately climb the second steep hill and return to the creek at a copse of hollies, mountain laurels, and oak saplings. Continue as the creek becomes gradually more turbulent and boulder strewn. Cross under Scenic Drive on a boardwalk.

At 2.9 miles, reach the intersection with Taylor Farm Road, and turn right to start following this blue-blazed trail. Travel gradually uphill for 0.6 mile to High Meadows Trail. Turn right onto this orange-blazed trail and meander downhill to Little Run. Turn left over the bridge and climb a sharp rise on a ridge where beeches cling tenuously to the edge. At 3.9 miles, reach Old Black Top Road. Turn right onto Old Black Top Road toward the ranger station, go 100 yards, and then turn left onto red-blazed Mary Bird Branch Trail. This 0.5-mile trail goes downhill to a bridge. Cross a short boardwalk and climb the facing ridge, which levels out on top. Upon reaching Scenic Drive (the end of Mary Bird Branch Trail), cross at the crosswalk and head right (south), to a sign marking the start of Quantico Cascades Trail.

Follow yellow-blazed Quantico Cascades Trail to Lake One Road, and turn left at a double-blazed tree to follow the road for a short distance. Turn right at the next intersection to keep following Quantico Cascades Trail. Go steadily downhill, crossing North Valley Trail and continuing on Quantico Cascades Trail toward a hill in the distance. Reach the "Fall Line" sign and head downhill on a series of tight switchbacks; this is the steepest elevation in the park. At 5.1 miles into the hike, drop onto the rocks of the cascades and note the sign reading "Power of Water." The slick, almost puttylike rock here is part of the Chopawamsic Formation, the result of volcanic eruptions 500 million years

Take time to enjoy the creek views while crossing the suspension bridge.

ago. Go right (south) along the creek on blue-blazed North Valley Trail (make sure not to head north on an unmaintained trail).

Continue on North Valley Trail. Pass a sign reading "Coastal Plain," and follow sharp bends in the creek, where massive upland boulders create boiling mini rapids—more dramatic than the cascades to the north. Stop at a sign reading "Pyrite Mine" and observe the concrete ruins of old mine buildings. Next, reach the bridge over North Fork Quantico Creek and turn left onto it to reach the north bank.

Follow the bank to a boardwalk bisecting a grove of tall pines. To the right is a denuded hill that was the site of the main pyrite mine, shut down in 1920. In 1995, the National Park Service built stormwater channels, planted 5,000 trees, filled the mine shafts, and buried the mine tailings (metal debris) in lime, all in an effort to regenerate plant and animal life. Continue on the boardwalk through more pines at the park's edge, following a depression from a narrow-gauge railroad that once served the mine. Turn right at a grove of rare redbuds and cross a bridge back to the south bank of North Fork Quantico Creek.

After the bridge, at 6.8 miles, turn left onto white-blazed South Valley Trail. Travel 0.9 mile back to the suspension bridge over South Fork Quantico Creek. Cross it and then retrace Laurel Trail Loop back to the parking lot.

MORE INFORMATION

Park entry is $20 per vehicle. Entrance fees are covered for visitors with Interagency annual recreation passes. In addition to the hiking trails, the park has 21 miles of bicycle trails, two large picnic pavilions, five historical cabins constructed by the Civilian Conservation Corps (see "Franklin D. Roosevelt's Tree Army: The Civilian Conservation Corps," on page 175) available for camping by advance reservation, and four campgrounds. For more information, visit nps.gov/prwi or call 703-221-7181.

NEARBY

The National Museum of the Marine Corps, with its slanted spire evoking the flag-raising at Iwo Jima and visible from I-95, is a state-of-the-art facility with galleries that take visitors through the history and traditions of the Marine Corps. It's adjacent to Marine Corp Base Quantico, home of the officer candidate school. See usmcmuseum.com.

The historical riverside town of Occoquan oozes a quaint yet eclectic vibe and offers waterside dining and shopping options. Rippon Lodge Historic Site in nearby Woodbridge is a peaceful location with a circa-1747 house, old family cemeteries, formal gardens, walking trails, and Potomac River vistas spread across 43 acres. Tours and special programs are offered seasonally. Visit discoverpwm.com to learn more about these and other local attractions.

UNDER COVER: SPIES IN THE PARKS

In the days of the New Deal under President Franklin Delano Roosevelt (FDR), the Civil Conservation Corps and Works Progress Administration built camps at Chopawamsic Creek (now Prince William Forest Park, Trip 33) and Catoctin Mountain Park and Cunningham Falls State Park (Trip 3). The newly created Office of Strategic Services (OSS), the precursor to the Central Intelligence Agency (CIA), appropriated these facilities in 1942 to train spies for World War II.

FDR wanted an American special operations and secret intelligence force to rival Great Britain's MI6, even though as recently as 1929, Secretary of State Henry Stimson had insisted, "Gentlemen do not read one another's mail." Long-standing U.S. policy eschewed peacetime espionage, so when FDR sought to establish the OSS (initially called COI, for Coordinator of Information) in July 1941, before Pearl Harbor's bombing, he had to proceed with caution. He tapped an old law school classmate, the decorated World War I colonel William "Wild Bill" Donovan, to lead the new organization.

The cabin camps (some of which are available today by reservation) served the OSS's top-secret needs well: close to Washington, D.C., yet semi-isolated, with plenty of rugged terrain surrounding them. Recruits—mostly young, college-educated men—lived in the bugged (and probably buggy), heavily guarded cabins and learned skills including forgery, forest parachuting, covert radio operations, and killing an enemy with a rolled-up newspaper. The Maryland and Virginia forests provided literal cover for fledgling undercover agents developing skills in stealth, concealment, and base station setup. Recruits entered the Pistol House—also known as the House of Horrors—to practice close-range pistol-fire combat as they navigated a pitch-black house with hidden phonographs that made realistic noises. The building was designed by British Special Operations—and at $6,000, it was the most expensive building constructed by the OSS.

Recruits practiced subtler covertness, too: befriending unsuspecting nearby townspeople, picking locks, spreading black propaganda (false information about an enemy), and using sabotage tactics, such as planting sham explosives under local bridges. Known by code names only and restricted to gathering in groups of four or fewer, recruits were forbidden to discuss their assignments. Their purported final exam involved infiltrating an industrial target by gathering information on production and supply or by planning sabotage. The OSS graduation parties were yet another test—liquor flowed liberally, and candidates were unwittingly evaluated on how much they would reveal under the influence. Utter loyalty was the ultimate test and the final cover they would need to carry out their dangerous work.

34 WASHINGTON AND OLD DOMINION TRAIL, GERRY CONNOLLY CROSS COUNTY TRAIL

This out-and-back hike covers a good distance of mostly level ground on two county-spanning trails, ideal for setting a steady, easygoing pace. At its midpoint is a well-preserved eighteenth-century mill.

Features 🐕 ♿ 💧 🚴

Location Vienna, VA

Rating Moderate to Strenuous

Distance 12 miles round-trip

Elevation Gain 230 feet

Estimated Time 4.5–5 hours

Maps USGS Vienna; official Northern Virginia Regional Park Authority Washington and Old Dominion Trail guide; online: wodfriends.org/maps/MainMap.html; novaparks.com/parks/washington-and-old-dominion-railroad-regional-park/wod-interactive-map; fairfaxcounty.gov/parks/cct

GPS Coordinates 38° 54.037′ N, 77° 15.607′ W

Contact Washington and Old Dominion Railroad Regional Park, Northern Virginia Regional Park Authority, novaparks.com/parks/washington-and-old-dominion-railroad-regional-park, 703-273-0596; Gerry Connolly Cross County Trail, fairfaxcounty.gov/parks/trails/cross-county-trail, 703-324-8700

DIRECTIONS

From I-495 (Capital Beltway), take Exit 49 to I-66 west. Take Exit 62 to VA 243 (Nutley Street) north toward Vienna. Go 1.0 mile and turn right onto Maple Avenue (VA 123). After 1.0 mile, turn right onto Park Street. Travel two blocks and turn right into the Vienna Community Center parking lot.

TRAIL DESCRIPTION

Washington and Old Dominion (W&OD) Trail is a paved hike-bike path that follows the former roadbed of the Washington and Old Dominion Railroad for 45.0 miles through northern Virginia. The full trail's southeastern end is at Arlington in the Shirlington business district, and the northwestern end is in the small town of Purcellville, approximately 9 miles from the Blue Ridge Mountains. Fairfax County's full Gerry Connolly Cross County Trail (CCT) travels through 40.5 miles of parkland with streams and valleys from the Occoquan River to the Potomac River at Difficult Run. The hike described here starts in Vienna and leaves W&OD Trail at Difficult Run to follow CCT. It ends at historical

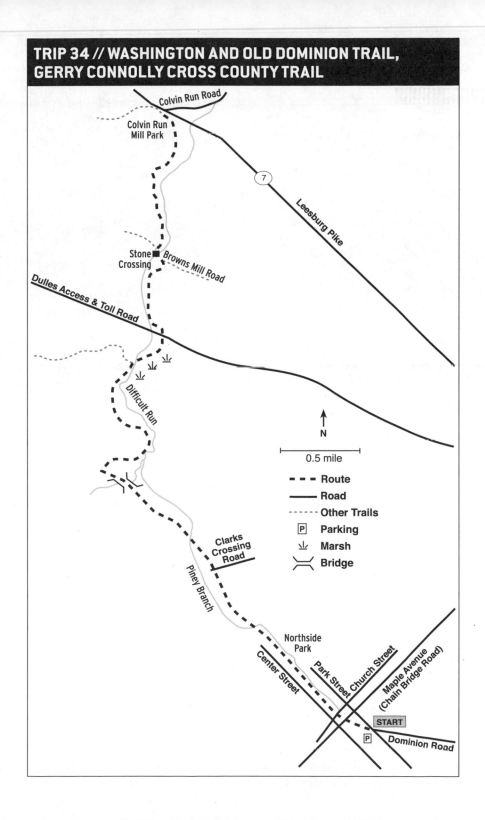

TRIP 34 // WASHINGTON AND OLD DOMINION TRAIL, GERRY CONNOLLY CROSS COUNTY TRAIL

Colvin Run Road

Colvin Run Mill Park

7

Leesburg Pike

Stone Crossing

Browns Mill Road

Dulles Access & Toll Road

Difficult Run

N

0.5 mile

- - - Route

——— Road

- - - - - Other Trails

P Parking

Marsh

Bridge

Clarks Crossing Road

Piney Branch

Northside Park

Center Street

Park Street

Church Street

Maple Avenue (Chain Bridge Road)

START

P

Dominion Road

Colvin Run Mill, circa 1813, serves as this hike's turnaround point. The working mill makes a pleasant spot for a picnic, with tours and a gift shop available. *Photo by Mike Bryan, Creative Commons on Flickr.*

Colvin Run Mill. Keep in mind that portions of CCT flood after heavy rains, so water-proof hiking boots are ideal.

From the community center parking lot, turn left onto asphalt W&OD Trail, hiking below large electric transmission towers. At 0.2 mile, cross Maple Avenue (Chain Bridge Road), which is the main north–south artery through Vienna. One block beyond Maple Avenue is Church Street, site of the historical Freeman House, a town museum and gift shop selling regionally produced books and crafts (open afternoons from Wednesday to Sunday). At 0.6 mile is another well-preserved structure, the eye-catching Vienna train station (circa 1859). The last train departed from here in 1967. Today, the station houses items from its heyday and a scale-model version of a railroad; the site is open to the public just a dozen times per year (visit nvmr.org for more information). A nearby building has a brightly painted mural—also look for the red caboose.

At mile marker 12 (12.0 miles from the full trail's start in Arlington County), an equestrian trail begins, paralleling the asphalt walkway and, in sections, offering a nice alternative path with some elevation change. Pass the entrance to Northside Park at the 1-mile mark of this hike. Here the trees are nestled close to the trail on the right; an open hill studded with power lines falls away to the left and offers little shelter on sunny days. Informative signs make it worthwhile to stop on this portion of the trail.

Two miles into the hike, the green space increases on either side of the trail, indicating Clarks Crossing and Tamarack parks. At 3.0 miles, cross a bridge over Difficult Run and go about 100 yards before swinging off the asphalt path and making a right onto CCT. The

40-mile trail (begun in 1999) connects Fairfax County north to south. This section of the hike is known as Difficult Run Stream Valley Trail because it adheres to Difficult Run until that stream's confluence with the Potomac River in Great Falls. The trail is red blazed and well marked with metal poles sporting the CCT logo but is intermittently maintained; in spring and after heavy rains, Difficult Run often overflows and can leave low-lying sections of the trail under several inches of water.

For the first mile after leaving W&OD Trail, the route snakes along the side of a hill with pleasant views of Difficult Run below to the right and suburban homes above to the left. After crossing a tributary of Difficult Run, turn right onto a gravel path and then traverse fast-moving Difficult Run over a series of round, concrete steps. Cross a small bridge over swampy lowland before forging a trail intersection to reach the Dulles Toll Road overpass. North of the toll road, turn left at a T intersection in a suburban neighborhood and follow a fairly level asphalt path.

At about three-quarters of a mile north of the toll road, cross Difficult Run for the final time, over a series of boulders. Immediately after, pass Browns Mill Road. The trail gradually edges westward away from Difficult Run and soon reaches a pleasant grove of pines and cedars that makes for the quietest and most secluded section of the hike. At the 6-mile mark, come to Colvin Run Road and its intersection with busy Leesburg Pike. The stream called Colvin Run once powered Colvin Mill, an early-eighteenth-century mill that has been restored and sits just across the pike and up Colvin Run Road. Decide here if you'd like to stop and explore. After visiting the mill and its surroundings, return to the main trail to retrace your steps to finish the hike.

MORE INFORMATION

Washington and Old Dominion Railroad Regional Park is open year-round, from dawn to dusk. The trail is generally open from dawn till dusk, but from Crestview Drive in Herndon east to Shirlington, the "closing time" has been extended to 9 P.M. to accommodate commuters. Admission is free. Leashed dogs are permitted. For more information, visit novaparks.com/parks/washington-and-old-dominion-railroad-regional-park. Also visit the Friends of the W&OD Trail at wodfriends.org to learn more about the trail and to see an updated list of available parking areas. Parking lots have accessible parking. See the Fairfax County Park Authority website (fairfaxcounty.gov/parks/trails/cross-county-trail) for information relating to CCT.

NEARBY

Colvin Run Mill Historic Site includes a circa-1811 gristmill, a miller's house, a charming country-style general store, and a barn. The park grounds are open from dawn to dusk daily. There is no admission fee for the grounds. Entry to the mill is by tour only—this worthwhile tour of the milling process costs $10 for adults and $8 for children, students, and seniors. Children under the age of 4 are free. Tours are offered on Saturdays and Sundays and include two ADA-compliant floors. At certain times of the year, actual grain milling, open to the public, occurs at the site. The general store sells freshly ground wheat, cornmeal, and grits; visit the website to see the latest hours of operation. For more information and to book a mill tour, visit (fairfaxcounty.gov/parks/colvinrunmill) or call 703-759-2771.

Bull Run Occoquan Trail, traveling through a swath of rural land in the Bull Run and Occoquan river watersheds, can seem as remote as the Appalachian Trail in some places.

Features 🐕 💧 $ 🏇

Location Manassas, VA

Rating Moderate

Distance 7.8 miles one way

Elevation Gain 470 feet

Estimated Time 4 hours

Maps USGS Manassas; map in Northern Virginia Regional Park Authority brochure available at available on-site; online: novaparks.com/parks/bull-run-occoquan-trail

GPS Coordinates 38° 46.007′ N, 77° 24.302′ W

Contact Bull Run Occoquan Trail, Northern Virginia Regional Park Authority, novaparks.com/parks/bull-run-occoquan-trail, 703-250-9124

DIRECTIONS

This hike requires a car shuttle between two points: Bull Run Regional Park and Hemlock Overlook Regional Park. Go to Hemlock Overlook first. From I-495 (Capital Beltway), take Exit 49 to I-66 west. From I-66, take Exit 53 (Centreville) to VA 28 south. Stay on VA 28 (Centreville Road) for 2.5 miles and then turn left onto Compton Road. At a T intersection, turn right onto Clifton Road. Go 1.8 miles, through the town of Clifton, turn right onto Yates Ford Road, and travel 1.4 miles to the parking lot at the Hemlock Overlook Regional Park entrance.

To reach Bull Run Regional Park, return north on VA 28 and turn left onto US 29 south (Lee Highway). Go 2.3 miles and then turn left onto Bull Run Post Office Road. Stay straight where the road jogs slightly left (avoiding a sharp left); go over I-66 and past the park's entrance station. Continue 1.6 miles and then park at the water park on the left. The trail begins just ahead to the right.

TRAIL INFORMATION

Bull Run Occoquan Trail is a 19.7-mile route that follows Bull Run in the north and the Occoquan River farther south, through the longest stretch of undeveloped land within an hour of Washington, D.C. The Northern Virginia Regional Park Authority (NVRPA) manages 4,000 woodland acres in these watersheds, including, from north to south, the

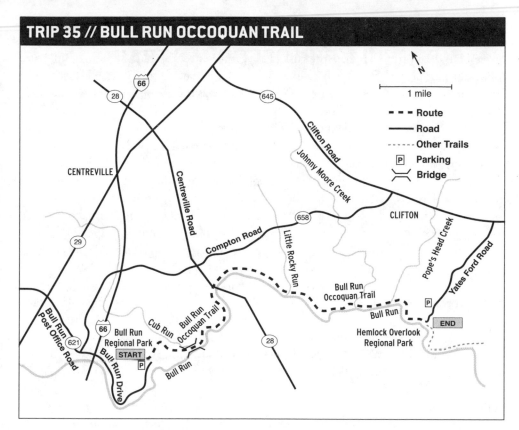

regional parks Bull Run, Hemlock Overlook, Bull Run Marina, Fountainhead, and Sandy Run. Bull Run Occoquan Trail, maintained by the Potomac Appalachian Trail Club, goes through all the parks except Sandy Run. The trail's terrain alternates between flat river bottomland and rocky hills and ravines, with dramatic elevation changes especially evident in the northern section described in this hike, between Bull Run and Hemlock Overlook regional parks.

From the water park parking lot, walk 100 feet down the road to an informational sign and a small wooden bridge beneath a willow oak. This is the start of blue-blazed Bull Run Occoquan Trail. Begin on the path, taking the boardwalk that leads through swampy areas, and turn right at the intersection with Cub Run. In April and early May, the forest floor here erupts in thousands of Virginia bluebells, shade-loving wildflowers that Native Americans used as a dye. The purple flowers of the pawpaw tree—looking like faded dark red roses—and the white flowers of the dogwood tree add springtime color here and elsewhere on the trail. Cross a clearing for electricity pylons; after 0.8 mile turn left at the second intersection, and cross Cub Run on a suspension bridge near its confluence with Bull Run. Notice the steep, rocky opposite bank of Bull Run—the uneven terrain here differs from the gentle course of the river near its origin west of Dulles Airport. From its headwater, Bull Run drops 1,280 feet through the Piedmont plateau to the coastal plain of the Potomac River.

Start along Bull Run's eastern shore, alive with scraggly river birch, tall sycamore, and stout Shumard oak. At 1.4 miles, go beneath Ordway Road and across a warped bridge. Several hundred yards on, where the husk of a sycamore stretches halfway across Bull Run, follow the blue blazes left and uphill. Climb to a cedar grove and then descend back to Bull Run as it flows under Centreville Road (VA 28). This was the site of the Civil War battle of Blackburn's Ford, where inexperienced New York troops under Israel B. Richardson stumbled into a brigade of Confederates concealed in the woods. The Union loss forced Richardson to find a new point of attack, leading to the First Battle of Bull Run.

Continue to an intersection and turn left uphill (marked by double blazes). Moving from the water, proceed up and down steep terrain on a twisting path. Pass a Civil War artillery emplacement under large tulip trees and then, at 3.7 miles, cross concrete steps over fast-flowing Little Rocky Run, where clear water snakes its way around dirt shoals. Turn left at double blazes, and soon cross a fire road under old-growth giants. Proceed up and down a series of broad hills carved by trickling, rocky streams. A green canopy of chestnut oak, pawpaw, and mountain laurel color the steep landscape.

Reach Bull Run again a little past the 5-mile mark of the hike—more bluebells flourish here in spring—and follow the riverside hornbeams, birches, sycamores, and oaks for 0.3 mile before veering left, away from the river. Climb alongside gurgling miniature waterfalls, cross the rocky stream on wood planks, and mount wooden steps up a steep-sided draw. Loop around a small hilltop and head back down to a low floodplain where old rusty engine parts share the forest floor with low-growing, foul-smelling skunk cabbage. At 5.7 miles, cross Johnny Moore Creek.

Return to Bull Run at an embankment where a side stream flows in. At the 6-mile mark, reach the rusting but still operating railroad bridge of the Norfolk Southern Railroad (Amtrak and Virginia Railway Express trains cross here on their way to Washington, D.C.). Inspect the crumbling stone foundations of the Civil War–era Orange & Alexandria Railroad trestle, a strategic point only a few stops from the vital hub of Manassas Junction (see Trip 42: Manassas National Battlefield Park). Go underneath the trestle, past small but sporting rapids, and then traverse a grassy, open expanse with the railroad tracks on the left and Bull Run on the right. Cross Pope's Head Creek near its confluence with Bull Run, taking care on its steep banks and slick stone pillars.

Continue on crumbly substrate at the bottom of a sharp, hemlock-lined cliff to the left. The dark green, conical hemlocks are complemented by diamond-barked flowering dogwoods. At 7.1 miles, arrive at what looks like a hollowed-out concrete bunker—the remains of the first hydroelectric plant in Virginia, built in 1925. This plant supplied power to Clifton, the first town in Fairfax County to receive electricity.

Go uphill alongside the plant (downriver) and then head left uphill at a blue blaze on a sharp rock. Curve along a narrow stretch lined with mountain laurel and go left at a sign for Hemlock Overlook/Yates Ford Road, leaving the blue blazes to follow yellow blazes directly atop a rocky streambed. Go 0.5 mile uphill to the parking lot at Hemlock Overlook Regional Park.

Bull Run Occoquan Trail provides stretches of peaceful hiking that can feel nearly as remote as the Appalachian Trail. *Photo by TrailVoice, Creative Commons on Flickr.*

MORE INFORMATION

Bull Run Occoquan Trail is open to horseback riders as well as hikers. Biking is prohibited on this segment of the trail (but is allowed on a 6.4-mile leg farther south, from Bull Run Marina to Fountainhead Regional Park). Leashed dogs are permitted. Bull Run and Hemlock Overlook regional parks are open year-round; admission to Bull Run is free for residents of Fairfax, Loudoun, and Alexandria counties; nonresidents pay $8 per vehicle.

Bull Run Regional Park offers a water park, among other attractions, and Hemlock Overlook Regional Park boasts an outdoor education center with zip lines and a ropes course (advance booking usually necessary). Both Bull Run and Hemlock Overlook parks have shooting centers, and rifle reports can be heard in the vicinity. For more information on Bull Run Regional Park, visit novaparks.com/parks/bull-run-regional-park or call 703-631-0550; for Hemlock Overlook Regional Park, visit (novaparks.com/parks/hemlock-overlook-regional-park or call 703-352-5900.

NEARBY

Occoquan Water Trail comprises 40 miles of Bull Run and the Occoquan River. Kayak and canoe access points along Bull Run Occoquan Trail include Bull Run Regional Park, the VA 28 intersection, Bull Run Marina, Fountainhead Regional Park, and Lake Ridge. (Fees may apply.) Occoquan Water Trail continues around Mason Neck to Pohick Bay Regional Park. Visit the Occoquan Regional Park website (novaparks.com/parks/occoquan-regional-park/things-to-do) for more details. Also worth a visit is the nearby Turning Point Plaza and Suffragist Memorial—these sites commemorate the women who were imprisoned at the Occoquan Workhouse in 1917 after protesting outside the White House for the right to vote.

FRANKLIN D. ROOSEVELT'S TREE ARMY: THE CIVILIAN CONSERVATION CORPS

In March 1933, new president Franklin D. Roosevelt (FDR) knew unrest was brewing as the Great Depression grew more severe. The previous year, his predecessor, Herbert Hoover, had faced a crowd of desperate World War I veterans (estimates of the group's size range from 10,000 to 20,000) protesting in Washington, D.C., to insist upon immediate payment of a service bonus promised to them but not redeemable until 1945. The regular U.S. Army soon forcibly evicted this "Bonus Army." One veteran was killed, and many were wounded.

FDR also felt grave concern about the soil erosion then decimating midwestern farmlands (due largely to logging and plowing), leaving their inhabitants in a swirling dust bowl without livelihood or sustenance. Appreciative of outdoor life, FDR also wished to make nature's benefits available to more Americans. To address these issues, he proposed to Congress on March 21, 1933, the creation of the Civilian Conservation Corps (CCC), to be used in "simple work, not interfering with normal employment and confining itself to forestry, the prevention of soil erosion, flood control, and similar projects. . . . [T]his type of work is of definite, practical value, not only through the prevention of great present financial loss but also as a means of creating future national wealth."

The legislative process moved swiftly. The Emergency Conservation Work Act was introduced into Congress the same day as Roosevelt's speech and approved by voice vote within days. Roosevelt issued Executive Order 6106 on April 5 to establish the CCC. The first worker enrolled on April 8, and the first camp—named Camp Roosevelt—was set up on April 17 in George Washington National Forest near Luray, Virginia. Camps were soon in all 48 states and several territories.

Members of the new CCC were paid $30 a month ($25 of which was sent directly home); they lived under military-style conditions. Single men 18 to 25 from families on relief could enroll for six months—eventually this was extended to two years. Veterans of World War I, single or married, soon were allowed to join. By summer 1933, 250,000 men had been mobilized. While camps in the northern states were initially integrated, the camps eventually became racially segregated. Black workers were housed in separate camps, receiving equal pay but barred from leadership roles aside from serving as education directors. A distinct division, mostly working in western states, was established for 85,000 American Indians.

Organized labor objected to low CCC wages and government-paid skills training that allowed these young men to compete unfairly with union members. Some complained that CCC workers would bring trouble to host communities.

But for many CCC workers, this program offered them their first chance of employment. About 70 percent of enrollees arrived malnourished and poorly clothed. Interviewed later, they universally recalled the muscles, skills, and pride they developed; the tangible results of their work; and the abundant food provided to them. One laborer interviewed for a PBS television documentary reminisced that it was "the only time in my life I'd ever had two pairs of shoes! And three squares [meals] a day. . . . I really had it made!"

Several camps were eventually established in and around Washington, D.C. In Fort Dupont, the list of completed projects included one comfort station, 64 yards of log guard-rails, 30 park and directional signs, 3.5 miles of foot trails, and 79 picnic tables. Another camp—Camp NA-DC-1—was in the National Arboretum. This camp was the first composed of Black men in the National Capital Parks area. The men—many from Washington, D.C., and Maryland, Virginia, and Pennsylvania—cleared brush and debris from 149 acres of the arboretum and worked on construction of an access road. Cedarville State Forest also housed CCC members who worked to develop the park's roads and trails—160 men worked at the park from 1933 to 1935, many of them Black men from Baltimore, Maryland, and Washington, D.C. The park had five barracks for housing.

The CCC was 3 million strong at the program's peak. Then came another world war, which led to the program's end; many CCC workers joined the armed forces as their corps were demobilized. Never formally authorized as a permanent agency, Congress ceased funding the program in 1942 and the program was disbanded during the following year. The camps were used to house conscientious objectors; interned Japanese Americans, German Americans, and Italian Americans; and Axis prisoners of war.

Today, the CCC's impact can be seen and experienced in parks nationwide. Workers helped create hundreds of parks, planted more than 3 billion trees, fought forest fires, carved erosion-control channels, built retaining walls, dug irrigation waterways, erected fire towers, quarried stone, stocked fishponds, and aided in disaster relief and cleanup. They helped build the presidential retreat Shangri-La (now Camp David) and portions of the Appalachian Trail. The CCC became a model for similar community service and conservation programs run at the federal, state, and local levels.

36 MASON NECK STATE PARK

Mason Neck State Park provides sanctuary for a stunning array of winged predators, including bald eagles, ospreys, herons, and hawks. Its trails traverse sandy beaches, a tidal marsh, and dense woodland.

Features 👣 🐕 💧 ⛱ 💲

Location Lorton, VA

Rating Easy

Distance 4.5-mile loop

Elevation Gain 196 feet

Estimated Time 2–2.5 hours

Maps USGS Fort Belvoir; map available at park's visitor center; online: dcr.virginia.gov/state-parks/document/data/mason-neck-avenza-map.pdf

GPS Coordinates 38° 38.743′ N, 77° 10.330′ W

Contact Mason Neck State Park, Virginia Department of Conservation and Recreation, dcr.virginia.gov/state-parks/mason-neck, 703-339-2385

DIRECTIONS

From the Capital Beltway, go south on I-95 for about 7 miles and take Exit 163 to Lorton Road (VA 642). Turn left onto Lorton Road, travel 1.0 mile, turn right onto Armistead Road, and take the second right onto Richmond Highway (US 1). Go about 1 mile and turn left onto Gunston Road, which heads east onto Mason Neck. Drive 4.5 miles, past Pohick Bay Regional Park and Gunston Manor, and turn right onto High Point Road, which leads to both the state park and Mason Neck National Wildlife Refuge. Pass the park entrance and follow the road straight to the picnic area parking lot and visitor center.

TRAIL DESCRIPTION

Mason Neck State Park contains 1,825 acres of shoreline, marshland, and mixed hardwood forest on a peninsula that juts into the Potomac River approximately 20 miles south of Washington, D.C. Nearby, Mason Neck National Wildlife Refuge (to the south and east), Gunston Hall and Pohick Bay Regional Park (to the northeast), and Meadowood Special Recreation Management Area (to the north) combine to protect 6,400 acres of the 8,000-acre peninsula. All the destinations offer hiking trails (in addition to canoe and kayak launches, bike paths, picnic areas, and nature overlooks), but the state park has the best-maintained and most extensive trail system. It also has one of the highest concentrations of bald eagles in northern Virginia, with approximately 50 pairs nesting year-round.

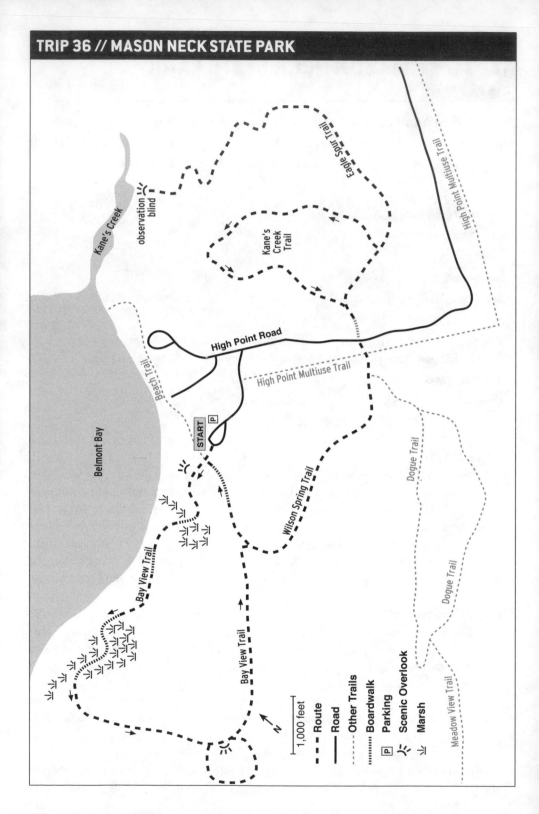

Kane's Creek

observation blind

Eagle Spur Trail

Kane's Creek Trail

High Point Multiuse Trail

High Point Road

Beach Trail

High Point Multiuse Trail

Belmont Bay

START

P

Wilson Spring Trail

Dogue Trail

Dogue Trail

Bay View Trail

Bay View Trail

Meadow View Trail

N

1,000 feet

- - - Route
——— Road
········· Other Trails
·········· Boardwalk
P Parking
Scenic Overlook
Marsh

Mason Neck State Park's elevated boardwalks offer hikers the chance to observe waterfowl and other marshland species up close. *Photo by Virginia State Parks, Creative Commons on Flickr.*

(*Note*: Because federal law mandates a 750-foot berth for bald eagle nests in national and state parks, trails are often relocated. Check with the visitor center for recent changes.)

Begin the hike on 1-mile, red-blazed Bay View Trail, which you can enter at the back left corner of the picnic area parking lot. This trail traces the shoreline of Belmont Bay, follows a creek upstream to a large tidal marsh, and passes into the forest. Follow the broad dirt-and-mulch path a short distance along the cliff above the shore and then ascend a series of wooden steps to a small bridge over a wet area. Continue on the sandy trail across a wooden walkway, where stands of honeysuckle enliven the meeting of land and water. The walkway affords an excellent view of Belmont Bay. Note the gabion barriers slowing erosion on the shoreline. Mason Neck suffers from wave erosion caused by polluted water, with many shore trees clinging to the tops of the sandy cliffs. Bay View Trail has to be periodically shifted inland due to cliff erosion. (Make sure to heed the postings for restoration areas.)

Arc back inland along a wooden fence and come to a boardwalk over a creek, where bay water flows into and out of the tidal marsh system, supporting a diverse wildlife population. Enter a variegated tidal zone of spatterdock, wild rice, and cattail, punctuated by wood duck habitats constructed as part of an Eagle Scout project. Take time to look for birds and other wildlife. During high tide, you might observe fish, including largemouth bass, longnose gar, and carp, swimming underneath the planks of the boardwalk. At low tide throughout the year, you sometimes can see frogs, snakes, and salamanders.

At the end of the boardwalk, enter the woods and ascend wooden steps that transition to gnarled roots; forge straight ahead to an observation blind for more views of the freshwater marsh. Loop back around and follow the trail's winding path through a mature upland mixed-hardwood forest, past an area that bears evidence of a 1986 fire. Burn marks still scar the trees, and the reduced understory growth has given rise to thriving blueberry and huckleberry bushes.

After taking in the views at the observation blind, return to main Bay View Trail, and then bear right onto 0.6-mile, yellow-blazed Wilson Spring Trail. Walk along the leafy and root-covered path as it alternately gains and loses elevation, crossing two wooden bridges over swampy runoff. Soon after the second bridge, cross High Point Multi-Use Trail, a parking area, and the main entrance road. Continue on an elevated walkway and turn right onto blue-blazed Kane's Creek Trail. Walk 200 feet and then turn right onto 1.3-mile, white-blazed Eagle Spur Trail. This out-and-back trail may be the most strenuous section of the hike. It hugs ridgelines and plunges into small valleys, traversing wooden planks over intermittently flowing streams. Oak, beech, and sweet gum trees—the latter with their ubiquitous, spiky, ball-shaped seedpods—line the way, and red-backed salamanders swarm over dead logs and scamper away from stomping feet, especially after a rainfall.

At the end of Eagle Spur Trail is an observation blind over Kane's Creek, a year-round nesting and roosting area for the magnificent bald eagle. Bald eagles are best spotted in the morning hours or at dusk, when park rangers lead guided tours to assist in observation. When ready to return, retrace the 1.25-mile hike down Eagle Spur Trail. Arrive at the intersection with Kane's Creek Trail and bear right to start this pleasant segment. Follow the loop, staying to the left at an intersection, and enjoy the level walk. Reach the same intersection that leads to Eagle Spur Trail, and stay straight to return to Wilson Spring Trail. Retrace the path down Wilson Spring Trail. Turn right at the intersection with Bay View Trail. Follow that trail over a boardwalk and back to the starting point.

MORE INFORMATION

Mason Neck State Park's trails are open year-round, 8 A.M. to dusk. Visitors pay a $10 per-vehicle fee to enter the park. All pets must be on a leash no longer than 6 feet at all times. The picnic area parking lot can fill on weekends or holidays; hikers can also start this trip at the Wilson Spring Trail parking lot, a short distance south on the entrance road. The park offers canoe and kayak rentals for access to Kane's Creek (April through October, weather permitting), a perfect opportunity to spot bald eagles, ospreys, great blue herons, beavers, and even otters. Bicycle rentals are available for High Point Multi-Use Trail. For more information, visit dcr.virginia.gov/state-parks/mason-neck or call 703-339-2385.

The park has a variety of accessible trails. Beach Trail is 300 yards long and ends at an accessible observation platform that offers stunning views over Belmont Bay. Those looking to explore the forest can consider Dogue Trail, which has a hard-packed dirt surface and is about 0.8 mile long. Paved High Point Multi-Use Trail parallels the park road. To learn more, visit dcr.virginia.gov/state-parks/mason-neck#other_info.

NEARBY

Pohick Bay Regional Park has excellent recreational facilities, including a water park, disc golf, and a miniature golf course. Also nearby is Gunston Hall, a restored Georgian-style mansion that is open for tours and offers a riverside bird walk (see Trip 37).

37 GUNSTON HALL: RIVER TRAIL

Nestled within this historical Virginia plantation is a brief, peaceful ramble to the Potomac River that brings you face-to-face with deer, herons, and bald eagles.

Features 🚶 💧 🏕 ⛺ 💲

Location Lorton, VA

Rating Easy

Distance 2.5 miles round-trip

Elevation Gain 86 feet

Estimated Time 1.5 hours

Maps USGS Fort Belvoir; free map available at the visitor center; online: gunstonhall.org/visit/guide/hiking-trails

GPS Coordinates 38° 39.922′ N, 77° 09.618′ W

Contact Gunston Hall, gunstonhall.org, 703-550-9220

DIRECTIONS

From I-495 (Capital Beltway), take I-95 south to Exit 163 and turn left onto VA 642 toward Lorton. Drive 0.4 mile and then turn right onto Lorton Market Street. After 0.6 mile, continue onto Gunston Cove Road, which then turns into VA 242 East/VA 600/Gunston Road. The entrance to Gunston Hall, 10709 Gunston Road, is on the left after 3.4 miles.

TRAIL DESCRIPTION

George Mason wrote the Virginia Declaration of Rights in 1776, during the midst of the American colonists' struggle for independence from Britain. James Madison later adapted the wording of the articles in Mason's declaration into the U.S. Bill of Rights. Mason's ideals of liberty and justice seem to have stood in contrast to his status as the owner of an active plantation; an apparent distaste for the institution never compelled him to offer his enslaved workers freedom. Today, the former plantation is maintained as a historic site, recognizing the paradox between Mason's ideals and the harsh realities of a plantation.

The property's River Trail is a short but rewarding trip to the shores of the Potomac River. Park in the large lot in front of the visitor center. Purchase your grounds pass—$5 for visitors over the age of 6—in the visitor center. This ticket entitles you access to the grounds, trails, and museum shop. If you would like to tour the house—a restored Georgian-style mansion—and the exhibitions in the visitor center, admission is $10 per adult.

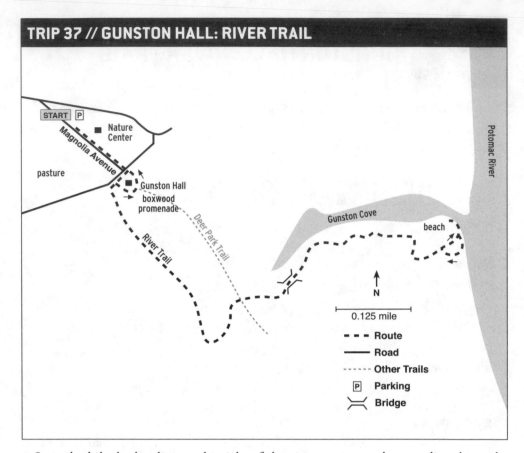

START P

Nature
Center

Magnolia Avenue

pasture

Gunston Hall
boxwood
promenade

Deer Park Trail

River Trail

Potomac River

Gunston Cove

beach

N

0.125 mile

- - - Route
—— Road
······ Other Trails
P Parking
⋈ Bridge

Start the hike by heading to the right of the visitor center and proceeding down the magnolia-lined carriage road to Gunston Hall. In George Mason's days, cherry trees, not magnolias, stood along this central road, which was mimicked by a wide hallway inside the house—this carriage road was the property's backbone. Go to the right of the residence; at the site of the Old Barn, depart the gravel path and turn left onto the grass. Look for a rutted dirt path that leads downhill to a clearing with a bluebird house in the middle—an orange blaze, a bit hard to spot at first, will help point you in the right direction. Several birdhouses line a large section of the grounds; they are an effort by a group of volunteers, including members of the Virginia Bluebird Society, to support a once-common bird whose natural habitat has been diminished by agriculture.

Continue into a mowed clearing fringed with forest and cross it toward the sign for River Trail. Look left for an attractive view of the slope up to the main house and the fenced fields that surround it. Orange-blazed River Trail curves to the right through patches of holly plants and ferns and then crosses a narrow creek, marked by wooden posts on either side.

Pass the intersection with the trail that leads to the deer park about 0.7 mile into the hike. Like many of his contemporaries, George Mason kept an area stocked with native deer, and several still populate this vicinity. Continue to the right on River Trail, now blazed yellow; head slightly downhill and then cross a wooden bridge with rails over a dry creek bed. The trail curves sharply to the left soon after, and water comes into sight on your left. This wetlands inlet, branching off the Potomac, is home to lush plant life and many birds, including herons, bald eagles, hawks, and ospreys. The undisturbed nature of the trail and the presence of fish in the water make it an excellent place to spot birds of prey. Listen for frogs as well.

The trail follows the edge of a low ridge, elevated above the inlet, with the plantation on the left as you climb the rooted, mossy slope. It descends to the right before circling and climbing again; you may begin to hear the hum of motorboats on the Potomac. As you near the river, the trail splits into a loop. Bear left for a lovely view of the wetlands before emerging at a beach with soft sand. Pause to admire the excellent vista from this vantage point. When the water is low enough, a few steps to the left bring you to the mouth of the wetlands inlet, offering the chance to see myriad birds.

When you are ready to return, head up a short and steep slope toward an old picnic area with an elevated view of the river—a pleasant spot to take a break and enjoy more scenery before completing the loop and then retracing your steps along River Trail to go back to the visitor center parking lot.

As you descend from the higher ground, look for an alternate return route for the last portion of the hike. If you veer to the right onto Deer Park Trail, marked by a sign, you can follow it through the woods to the far side of the deer park's grassy clearing. When you reach the meadow, enjoy a splendid view of the re-created Mason-era terraces and the garden fence. Walk across the grass to the remnants of an eighteenth-century road and follow the path up the ravine. The terraces and fence will be on your left. As the trail ascends, you will start to see the buildings in the reproduction kitchen yard.

The trails at Gunston Hall offer pleasant walking.

If you retraced the complete River Trail, head straight up the hill and turn right at the birdhouse at the top of the rise to follow the path back to the parking lot. If you used Deer Park Trail, walk past the kitchen yard to the lane and then continue through Magnolia Avenue to the parking lot.

MORE INFORMATION

Gunston Hall is open daily except Thanksgiving Day, December 25, and the first two weeks of January. The grounds are open from 9:30 A.M. to 6 P.M. or dusk, whichever is earlier. Guided tours, beginning at 10 A.M. and ending at 4 P.M., can be reserved online at gunstonhall.tix.com. Bathrooms and a water bottle filling station are available in the visitor center. The museum shop has snacks.

NEARBY

Consider adding Bluebird Trail, a 0.9-mile route that loops around the grounds. It's easy to stay on course—just follow the birdhouses. Bluff Trail is a 0.6-mile out-and-back route that takes visitors to an overlook of Pohick Bay and the Potomac River. To add some variety to a longer day trip, Mason Neck State Park (see Trip 36) and Pohick Bay Regional Park are both close by.

38 SIGNAL KNOB

This challenging but rewarding loop follows rugged trails, with viewpoints overlooking the Shenandoah Valley and Strasburg, Virginia.

Features

Location Fort Valley, VA

Rating Strenuous

Distance 10.6-mile loop

Elevation Gain 2,680 feet

Estimated Time 7–7.5 hours

Maps USGS Fort Valley West; National Geographic Trails Illustrated Maps, #792, Potomac Appalachian Trail Club Map G: Trails in the Massanutten Mountain

GPS Coordinates 38° 56.102′ N, 78° 19.174′ W

Contact Lee Ranger District, George Washington and Jefferson National Forests, U.S. Forest Service, fs.usda.gov/recarea/gwj/recarea/?recid=77721, 540-984-4101

DIRECTIONS

From I-495 (Capital Beltway), take Exit 49 to I-66 west heading into Virginia. Take Exit 6 for US 340/US 522 toward Front Royal/Winchester. Turn left onto US 340/US 522 south and continue for 1.2 miles. Turn right onto VA 55 West/West Strasburg Road and continue for 5.1 miles. Turn left onto VA 678/Fort Valley Road and continue for 3.4 miles. The parking lot is on the right off VA 678.

TRAIL DESCRIPTION

Signal Knob was a strategic lookout point during the Civil War, used by the Confederate army to observe Union troop movements in three counties in the Shenandoah Valley and to plan attacks, including an unsuccessful surprise attack attempted by General Jubal Early in 1864. Signal Knob traded hands several times during the war as both sides attempted to control the important site. This rugged loop takes hikers up Massanutten Trail past the Buzzard Rocks overlook and the Signal Knob viewpoint, which is the northernmost point of Massanutten Mountain; it then joins with Tuscarora Trail, climbs across the ridgeline, and returns to the parking lot. The loop comes in just shy of 10 miles; the terrain is, at times, an all-rock treadway requiring hikers to hop from rock to rock, so it is best to allow ample time to complete the trip. Be aware that the mileage on signs in the Elizabeth Furnace Recreation Area is rounded; refer to this guide for more accurate mileage.

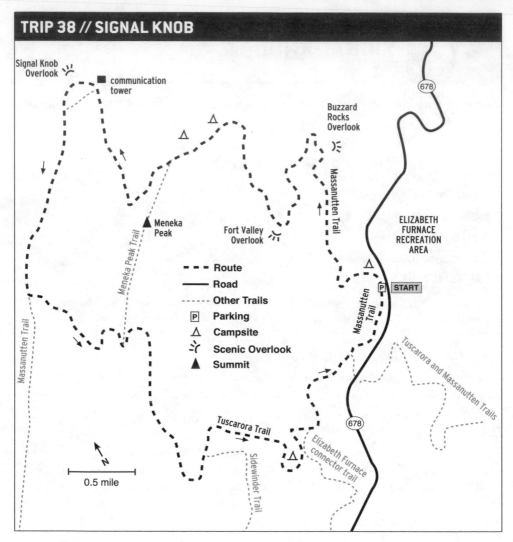

Orange-blazed Massanutten Trail begins to the right of the parking lot and climbs moderately through a deciduous forest. Pass a camping area on your right and an old stone house as you follow the narrow, rocky trail; continue to ascend as a streambed drops away on the right.

Turn right to cross an often-dry streambed bordered by a rock wall; continue climbing a sandy slope with rocky areas mingled with mossy forest on either side. You are now on the east side of Massanutten Mountain, with a steep slope dropping to your right, where glimpses of the valley come into view.

The trail continues to ascend as it curves up the mountainside and gradually grows rockier as it emerges into a more open section, with several pleasant views of the valley on your right. After climbing steadily for the first 1.5 miles, take a break at the unmarked but impressive Buzzard Rocks overlook, which provides a view over the valley at the distant cliffs. Pay careful attention here because the trail can be confusing to follow—the correct path takes a sharp hairpin turn to the left at Buzzard Rocks. Watch the orange blazes to stay on track.

Climb on a gently rising, pitch-pine-flanked upper switchback. The treadway becomes increasingly rocky, requiring some rock-hopping across several stretches. Use caution in this section. As the trail takes a tight turn in a leafy grove, look for a view of the valley. The climb eases out as the grade becomes less steep, but the trail remains rocky. Curve to the right on the ridge, passing the Fort Valley Overlook at 2.2 miles to see a slightly overgrown but far-reaching view of Fort Valley. At the overlook, the trail curves sharply to the right to head north.

Massanutten Trail rises gently on rocks through another open area; pick your way over the rough terrain with the valley now to the left. The trail continues to climb, although more gently, entering a thick forest of mountain laurels. In spring, these shrubs are festooned with pink blossoms. Here, the path narrows and becomes gentler, occasionally widening as the view of the valley disappears. Pass several campsites as the trail once again becomes slightly steeper and rockier.

Soon after, orange and white blazes appear together, heralding the intersection with white-blazed Meneka Peak Trail. This route goes left to the summit of Meneka Peak, cutting off the Signal Knob viewpoint. Continue straight on orange-blazed Massanutten Trail for the 1.1 miles remaining to Signal Knob. Pass through varied sections of forest and lush beds of ferns. The trail descends slightly to curve around the ridge; it then rises and falls, flanked by a carpet of blueberry bushes.

The trail flattens for a section that is open on both sides, although the view is obscured by young trees. Soon after, the WVPT public television tower comes into view. A sign indicates that you have hiked 5 miles (at this point you have actually traveled approximately 4.5 miles). Behind the tower is a view of the valley, partially obscured by power lines—this is not the view you are looking for; follow the trail past the tower and bear right at the fork to continue on the orange-blazed trail. Very soon, arrive at the marked Signal Knob overlook with its stunning view of Strasburg, Virginia, and the Shenandoah Valley. Wide, flat rocks offer tempting spots for a break to take in the views.

Head to the left to continue on Massanutten Trail, which soon joins the wide, descending gravel fire road. Look right and left to see thistles and, in August, Queen Anne's lace. At 1.3 miles from Signal Knob, the blazes turn from orange to blue and orange to mark the intersection with the blue-blazed Tuscarora Trail. Turn left onto this trail, which delivers a stout 0.8-mile climb to the wooded ridgeline of Meneka Peak.

Cross a shallow creek and then climb on the narrow path. The Tuscarora Trail rises through lichen-covered, boulder-strewn areas, becoming steadily steeper and rockier for the loop's last major ascent. Loop left and right on well-placed switchbacks, curving around the ridge and climbing steadily as the view begins to open up behind you.

At the top, the Tuscarora Trail intersects with white-blazed Meneka Peak Trail. Continue on the Tuscarora Trail, descending and occasionally climbing on the rocky path, which narrows as it dips back into the forest. The rocks gradually diminish. As the trail flattens out, a view opens up through the trees ahead and the valley comes into sight on the

A hiker approaches the Signal Knob overlook at the northernmost summit of Massanutten Mountain. During the Civil War, Confederate troops used this strategic viewpoint to observe battles in the Shenandoah Valley below.

left. The trail, descending again on switchbacks, winds past occasional dizzying glimpses of the valley, framed by pitch pines laden with pinecones.

The trail continues to wind downhill, passing an intersection with pink-blazed Sidewinder Trail, which departs to the right—stay straight on the blue-blazed Tuscarora Trail. In another mile, pass an intersection with the white-blazed connector trail to Elizabeth Furnace; again, stay on the Tuscarora Trail.

Cross a shallow brook on a large, flat rock; the trail curves to the right and soon passes a campsite on the left. Continue to descend more gently on switchbacks, circling around a deep valley on the right with a view of a rocky streambed. The trail parallels VA 678 for the last stretch (you may hear distant traffic noise). The trail widens as it passes a deep pit on the left; shortly after, it intersects a shallow gorge on the left.

When the Tuscarora Trail intersects again with Massanutten Trail, bear left to rejoin the orange blazes for the remaining 0.5 mile back to the parking lot. The trail has been rerouted in several areas to deter ATVs, but it is well marked. Pass a turnoff on the right for group camping; continue straight and cross a rocky streambed. To the right, VA 678 comes into view. Hike parallel to the road until you arrive back at the parking lot.

MORE INFORMATION

Bears are present throughout George Washington National Forest. Seeing them can offer the thrill of wilderness within a short drive of the city, but respect these impressive animals by keeping your distance and not leaving food unattended. Never come between a mother bear and her cubs.

NEARBY

The Elizabeth Furnace Recreation Area includes opportunities for family camping, group camping (by advanced reservation), picnicking, fishing, and hiking two interpretive trails that highlight the art and science of making pig iron and charcoal. Pig Iron Trail features the remnants of the Elizabeth Pig Iron Furnace. For those seeking more hiking adventures, Shenandoah National Park's Skyline Drive beckons a short distance away. And for those seeking food to fuel their explorations, the nearby towns of Strasburg and Front Royal offer a variety of dining options.

39 SKY MEADOWS STATE PARK

Saved from development by the noted philanthropist Paul Mellon in 1975, Sky Meadows State Park offers an incredible blend of pastures and woodlands in Virginia's Piedmont region.

Features

Location Delaplane, VA

Rating Moderate

Distance 5.8-mile loop

Elevation Gain 1,000 feet

Estimated Time 3 hours

Maps USGS Upperville; Potomac Appalachian Trail Club Map 8; map available at park; online: dcr.virginia.gov/state-parks/document/data/sky-meadows-avenza-map.pdf

GPS Coordinates 38° 59.118′ N, 77° 57.523′ W

Contact Sky Meadows State Park, Virginia Department of Conservation and Recreation, dcr.virginia.gov/state-parks/sky-meadows, 540-592-3556

DIRECTIONS

From I-495 (Capital Beltway), take Exit 49 to I-66 west, and then take Exit 23 toward Delaplane/Paris to US 17 (Winchester Road) north. Go 6.5 miles and turn left onto VA 710 into the park. The road ends at a parking lot near the Mount Bleak House and the visitor center.

TRAIL DESCRIPTION

Sky Meadows State Park is composed of 1,864 mountain acres on elevations ranging from 600 to 1,800 feet. The park's trails ascend hilly, open meadows and travel through alternating woodlands and pastures at the top of the ridge, which affords stunning vistas of the surrounding countryside. Throughout the hike, note the great diversity in butterfly species (best enjoyed with close-focusing binoculars and a good field guide). Zebra swallowtails regularly flutter across the trails, catching a hiker's eye with their bright pattern of black-and-white stripes and splashes of red on their tails. Monarch butterflies are common in July and August; the ultra-rare giant swallowtail appears only in August.

Begin your hike at the northwest corner of the parking lot. Follow a connector path that immediately veers left onto gravel-surface Boston Mill Road. After a few hundred feet, climb the stone steps to the right and begin the 0.7-mile ascent on red-blazed Piedmont Overlook Trail. Cross a wooden bridge over a brook and pass an old farm building.

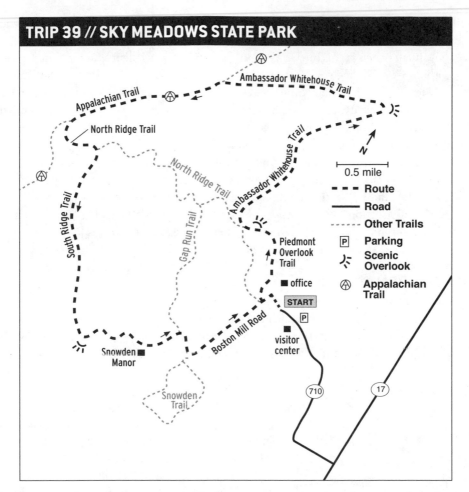

Continue up along the open pasture before arriving at benches that give a breathtaking view from Piedmont Overlook; survey the patchwork quilt of pastures and farm fields, interspersed with lakes and streams, stretching across Crooked Run valley below. George Washington mapped this area in the 1740s. In 1861, the valley served as the jumping-off point for Confederate soldiers en route to the Battle of Bull Run.

Continue on Piedmont Overlook Trail into a patch of woods. Go up and then down wooden steps to reach an intersection with blue-blazed North Ridge Trail. Turn right onto this trail and follow it 0.2 mile. Turn right onto 1.1-mile Ambassador Whitehouse Trail. This route arcs northward to another overlook and then bends to the left.

Keep your eyes and ears open for the ubiquitous red-headed woodpecker, a year-round resident whose drumbeat mating call reverberates through the park in spring and early summer. Blue jays, mockingbirds, and cardinals also abound all year. The trail ends at the intersection with the white-blazed Appalachian Trail (AT), which stretches along the ridgeline. Turn left onto the AT and sample a somewhat rocky mile—at least in comparison to the previous trails—of this famed long-distance trail. The AT then reenters the woods. Pass an intersection with Old Trail and then arrive at the intersection with North Ridge

Trail. Turn left onto North Ridge Trail and make your way downhill to the intersection with South Ridge Trail.

A convenient bench at this intersection provides another excellent spot for a short break, even without views. When you're ready to continue, turn right onto 1.6-mile, yellow-blazed South Ridge Trail and ease downhill on a wide, soft-packed path. The South Ridge Overlook offers another excuse to stop—this time to enjoy the views—before continuing downhill. About halfway down the ridge, make a short side trip to the ruins of Snowden Manor, a Federal-style house built in the 1860s and mostly consumed by fire in 1913, leaving only a fireplace and a chimney behind. Arrive at the intersection with a path that leads to overnight campsites. Turn right here and quickly arrive at an intersection with Boston Mill Road. Turn left and follow the gravel road 0.5 mile to the parking lot.

Near the intersection of South Ridge Trail and Boston Mill Road is Snowden Trail, which loops through a mature oak forest. Hikers can easily attach this loop to the day's itinerary, adding 1.0 mile to the overall route.

MORE INFORMATION

Sky Meadows State Park is open daily, 8 A.M. to dusk. Admission is $4 per vehicle on weekdays and $5 per vehicle on weekends. The park is home to a red-headed woodpecker sanctuary near the contact station at the southern end of the property, just off VA 710. The visitor center has nature and history exhibits, as well as a gift shop. Camping is also available.

With views like these, everyone—even dogs—need to take a break and soak them in. *Photo by David Posey.*

The park offers several opportunities for visitors to learn more about the area. Some programs are offered throughout the year, but the main programs run from March to December. The park is also a designated International Dark Sky Park, and has monthly programs led by volunteer astronomers. For more information and to see a list of upcoming programs and events, visit dcr.virginia .gov/state-parks/sky-meadows or call 540-592-3556.

Sensory Explorers' Trail at Sky Meadows State Park has adaptions for visually impaired, hearing-impaired, and mobility-impaired visitors. This 0.3-mile trail is minimally graded with packed gravel and has clay models of animals along the route. A printed guide is available at the trail entrance, and instructions for downloading an audio guide are on the park's website at dcr.virginia.gov/state-parks /sky-meadows#recreation. Braille signs along the route, signaled by changes in the trail's surface, work in conjunction with the audio guide.

NEARBY

The neighboring hamlet of Delaplane holds its Strawberry Festival every Memorial Day weekend. G. Richard Thompson Wildlife Management Area (Trip 40) is a short drive from Sky Meadows, and Signal Knob (Trip 38) is about 30 miles to the west, making for a nice weekend-getaway combo. This area of Virginia's Piedmont is also home to wineries, antiques shops, and historical bed-and-breakfasts in its many small communities.

40

G. RICHARD THOMPSON
WILDLIFE MANAGEMENT AREA

The trails at G. Richard Thompson Wildlife Management Area crest the Blue Ridge Mountains to reach heights of 2,200 feet above sea level. In springtime, the property is adorned with Virginia's best display of trillium flowers.

Features 🐕 💧 $

Location Delaplane, VA

Rating Strenuous

Distance 8.8-mile loop

Elevation Gain 1,750 feet

Estimated Time 4.5–5 hours

Maps USGS Linden, USGS Upperville; Potomac Appalachian Trail Club Map 8: Appalachian Trail in Northern Virginia—South Half, Snickers Gap to Chester Gap; online: dwr.virginia.gov/wp-content/uploads/media/Thompson-WMA -Map.pdf

GPS Coordinates 38° 57.446′ N, 77° 59.327′ W

Contact G. Richard Thompson Wildlife Management Area, Virginia Department of Wildlife Resources, dwr.virginia.gov/wma/thompson, 866-721-6911

DIRECTIONS

From I-495 (Capital Beltway), take Exit 49 to I-66 west, and then take Exit 23 toward Delaplane/Paris to US 17 (Winchester Road) north. Go 6.5 miles and then turn left onto VA 688 (Leeds Manor Road) into the wildlife management area. After 2.5 miles, turn right into the Lake Thompson parking area, which contains two lots. Park in the northern lot near Lake Thompson.

TRAIL DESCRIPTION

The Virginia Department of Wildlife Resources stewards 36 wildlife management areas (WMAs) across the state that encompass 200,000 acres of public land. To maximize hunting and fishing opportunities, WMAs introduce species, burn undergrowth, plant edible wildflowers, develop hedgerows, and stock ponds. Hunting is allowed, but hikers can enjoy one of northern Virginia's largest and best natural areas during open seasons by wearing bright safety clothing and staying on designated trails.

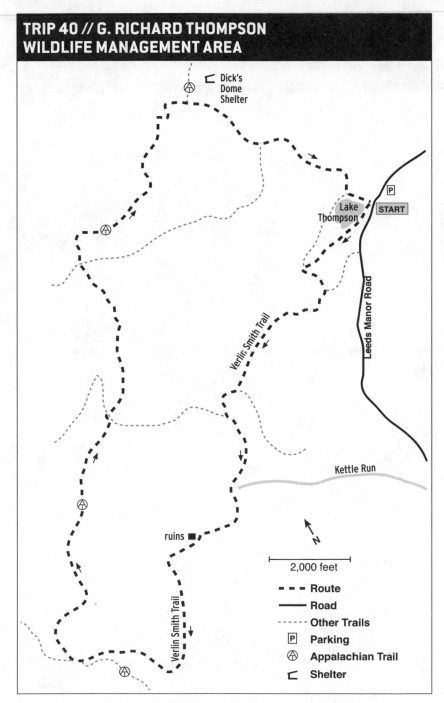

G. Richard Thompson WMA is broken into two tracts; the much larger southern tract has elevations between 700 and 2,200 feet above sea level, with the Appalachian Trail (AT) spanning the ridgeline for 7.0 miles on its western boundary. This hike is within the southern tract. Generally speaking, as the trail goes west, it goes uphill. Eleven parking

A rugged dirt road in G. Richard Thompson Wildlife Management Area testifies to the preserve's unspoiled atmosphere. Mid-spring, look for abundant trillium blooming along the trails. *Photo by Stephen Mauro.*

spots surround the area, and several trails running east to west connect the parking lots on either side.

One of this hike's main attractions is the large-flowered trilliums that bloom along the route from late April to early June. Added to the trilliums are dozens of other vibrant wildflowers: an impressionistic blend of showy orchids, yellow lady's slippers, sweet cicely, golden ragwort, lousewort, wild hydrangeas, buttonbush, and fleabane. The final feather in Thompson's bountiful cap is 10-acre Lake Thompson, which is stocked with trout, bluegill, sunfish, catfish, and bass.

From the parking lot, walk 100 yards down the gravel path to the lake and continue along the south shore. At the end of the lake, a deep ravine cradles a streambed, opening to the right. The ascent gradually becomes steeper until, at 0.6 mile from the starting point, another trail joins from the right, signaling the beginning of steep and rocky terrain.

Turn right at the intersection onto unmarked Verlin Smith Trail, which runs along a wire fence at the border of the WMA. Beyond are open hillsides with farms, vineyards, and solar-panel-equipped houses. Travel uphill along the fence for 200 yards and then veer right for a 0.5-mile climb, gaining 300 feet of elevation on the widening red-dirt trail to a clearing where another trail comes in on the left. Continue on Verlin Smith Trail past granite boulders and curve gently to the left. At a dilapidated sheet-metal shack, turn left to stay on Verlin Smith Trail.

As the trail goes downhill, Kettle Run, a shaded stream, glides across the path. This is a good place to see birds, box turtles, and snakes. Cross the stream and trek uphill again, passing through a clearing with dense, chest-high flowering plants. The trail levels out; at 0.2 mile from the clearing, it follows a rocky streambed for about 15 yards. Turn right to reach Wildcat Hollow Spring, which flows through granite boulders strewn across the treadway. Proceed on more sharp-edged rocks, traveling back uphill out of the ravine and along a gradual, narrow, and pleasant dirt trail. Swing abruptly right at a large clearing that on sunny days affords attractive views of the surrounding area. Soon the trail widens and becomes gravelly.

Under a grove of large-leafed yellow poplars, the white-blazed AT enters from the left to meet Verlin Smith Trail. This point marks the beginning of the journey along the rocky spine of the mountain. The smooth rock here makes this a pleasant perch, offering a moment of tranquility before you turn right to start hiking the AT. A little way ahead, the AT follows a rocky streambed along a gentle curve. Continuing on, the trail becomes rocky and steep, as hickory, white ash, chestnut oak, and a few sassafras trees crowd the path.

A blue-blazed trail (leading to more parking and a view of microwave/radio towers) breaks away to the left. Go straight on the AT (several side paths connect to parking lots), keeping an eye on the white blazes to stay on track. Enjoy the sight of tall hickories spreading horizontal limbs of thick foliage overhead—what AT thru-hikers call the Green Tunnel.

Just after a clearing, another side path intersects the AT. Go straight here to stay on the AT, and pass a large, smooth boulder that looks like a Martian spacecraft. After an uphill stretch, a small, narrow path breaks off to the left to yet another parking area. Stay on the AT as it veers right and begins a long, gradual descent. The terrain alternates between sharp rocks and soft-packed dirt, with some dramatic granite boulders. Near the boundary of the WMA, reach an intersection with an unmarked trail to the right—this is your return route. For a brief side trip, follow the AT past this intersection for a short distance and turn onto the blue-blazed spur path that leads to the Dick's Dome shelter. Return to the intersection and turn to the left down the trail to continue the hike. In summer, this section, unofficially known as Stone Wall Trail, is overgrown, requiring extra effort to move through the junglelike mass of clothes-grasping raspberry bushes and devil's-walking-stick. At points, the trail is completely consumed, making it difficult to locate its twists and turns.

After a scramble over some old stone ruins, watch for a connector trail that intersects from the right, which signals the opening of a bigger, less dense path ahead. On this downhill stretch, the trail alternates between dense vegetation and open areas. Descend to the lake and turn left along its eastern edge to return to the parking lot.

MORE INFORMATION

Access permits are required to visit G. Richard Thompson WMA. A daily pass is $4 per person and an annual pass is $23. Passes can be purchased online or by calling 866-721-6911 during regular business hours. Hunting is permitted in the WMA, so wearing blaze orange during hunting season is a must. To learn more about Thompson WMA and how to purchase access permits, visit dwr.virginia.gov/wma/thompson.

NEARBY

More hiking can be found nearby at Sky Meadows State Park (Trip 39) and Signal Knob (Trip 38), if you're looking to build a weekend getaway. Many unexpected treasures await visitors along the side roads in these parts, such as the Apple House on VA 55 in Linden, a good choice for a hearty Virginia breakfast or lunch—with or without cider donuts. If you have time, consider driving along scenic US 50 to reach Thompson WMA with a trip through beautiful horse country.

41 VIRGINIA OUTDOORS FOUNDATION'S PRESERVE AT BULL RUN MOUNTAINS

Bull Run, the closest mountain range to Washington, D.C., provides hikers with mild terrain as they explore a living laboratory dedicated to protecting a host of plant and animal species along with cultural history sites.

Features

Location Broad Run, VA

Rating Easy

Distance 2.2-mile loop

Elevation Gain 250 feet

Estimated Time 1–1.5 hours

Maps USGS Thoroughfare Gap; free map at trailhead; online: vof.org/wp-content/uploads/2019/07/VOF-BRMNAP-Trail-Map.pdf

GPS Coordinates 38° 49.516′ N, 77° 42.183′ W

Contact Bull Run Mountains Natural Area Preserve, Virginia Outdoors Foundation, vof.org/protect/reserves/bull-run-mountains, 844-863-9800, ext. 460

DIRECTIONS

From I-495 (Capital Beltway), take Exit 49 to I-66 west. Go 27.0 miles on I-66 and take Exit 40 (Haymarket). At the end of the exit ramp, turn left at the traffic light onto US 15 south (James Madison Highway). Go 0.5 mile to the next light and turn right onto VA 55 (John Marshall Highway) west. Go 2.7 miles (crossing railroad tracks at 2.0 miles) and turn right onto Turner Road. Follow it a short distance across I-66 and then turn left onto Beverley Mill Drive. Go 0.8 mile to the public trailhead on the right at the end of the road.

TRAIL DESCRIPTION

Bull Run Mountains Natural Area Preserve consists of 2,500 acres near Haymarket, Virginia. The Virginia Outdoors Foundation (VOF) owns and manages this state-designated natural area preserve as a living laboratory and open-air museum focused on stewarding and sharing the wonders of the landscapes' ten distinct plant communities and suite of cultural resources. Hikers will find it easy to make a full day of exploring this special location, which is open every Friday, Saturday, and Sunday year-round. This trip focuses on the center of the preserve's hiking area and includes a variety of historical sights.

From the parking lot, head toward the trail kiosk, which has a large-scale map of the preserve. Cross the railroad tracks and enter the trail system by walking north. The path is

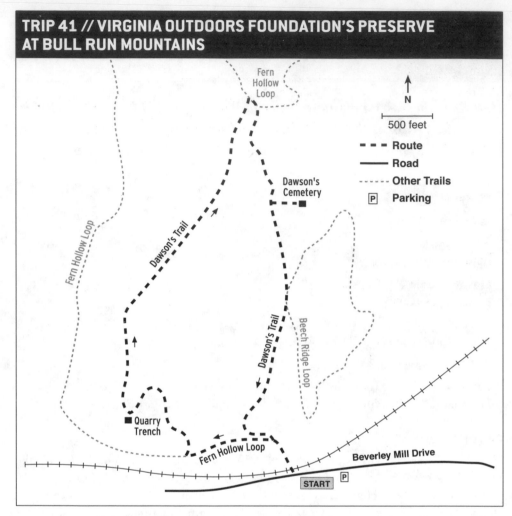

narrow but well defined. At a split, where Dawson's Trail goes uphill to the right, follow level, green-blazed Fern Hollow Loop straight ahead.

The trail stays mostly flat, passing over a boardwalk, and then reaches another intersection with red-blazed Dawson's Trail. Before turning right onto Dawson's Trail, take a few steps forward to check out the stone pit that was once used to store ice.

Once ready to resume, follow Dawson's Trail uphill, making a wide switchback to the left. At 0.5 mile, reach Quarry Trench, the site of well-preserved trenches that are remnants from the Battle of Thoroughfare Gap, which led up to 1862's Second Battle of Manassas (Second Battle of Bull Run).

After the trenches, the trail swings to the right, with a bit of gentle climbing as travels along the hilltop. Look for hickory and chestnut oak in this area. The trail gradually eases out for a short stretch and then begins to head downhill.

Near the bottom of the descent, roughly 1.3 miles into the hike, Dawson's Trail and Fern Hollow Loop intersect. Turn right to follow this briefly combined trail—it soon splits again, with Fern Hollow Loop departing to the left. Keep right to stay on red-blazed Dawson's Trail.

In 0.2 mile, look for an unmarked side path to the left that leads to Dawson's Cemetery. This is worth a detour—the carvings on the gravestones seem to have aged remarkably well. Marvel at the passage of time shown by the tree that has grown around one of the gravestones.

Return to the intersection and turn left to rejoin Dawson's Trail. The walking along this segment is mild as the trail rolls through a picturesque hollow. Pass the intersection with Beech Ridge Loop. (Hikers wanting a longer journey can easily include this loop—doing so adds 1.3 miles to the total distance.)

For the final 0.4 mile of the hike, the trail slopes gently downhill and then reaches the intersection with Fern Hollow Loop. Follow that trail to the left as it goes back over the railroad tracks and to the parking lot.

MORE INFORMATION

Pets are not allowed in the preserve. The preserve is open Friday, Saturday, and Sunday, year-round. VOF offers guided hikes to explore various aspects of the preserve—find more information on VOF's website (vof.org) or on its social media (@bullrunmountains on Instagram or Facebook). Planning is under way to develop a new parking lot, trailhead, and renovated trail system—see the preserve's website at vof.org for the latest

A tree wraps itself around one of the headstones in Dawson's Cemetery

updates. Chapman Mill Historic Site is open on weekends and some holidays. Visit chapmansmill.org to learn about the history of the five-story gristmill and ongoing restoration efforts.

NEARBY

The village of The Plains, a short distance to the west along VA 55 (John Marshall Highway), is an icon of northern Virginia's horse and hunt country. It hosts various equestrian events spring through fall at the Great Meadow venue, such as the Virginia Gold Cup steeplechase race the first Saturday in May. Visit theplainsvirginia.com and greatmeadow.org for current information.

For one of the region's most enchanting scenic drives in any season, continue north from The Plains on VA 626 (passing several wineries on the way) to another lovely country village, Middleburg, where you'll find taverns and antiques shops to enjoy. See visitmiddleburgva.com for details. Then take US 50 east back toward Washington, D.C., pausing in the hamlet of Aldie to view the restored Aldie Mill; visit aldieheritage.com for information.

42 MANASSAS NATIONAL BATTLEFIELD PARK

The rolling hills of Manassas National Battlefield Park offer the perfect mix of nineteenth-century historical interpretation and opportunities for forested solitude.

Features

Location Manassas, VA

Rating Moderate

Distance 5.4-mile loop

Elevation Gain 900 feet

Estimated Time 3–3.5 hours

Maps USGS Gainesville; online: nps.gov/mana/planyourvisit/maps.htm

GPS Coordinates 38° 48.761′ N, 77° 31.300′ W

Contact Manassas National Battlefield Park, National Park Service, nps.gov/mana/index.htm, 703-361-1339

DIRECTIONS
From I-495 (Capital Beltway), take Exit 49 to I-66 west to Exit 47 (Manassas). Go north on VA 234 (Sudley Road). The park entrance is 1.0 mile ahead on the right.

TRAIL DESCRIPTION
The open hills and forested patches of Manassas National Battlefield Park offer the intrepid hiker food for thought and memory as well as a physical workout. The lay of the terrain in this hike played a major role in the First Battle of Manassas on July 21, 1861—the first major land battle of the Civil War. Bull Run, the small creek meandering through the area, forced advancing Union troops to waste valuable time searching for a ford where they could cross it with their artillery and supply wagons, and the hills to the south offered the Confederates high ground from which to inflict punishment and eventually drive the Union army back. First Manassas Trail, a 5.4-mile trek over this terrain, visits Bull Run and several of the most hotly contested points of the battle.

First Manassas Trail starts to the right of the visitor center. Follow the broad, grassy path straight ahead toward a line of cannons. The higher, unmowed grass on either side re-creates the sea of weeds through which the soldiers waded during the fighting. Bear right on the mulch path denoted by a blue-blazed marker. The cool, shaded covering here is courtesy of a diverse range of pines, cedars, hickories, American elms, persimmons, and a few black walnut trees. Soon the mulch changes into gravel, with ash trees set directly in the

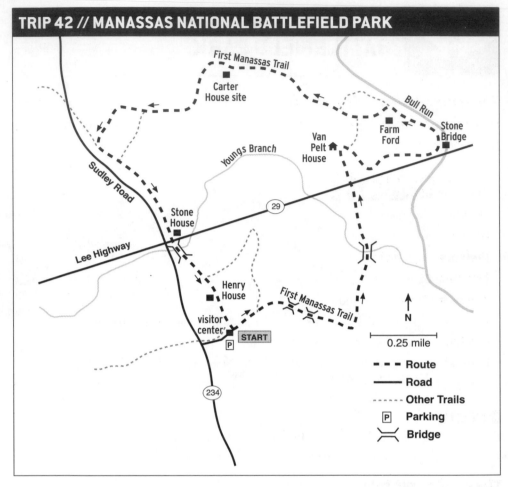

path. Cross two wooden bridges over streambeds (dry in summer). An old bench sits right before the bridges.

Turn 90 degrees left at the clearing. Make sure to take the second left onto the wider gravel road. (Do not take the first left onto a small dirt path—this is the horse path.) Ahead is a concentrated pine grove. Cedars, oaks, and a few sassafras shrubs mark the way on the right, and a small clearing opens on the left. Scattered trees in the clearing mark the early succession of field to forest. The trail returns to gravel here. At the end of the clearing, where a large black walnut unfurls its canopy of crowded compound leaves, turn left over a dry streambed toward another clearing and then immediately right (a marker denotes the turn). Travel over Youngs Branch (a tributary of Bull Run) on a wooden bridge shaded by elms and hickories. Turn left onto a gravel path near another marker and arrive soon in the middle of a large, open field. Rows of cedars and pines come and go on the right, and two benches sit under the shade of a single cedar—a perfect spot for lunch. Cross US 29 (Lee Highway—a major thoroughfare) and ascend a short rise. Make sure to go straight where a dirt path diverges sharply to the right. Pass a squat tree that gives off a silver sheen—an illusion maintained by the silvery underside of its leaves—and turn right up a rise to the

Van Pelt House site, a small clearing surrounded by big-leafed redbud trees. This site served as the battle headquarters of the Confederate colonel Nathan Evans, whose South Carolinians cleared timber from the ridge on the western slope all the way to Bull Run. Follow a sign for Stone Bridge pointing right and descend a sharp slope to a raised walkway over damp lowland.

Turn left on the gravel trail in front of the bridge and follow Bull Run. Walk upstream and cross a small footbridge. Ascend the steep slope to the site of Farm Ford (marked by a wayside exhibit). As you exit the woods, turn right back onto the larger trail that comes directly from the Van Pelt House site. This habitat where trees and grass meet is replete with chickadees, bluebirds, mockingbirds, sparrows, robins, and red-tailed hawks. Travel slowly downhill past a law enforcement office on the left and plunge into the woods on a mulch path that travels by giant yellow poplars, a few sycamores, and, a rare chestnut oak. The trail passes the Carter House site, a few ruins standing in a depression. After 4.0 miles on the hike and 0.75 mile on the broad mulch path in the woods, on the left pass a marker memorializing George Stovall, a Georgian who died here and whose last words, according to the marker, were "I am going to heaven." This is the wooded saddle of Matthews Hill. Emerge from the woods and proceed straight onto a mowed portion of grass. Head toward a few cedars on the rise ahead and continue down Matthew's Hill to Stone House, which was in the thick of the carnage and served as a Union hospital through numerous engagements. Cross US 29 at the traffic light and then cross a wooden bridge over Youngs Branch, heading uphill over ground where Union forces retreated. Arrive at Henry House, which is a postwar structure—the original house was destroyed. Octogenarian Judith Henry was mortally wounded by artillery fire when Union gunners attempted to flush out Confederate sharpshooters from the yard. Continue past the structure, back to the visitor center.

MORE INFORMATION

Visitors pay no admission fee at Manassas National Battlefield Park, but donations are accepted. The Henry Hill Visitor Center, open daily from 8:30 A.M. to 5 P.M. (closed Thanksgiving Day and December 25), offers an in-depth, 45-minute orientation film that plays hourly until 4 P.M.

The visitor center is accessible to wheelchairs. Park rangers can lead talks and short tours to accommodate all visitors, including those with any mobility impairments. The visitor center also offers tactile exhibits for the visually impaired, and the map program is closed-captioned. The park has several paved trails, including one to Stone House (although the house itself is not accessible) and Chinn Ridge Trail. The path from the parking lot to the Brawner Farm Interpretive Center (open seasonally) is paved and accessible. The center includes exhibits and a fiber-optic battle map about the Second Battle of Manassas. To learn more, visit nps.gov/mana/planyourvisit/accessibility.htm.

During winter, the hiking trails, rolling hills, and bridle paths draw cross-country skiers and snowshoers.

Stone House on Manassas National Battlefield served as a refuge for soldiers wounded in the first conflict here, in July 1861. Today, the house is flanked by a pair of silver maple trees. *Photo by Stephen Mauro.*

NEARBY

The historical downtown district of Manassas, a few miles south on VA 234 (Sudley Road), boasts an appealing array of eateries, brewpubs, and shops, along with the Manassas Museum and the James and Marion Payne Memorial Railroad Heritage Gallery—the latter in the city's renovated train station and showcasing 150 years of railroad history in the Manassas area. For local African American history, stop by the Manassas Industrial School and Jennie Dean Memorial, a 5-acre archaeological park on the original site of a school founded through the efforts of Jennie Dean, a former enslaved person.

Also nearby is the inviting fieldstone Ben Lomond Historic Site, a farmhouse turned Civil War hospital, where visitors can view handwritten notes from soldiers. Garden enthusiasts will enjoy the site's 5,200-square-foot Old Rose Garden, one of the nation's largest public gardens devoted to antique rose cultivars. Check out visitmanassas.org and discoverpwm.com for more information on these and other attractions.

"FIRSTS" OF THE FIRST BATTLE OF MANASSAS

The picturesque rolling hills around Manassas Junction, or Bull Run, in Virginia were the site of many military firsts. Most notably, the first major land engagement of the Civil War took place here on July 21, 1861. Many people expected the battle to be an occasion for celebration—each army was certain that it could easily beat the enemy in one battle. However, both sides were, in President Lincoln's words, "green alike." Drilling, discipline, and practice were sorely needed.

Major changes to battlefield strategy and tactics were also necessary, and possible, because railroads had recently become an important aspect of the American landscape and economy. Military leaders were just beginning to appreciate the iron lines' value and utility in wartime. Wanting to control the railroads as a step toward capturing the Confederate capital at Richmond, Union general Irvin McDowell moved his army of 35,000 volunteers—the largest army ever fielded in America at that time—southwest from Washington, D.C., toward the Manassas rail junction, where 21,000 Confederate troops under Brigadier General Pierre G. T. Beauregard (McDowell's West Point classmate) were encamped.

Some of the Union soldiers, marching slowly to their first face-off with the Confederate army, dawdled in the sultry heat to pick blackberries. But soon both sides, at their first taste of war, quickly realized the seriousness of their situation. The ensuing battle demanded the first train movement of troops into combat in U.S. history, as the Confederates hurried in Brigadier General Joseph E. Johnston's brigade from the Shenandoah Valley to reinforce Beauregard. Well-to-do civilians, including members of Congress, drove out to the battleground in carriages laden with picnic baskets and champagne, and then—as defeat loomed—they clogged the roads while fleeing alongside frantic Union soldiers toward the safety of their capital (in perhaps the earliest recorded American traffic jam). The routed Union army handed the Confederate army its first major land victory, although both sides made serious errors and sustained unexpectedly heavy losses.

Another transportation mode first entered American military usage at the First Battle of Manassas, when General McDowell requested aerial reconnaissance by Professor Thaddeus Lowe's balloon *Enterprise*, which was then on a demonstration tour in Washington, D.C. Lowe was one of several aeronauts seeking a Union government contract to create an army balloon corps. From a tethered balloon, airborne telegraphy was even possible. On July 24, after the battle, a second balloon recon mission by Lowe relieved northern terrors by reporting that the victorious Confederates weren't massing for attack, and President Lincoln appointed Lowe the Union army's chief aeronaut.

Back on the ground, wigwag semaphore signaling—the use of large, square, colored flags waved in code patterns—was being employed in combat for the first time.

First mentioned in accounts of the 1861 battle at Manassas was the Confederates' infamous, unnerving Rebel yell. No one is sure today how the yell really sounded, but it has been described as a high-pitched shout—possibly similar to a fox hunter's cry. One witness claimed that when it sounded, "a peculiar corkscrew sensation . . . went up your spine," and another taunted, "If you claim you heard it and weren't scared, that means you never heard it!"

Local grocery merchant Wilmer McLean also learned about wartime beginnings, and endings, in a very personal way. McLean and his wife lived on land that became part of the Manassas battlefield. During the First Battle of Manassas, the McLeans' home was commandeered as a headquarters for Brigadier General Beauregard, who later recalled, "A comical effect of this artillery fight was the destruction of the dinner of myself and staff by a Federal shell that fell into the fireplace of my headquarters at the McLean House." The McLean family later moved south to Appomattox—to a house eventually chosen to host General Lee's formal surrender to General Grant in 1865. After the surrender, McLean reportedly said, "The war began in my front yard and ended in my front parlor."

43 BANSHEE REEKS NATURE PRESERVE

If you want to get off the beaten path and enjoy the beauty of northern Virginia, head to Banshee Reeks for a ramble through its mixture of fields and forests, where civilization feels a hundred miles away.

Features 🚶 🐕 💧 ⛺

Location Leesburg, VA

Rating Moderate

Distance 5.2-mile loop

Elevation Gain 215 feet

Estimated Time 2.5 hours

Maps USGS Leesburg; map is available for free at kiosk in front of the preserve's visitor center; online: bansheereeksnp.org/map

GPS Coordinates 39° 1.720′ N, 77° 35.972′ W

Contact Banshee Reeks Nature Preserve, Friends of Banshee Reeks, bansheereeksnp.org

DIRECTIONS

From I-495 (Capital Beltway), take Exit 45A to VA 267. Travel 22.5 miles and then take Exit 3. Turn left onto Shreve Mill Road/VA 653. After 0.8 mile, turn left onto Evergreen Mills Road and continue for 2.4 miles. Turn right onto The Woods Road/VA 771 and drive about 1 mile; the entrance to the preserve is on the left, at 21085 The Woods Road. Travel 0.75 mile to the parking lot near the visitor center.

TRAIL DESCRIPTION

Banshee Reeks is a 695-acre preserve with more than 20 miles of trails, ranging in difficulty from easy to moderate, an enclave of nature in sharp contrast to the subdivisions and housing developments springing up around it in Leesburg, Virginia. Despite the proximity to suburban neighborhoods, the landscape along these carefully maintained trails looks and feels remote, even a bit rough around the edges.

Reeks is a Gaelic term that refers to the area's rolling hills. But the preserve's unusual name has less to do with a haunting than with a different sort of spirit. According to the preserve's website, the nineteenth-century owner of the farm that became Banshee Reeks spent an evening at a saloon in nearby Leesburg and, in his intoxicated state upon returning to the farm, mistook the howling of the wind for the shrieks of a banshee.

Visitors will not encounter ghosts—only haunting beauty. They are likely to glimpse a variety of wildlife as they hike through successional fields, meadows, and mixed hardwood

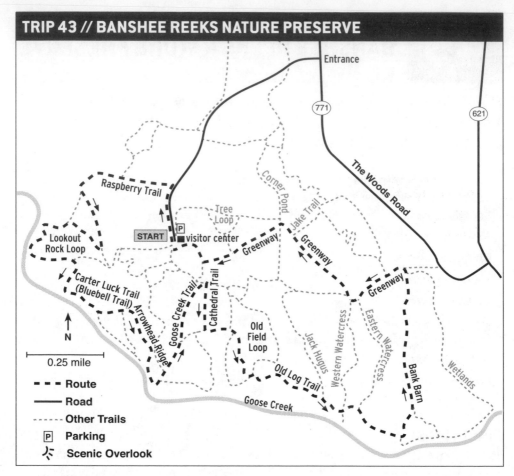

forests. Located in the Piedmont ecosystem, the preserve is home to white-tailed deer, beavers, foxes, skunks, and turkeys and many other types of birds. A list of some 141 bird species that may be seen in the preserve is available at the kiosk in the parking area.

Some residents of the preserve are unwelcome sights—ticks are prevalent here. As you drive in, you may see a sign reading "Designated tick area." Many of the trails pass through grassy fields where these pests may be abundant, particularly in spring and early summer. Wear long, tight-fitting pants or tuck loose pants into high socks, and check for ticks when leaving Banshee Reeks.

Parking is free near the visitor center, which features museum-quality specimens of local flora and fauna and also contains restroom facilities. From the parking lot, Raspberry Trail runs parallel to the road as a mowed path through the grass. At the first left turn, look left for a broad view of the southwest and the Bull Run Mountains. The trail climbs gently as you begin this loop, with thorny bushes and scrubby growth lining the way. Summer brings an explosion of almost 200 species of wildflowers. In August, look for fields of native goldenrod throughout the preserve.

At the intersection with Lookout Rock Loop, continue on Raspberry Trail. The path remains straight and flat. Look left here to see the visitor center in the distance as the field slopes slightly down from the trail. At the next intersection, turn right onto Lookout Rock Loop and leave the field behind, climbing gently on the rocky, rooted path. Pass another intersection with Raspberry Trail and in spring and summer enjoy abundant native wildflowers that line the path as the trail descends. A little way to the right is a view of Goose Creek, a designated Virginia Scenic River that borders the south end of the preserve. The creek is calm in some places, but bear in mind that swimming is not allowed in the preserve. Keep an eye out for great blue herons, kingfishers, ospreys, and bald eagles along the creek.

At the next intersection, turn right onto Bluebell Trail. (The preserve's map lists this trail as Carter Luck Trail, but it is labeled Bluebell Trail on markers.) Watch out for thorns along the path in this forested section. At an unmarked intersection, continue straight; soon the trail widens. At a marked intersection, turn left to continue toward Arrowhead Ridge. The trail curves left, then right, and heads into deeper forest. At the next intersection, turn left toward Goose Creek. Immediately cross a log bridge over a narrow tributary. From here, the trail snakes through thick forest.

At the intersection of Bluebell (Carter Luck) Trail and Goose Creek Trail, turn left onto Goose Creek Trail; turn left again at the next intersection (unmarked) to stay on this trail. At the intersection with Arrowhead Trail, turn right to stay on Goose Creek Trail, which climbs steeply. As you crest the slope on a broad, grassy path, look left for a view north, across the successional fields to the visitor center.

Goose Creek, a tributary of the Potomac River, flows for two miles alongside Banshee Reeks' southern border.

Arrive at a gate and turn sharply right onto Cathedral Trail; then immediately turn right again to keep following the trail. Descend a mowed corridor through a grassy field to a cluster of trees at the edge of a thick forest. Turn left here to head toward the south end of Old Field Loop, climbing gently at first and then more steeply for a time. The route travels through a forested grove and winds over a small rise before descending to an intersection. Turn right onto Old Log Trail and then immediately turn left. This dirt path, crisscrossed with roots, rises and falls before traversing a creek bed.

Soon after, turn right on the southern end of the Jack Hugus/Western Watercress loop. At the intersection with Western Watercress, stay right and cross a narrow creek. Arrive at the intersection with Eastern Watercress and Bank Barn trails and bear right to start following Bank Barn Trail. This trail, which takes you north to the top of the loop, passes through strikingly beautiful tunnel-like vegetation, giving the impression of a maze made of vines and trees.

At the next intersection, stay on Bank Barn Trail, turning left to head north. Climb moderately, emerging into a less forested area. When you reach the intersection with Wetlands and Greenway trails, take Greenway uphill to a cluster of old barns and buildings with attractive field views on either side. Turn left to stay on Greenway, which you'll take all the way back to the visitor center; this trail is as wide as a single-lane road. Pass the north terminus of both Eastern and Western Watercress trails on your left, as well as intersections with Woodchuck Trail, Jake Trail, Jack Hugus Trail, Corner Pond Trail, and Tree Loop. Stay straight, climbing gently and steadily. This part of the trail is very open—sunscreen may be a good idea here.

Pass through a field dotted with bluebird houses. Look left to see silos blanketed with native Virginia creeper vines. The trail crosses the access road that leads to the silos and ends at a gravel road as the visitor center comes into view. Turn right onto the gravel road, which shortly curves around to return to the visitor center and parking area.

MORE INFORMATION

Dogs are allowed but must be leashed (county ordinance). Bikes and horses are not permitted. The preserve is open Tuesday, Wednesday, Thursday, Saturday, and Sunday. Seasonal hours of operation are November to February, from 8 A.M. to 5 P.M.; March, from 8 A.M. to 6 P.M.; April to September, from 8 A.M. to 8 P.M.; and October, from 8 A.M. to 6 P.M.

Visitors can use the Avenza Maps app (see bansheereeksnp.org/map) to download a map of the preserve that shows their location in the preserve in real time.

Visit bansheereeksnp.org to learn more about the preserve, including how you can support it. Contact bansheereeks@loudoun.gov with inquiries.

NEARBY

Set in idyllic countryside, Banshee Reeks is surrounded by farms and vineyards. See virginia.org/winetrails for a vineyard near the preserve to sweeten your day trip.

44 MEADOWLARK BOTANICAL GARDENS

Meadowlark Botanical Gardens offers an ADA-accessible path that meanders among trees, shrubs, and wildflowers indigenous to Virginia's wetlands and Piedmont region. Take time to enjoy the Korean Bell Garden, the only one of its kind in the United States.

Features 👥 ♿ 💧 ⛺ 🚹 $

Location Tysons Corner, VA

Rating Easy

Distance 0.8 mile round-trip

Elevation Gain 70 feet

Estimated Time 1 hour

Maps USGS Vienna; online: novaparks.com/parks/meadowlark-botanical-gardens

GPS Coordinates 38° 56.250′ N, 77° 16.955′ W

Contact Meadowlark Botanical Gardens, Northern Virginia Regional Park Authority, novaparks.com/parks/meadowlark-botanical-gardens, 703-255-3631

DIRECTIONS

From I-495 (Capital Beltway), take Exit 47 (Tysons Corner) west to VA 7 (Leesburg Pike). Drive 3.0 miles (passing Tysons Corner Mall) and turn left onto Beulah Road. Then drive 1.0 mile to the garden entrance on the right.

TRAIL DESCRIPTION

Meadowlark Botanical Gardens, 3.0 miles west of Tysons Corner in the heart of northern Virginia, is a small suburban park (95 acres) managed by the Northern Virginia Regional Park Authority. It combines the beauty of botanical gardens with several miles of wooded trails and includes a rare native plant collection. Make sure your phone is charged for the many photography opportunities, or bring a camera to really capture all the splendor.

Exit the visitor center and follow the paved path around the garden area to the atrium building. This path is ADA accessible, starting near the visitor center and ending at the gazebo in Lake Caroline. Follow the path to the seasonal plantings and the herb garden—here, take a few minutes to enjoy a picturesque view of the Great Lawn. To the left is Lake Gardiner, and straight ahead is Lake Caroline, with its picturesque gazebo. To the right, hidden by the trees, is Lake Lina. Surrounding the waters are a multitude of gardens and nature areas.

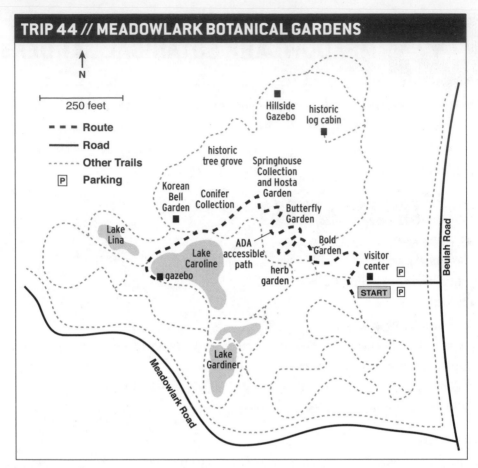

Follow the paved path downhill as it passes seasonal plantings to the left and the Bold Garden to the right. Just past the Bold Garden, the path makes a sharp turn to the right. It passes the Perennial Color Border and then bends to the right.

Reach the Butterfly Garden and turn sharply right to loop around it. To the right, the Springhouse Garden and the Hosta Collection come into sight. At the next intersection, turn right. Pass a mulch walking trail, and then turn left to travel past the Conifer Collection.

Just after the Conifer Collection, a side spur path (not accessible) on the right leads into the Korean Bell Garden, which boasts an ornately carved, hand-built pavilion containing the massive 3-ton *Bell of Peace and Harmony*, cast in Korea by masters of the art and donated to the park by the local Korean community. The bell is intricately engraved with the rose of Sharon (national flower of Korea) and the dogwood (state flower of Virginia). The words *Peace and Harmony* and the ten traditional symbols of longevity: sun, mountain, water, cloud, stone, pine tree, white crane, turtle, deer, and the mushroom of immortality (the *Ganoderma* mushroom, also called *reishi* or *lingzhi*). This bell garden is unique to the United States—in fact, it is the only one in the Western Hemisphere. Much of it can be seen from the paved path.

Follow the paved path to the bank of Lake Caroline—it's worth taking a moment to visit the gazebo and admire the views. Then retrace the path back to the start.

MORE INFORMATION

The park opens at 10 A.M. The gardens close at 4 P.M. from November through March and at 7 P.M. from April through October. The visitor center closes 30 minutes before the gardens do. The park is closed Thanksgiving Day, December 25, and January 1. The entrance fee is $6 for adults and $3 for visitors 6 to 17 and 55 and older. Children younger than 5 are free. Annual memberships are also available for purchase. Dogs are not permitted in the gardens.

The gardens offer ample facilities. In addition to the visitor center with a gift shop and educational programs, an atrium with an indoor tropical garden can be rented for weddings and other functions, as can the Korean Bell Garden pavilion. The park also offers gardening and horticulture workshops and summer concerts. During the "Winter Walk of Lights," the gardens are festively decorated and lit up. The site includes picnic areas, restrooms, a half dozen gazebos, and a large parking lot.

NEARBY

Wolf Trap National Park for the Performing Arts, a favorite live performance venue for musical acts, is just a stone's throw away in Vienna, Virginia. This is a perfect year-round destination for a picnic while enjoying wide array of musical styles, from classical and opera to hip-hop, folk, and jazz. Check out wolftrap.org for schedules and tickets.

The Korean Bell Garden at Meadowlark is the only one of its kind in North America.

RIVERBEND PARK AND GREAT FALLS PARK

A hike from Riverbend Park to Great Falls Park offers dynamic, changing views of the Potomac River as it churns through Class V rapids at Great Falls and then flows into narrow Mather Gorge.

Features 🐕 ♿ 〰 💧 ❄ ⛱ 🚶

Location Great Falls, VA

Rating Moderate

Distance 6.8-mile loop

Elevation Gain 1,100 feet

Estimated Time 4–4.5 hours

Maps USGS Seneca, USGS Vienna, USGS Falls Church; online: fairfaxcounty.gov/parks/riverbend-park, nps.gov/grfa/upload/GRFA-complete-map-508.pdf

GPS Coordinates 39° 01.123′ N, 77° 14.787′ W

Contact Riverbend Park, Fairfax County Park Authority, fairfaxcounty.gov/parks/riverbend-park, 703-759-9018; Great Falls Park, National Park Service, nps.gov/grfa/index.htm, 703-757-3101

DIRECTIONS

From downtown Washington, D.C., take US 50 (Constitution Avenue) west. Continue as it becomes I-66 and go over Theodore Roosevelt Bridge. Keep right at the end of the bridge, merging onto George Washington Memorial Parkway north. Proceed 9.0 miles to I-495 (Capital Beltway). Use the two left lanes to take the I-495 south exit toward Virginia. Go 1.0 mile and take Exit 44 west to Georgetown Pike (VA 193). Drive 4.6 miles on Georgetown Pike, passing Great Falls Park on the right and turning right onto River Bend Road. Go 2.2 miles on River Bend Road, turn right onto Jeffery Road, and turn right again onto Potomac Hills Street, which ends at the Riverbend Park visitor center.

TRAIL DESCRIPTION

Riverbend Park (Fairfax County Park Authority) and Great Falls Park (National Park Service) are only a few miles apart along the Virginia bank of the Potomac River. They are linked by the Potomac Heritage National Scenic Trail, also called the Potomac Heritage Trail.

Starting along the relatively calm waters at Riverbend Park, this southward journey takes hikers past Great Falls on the Potomac River and the equally dramatic Mather Gorge. This trail also skirts the well-preserved remains of the eighteenth-century Patowmack Canal, a

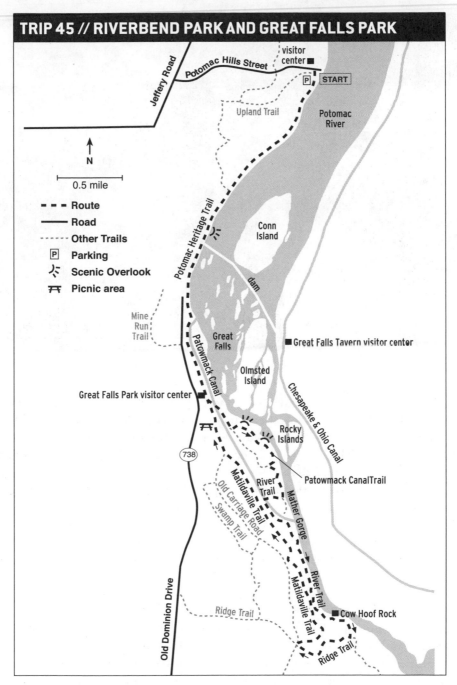

Map legend:
- **- - - Route**
- **—— Road**
- **····· Other Trails**
- **P Parking**
- **Scenic Overlook**
- **Picnic area**

Map labels: Jeffery Road, Potomac Hills Street, visitor center, START, Upland Trail, Potomac River, Potomac Heritage Trail, Conn Island, dam, Mine Run Trail, Patowmack Canal, Great Falls, Great Falls Tavern visitor center, Olmsted Island, Great Falls Park visitor center, Chesapeake & Ohio Canal, 738, Rocky Islands, Patowmack Canal Trail, River Trail, Matildaville Trail, Old Carriage Road, Swamp Trail, Mather Gorge, Old Dominion Drive, Ridge Trail, Matildaville Trail, River Trail, Cow Hoof Rock, Ridge Trail, N, 0.5 mile

remarkable engineering feat begun by George Washington and now recognized as a National Historic Landmark.

From the Riverbend parking lot, head toward the river and turn right on blue-blazed Potomac Heritage Trail to begin the 1.75-mile segment to the Great Falls Park visitor center. The trail enters the riverside forest, where sycamore trees lean almost horizontally above

The power of the falls never ceases to amaze visitors. *Photo by Karan Girdhani.*

the water, complementing the understory of tropical-looking pawpaw trees. Follow the trail as it ascends along a rocky ledge carved into the hillside. Note the exposed, 500-million-year-old metamorphic rock, formed when the African continent pushed into the North American continent and lifted the ocean floor. (See "Far Away in Time: The Geology of Great Falls," on page 220.)

At 0.6 mile, pass an intersection with a side path, and at 0.9 mile, cross a small bridge over a stream that marks the southern boundary of Riverbend Park. At the 1-mile mark is a small sign for Great Falls Park. An overlook offers a clear view of the aqueduct dam—the northern limit for boat traffic on the Potomac, due to the nearby falls—and of Conn Island in the center of the river. After the dam, the trail follows a wide gravel service road. Abandon it at 1.3 miles by veering slightly left onto River Trail, a blue-blazed, natural-surface trail that returns to the river (look for a river hazard sign at the split). At 1.5 miles, the remnants of the 200-year-old Great Falls Skirting Canal come into sight on the left. The first structure is the wing dam, which funneled water into the canal built by the Patowmack Company between 1786 and 1802. When completed, the canal was 1,820 yards long and had five lift locks to carry boats past the falls to the gorge below. Eventually, however, canals—including this one—were displaced by railroads, as year-round maintenance was too difficult and could not meet the demands of commercial transportation.

Follow the trail along the canal inland, crossing a bridge over Mine Run and reaching the Great Falls Park visitor center at 1.75 miles. South of the visitor center, go left across the canal bed and onto Patowmack Canal Trail, which offers access to three falls overlooks. All are well worth a visit, although overlook 1 gives only a partial view of the falls. Overlooks

2 and 3 are accessible, with overlook 2 giving a good view of the falls from a large platform, and overlook 3 delivering even better views from its two platforms. Churning rapids tumble 40 feet in 200 yards through a maze of jagged, weather-beaten rocks. At average flow, the river cascades to a 25-foot-deep pool just below the falls, but after a snowmelt or heavy rains, it can swell and overflow narrow Mather Gorge. A sign on Patowmack Canal Trail, near overlook 3, marks the water level during several heavy twentieth-century floods, including the 1996 flood that put portions of Alexandria, Harpers Ferry, and the Chesapeake & Ohio Canal towpath underwater.

Proceed past a picnic area and turn left back to blue-blazed Potomac Heritage Trail as it forges uphill and begins to navigate around granite boulders. At 2.4 miles, descend to a wooden footbridge over a steep feeder stream, cross it, and climb back uphill to the cliffs above Mather Gorge, named for Stephen T. Mather, the first director of the National Park Service. At 2.6 miles, a sign signals a right turn back over the canal cut. Upon leaving the canal, immediately turn left to continue on the Potomac Heritage Trail, following what becomes a tree-lined bluff above Mather Gorge. Soon the thin gorge widens into the larger Potomac Gorge, marking a point where the river crosses the fall line between the Appalachian Piedmont and the Atlantic Coastal Plain. At 2.9 miles, the blue-blazed trail reaches a road that leads down to Sandy Landing. Cross it diagonally to the right and follow the trail into a small ravine and up the opposite side, passing through a notch in a spine of boulders. With the river to the left, walk along the slope and climb steeply to Cow Hoof Rock. From here, follow the blue blazes uphill.

Continue to the intersection and turn right onto Ridge Trail. At 3.3 miles is a five-way intersection marked by a signpost. Turn slightly right here onto Old Carriage Road and then immediately turn right onto Matildaville Trail, which travels through the indistinct ruins of a town founded by the Revolutionary War commander "Light Horse" Henry Lee, who named it for his first wife. Just north of the town's remains, return to Old Carriage Road and pass the visitor center. (This is also an excellent opportunity to check out the overlooks again.) Look for the blue blazes past the visitor center to retrace the path back to Riverbend Park and to the parking lot.

MORE INFORMATION
Riverbend Park is open daily from 7 A.M. to dusk and offers canoe and kayak rentals from May to October. Leashed dogs are permitted. For more information, visit fairfaxcounty. gov/parks/riverbend or call 703-759-9018. Great Falls Park is open from 7 A.M. to 30 minutes after sunset, daily except for December 25. For more information about Great Falls Park, visit nps.gov/grfa or call 703-757-3103.

NEARBY
Visit the Maryland side of Great Falls with a hike along the famed Billy Goat Trail (Trip 21) and decide which state offers the best views. Or take time to further explore Riverbend Park, which has more than 10 miles of trails.

FAR AWAY IN TIME: THE GEOLOGY OF GREAT FALLS

If the rocky channel carrying the roiling Potomac River through Great Falls seems like a vision from an ancient time, that's only natural. More than 500 million years ago, the long-vanished Iapetus Ocean covered this spot. Its floor was a layer of graywacke, or mud and sand coalescing into sandstone. The ocean's underlying crust eventually shifted and sank, scraping against the hard edges of volcanic islands on a tectonic plate that was slowly moving toward present-day North America. The ensuing collision—known as the Taconian Orogeny—helped build the Appalachian Mountains 450 million years ago. Meanwhile, the approaching crust acted like a bulldozer, pushing chunks of graywacke into an underwater heap. Tectonic pressure and volcanic heat churned and melted this sedimentary rock into metamorphic rocks: metagraywacke, gneiss, and schist.

Migmatite, 460 million years old, is heavily folded layers of medium gray metagraywacke, with wispy swirls of other rock types (granite, schist, quartz) injected by volcanic activity deep beneath Earth's surface and then cooled as pressure pushed the mass away from its heat source. Also look for 530-million-year-old amphibolite, a metamorphic hornblende rock with an igneous protolith (source rock) and a dark gray hammered surface. Sedimentary graywacke still appears in bed formations; the coarser the grain of a layer within a bed, the longer ago the particles settled—as long as 600 million years back into Earth's past.

The rocks of the Mather Gorge Formation, just downstream from Great Falls, contain veins of whitish quartz, pink feldspar, deep red garnet, mica, and other minerals. Lamprophyre dikes—near-vertical layers of 360-million-year-old igneous rock forced upward by heat into cracks in surrounding rock—stretch across Mather Gorge from Maryland to Virginia, noticeably misaligned. One possible explanation is that a fault line beneath the river sliced through the gorge, making the lamprophyre shudder from side to side. Lamprophyre's presence is often linked with gold deposits; indeed, gold was mined for decades along the Maryland bank of Great Falls.

Much of this geological richness lay buried until the last ice age, 20,000 to 30,000 years ago. Before that time, the Potomac flowed across a higher, broad valley. Dropping sea levels and massive snowfalls caused the river to flow stronger and cut deeper, exposing the bedrock. Over the course of millennia, erosion formed successive river terraces that are still visible today.

46 SCOTT'S RUN NATURE PRESERVE

Scott's Run Nature Preserve offers strenuous hiking along bluffs and ridges overlooking the Potomac River near Washington, D.C.

Features 🐕 〰️ 💧

Location McLean, VA

Rating Strenuous

Distance 3.1-mile loop

Elevation Gain 710 feet

Estimated Time 2–2.5 hours

Maps USGS Falls Church; online: fairfaxcounty.gov/parks/sites/parks/files/assets/documents/nature-history/riverbend/scotts-run-trail-map.pdf

GPS Coordinates 38° 57.528' N, 77° 12.301' W

Contact Scott's Run Nature Preserve, Fairfax County Park Authority, fairfaxcounty.gov/parks/scotts-run, 703-759-9018

DIRECTIONS

From I-495 (Capital Beltway), take Exit 44 to VA 193 west (Georgetown Pike). Proceed past the first small parking lot for Scott's Run Nature Preserve (on the right, 0.3 mile from I-495) and turn right into the second main lot (1.0 mile from I-495). The turnoff is hidden from view just after the Swinks Mill Road sign on the left and just before a large sign on the right for Betty Cooke Bridge.

TRAIL DESCRIPTION

The swath of wilderness now called Scott's Run Nature Preserve was once known as the Burling tract and was the scene of controversy in the 1970s when housing developers came knocking. Determined local environmentalists and high school students saved it from suburban sprawl. This 385-acre preserve has scenic views of Scott's Run, the Potomac River, a small waterfall, the remains of an old homestead, and a grove of old-growth eastern hemlocks. The latter's ancestors arrived here during the last ice age, and the trees stand as a reminder that this region long ago was in a subarctic, or boreal, climate zone—equivalent to that of interior Alaska today. Geology lovers will find the preserve's wild, craggy rock formations appealing and fascinating. The preserve's southern section lies on a major fault line dating back 520 to 570 million years (see "Far Away in Time: The Geology of Great Falls" on page 220). Trailing arbutus, Virginia bluebell, and trillium bloom on the steep hillsides. Scott's Run itself starts near the parking lots of the Tysons Corner shopping

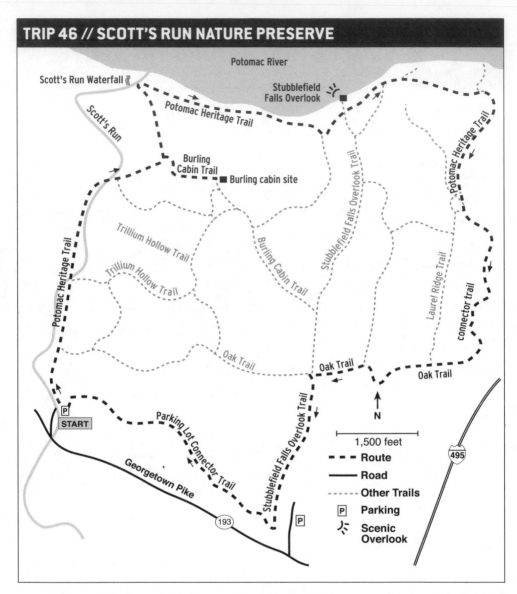

Potomac River

Scott's Run Waterfall

Scott's Run

Potomac Heritage Trail

Stubblefield Falls Overlook

Burling Cabin Trail

Burling cabin site

Potomac Heritage Trail

Trillium Hollow Trail

Trillium Hollow Trail

Burling Cabin Trail

Stubblefield Falls Overlook Trail

Potomac Heritage Trail

Laurel Ridge Trail

connector trail

Oak Trail

Oak Trail

Oak Trail

N

P
START

Parking Lot Connector Trail

Stubblefield Falls Overlook Trail

Georgetown Pike

193

P

1,500 feet

╍ ╍ **Route**

──── **Road**

········· **Other Trails**

P **Parking**

╱╷ **Scenic Overlook**

495

center, flows north through business parks and condominium complexes, and finally travels through the nature preserve and over the waterfall as it empties into the Potomac.

Scott's Run Nature Preserve is interlaced with trails—about 25 intersections and 40 segments, ranging from easy to very difficult. The trails are blazed to match the colors shown on the online trail map, but they are not signed. Maps are also posted near the parking lots and at several locations in the preserve. (*Note*: On weekends, the easier trails may be crowded with families and groups.)

This hike largely follows the looping Potomac Heritage National Scenic Trail (Potomac Heritage Trail), with a side visit to the Burling cabin site, and returns via Oak Trail and Parking Lot Connector Trail. From the main parking lot, start on the wide, rocky, light-blue-blazed Potomac Heritage Trail, which parallels Scott's Run through a small, steep-sloped valley. The wooded slopes are crowded with sycamore, yellow poplar, chestnut oak, American beech, and various pines. In 400 yards, the trail crosses Scott's Run on short concrete posts that act as stepping-stones. Continue for 600 yards, with the streambed on the right, until the trail splits. Take the left fork across Scott's Run and then climb a moderately steep hill.

Arrive at the intersection with green-blazed Burling Cabin Trail—turn right to follow steps that lead to a 300-yard out-and-back hike to a hilltop, where the chimney is all that remains of the Burling cabin. Edward Burling was one of the founders of the iconic Washington, D.C., law firm Covington and Burling. The cabin here hosted politicians seeking to escape the pressures of the capital. Return to the steps and turn right downhill, following the Potomac Heritage Trail to the Potomac riverbank. At water's edge, look left to see the 30-foot waterfall where Scott's Run flows over the rock ledges into the Potomac River.

Turn around and follow a narrower segment of the Potomac Heritage Trail that runs along the riverbank, enjoying the scenic views of the Potomac, where strong currents flow through the Stubblefield Falls. Take the small connector path on your left to visit the Stubblefield Falls overlook and then return by following yellow-blazed Stubblefield Falls Overlook Trail just 60 yards back to the Potomac Heritage Trail. Turn left on the Potomac Heritage Trail and walk through a grove of large pawpaw trees and past steep rock ledges on the right. Continue along the riverbank, cross an intermittent stream, and follow the light-blue blazes as the trail bends to the right.

Scott's Run cascades down a rocky ledge to flow into the Potomac River from the headwaters near Tyson's Corner shopping center. Because the stream picks up pollution from storm runoff and other sources, swimming and wading are prohibited. *Photo by Joseph Bylund, Creative Commons on Flickr.*

This section of the Potomac Heritage Trail runs sharply uphill at first, through some challenging, rugged terrain likely to put you on hands and knees. Crawl along a stream running through the rocks. Hike up the side of the hill to the first ridge, where you'll see red blazes for Laurel Ridge Trail on your right. Follow the Potomac Heritage Trail's light-blue blazes slightly left (southeast) about 100 yards to the next ridge. Then continue uphill to one of the higher elevations on the route, 276 feet above sea level. The topography eases approaching this vantage point.

Here, leave the Potomac Heritage Trail on a connector trail leading southwest toward the next high point. Follow this pleasantly curving trail 200 yards and then turn right on Oak Trail, blazed royal blue.

The terrain runs level to just slightly rolling for some 250 yards. At a downslope, the trail bends left; then it crosses a small stream and makes a hairpin turn to the right as it climbs the opposite bank. Pass a connector path on the right. Next, come to a four-way intersection with yellow-blazed Stubblefield Falls Overlook Trail and follow it to the left (south). This trail ascends toward the preserve's highest point. Arrive at the first, smaller parking lot on Georgetown Pike and then turn right onto purple-blazed Parking Lot Connector Trail, which leads back into the woods and parallels the road down a shallow ravine. Cross the streambed and walk up the other side of the ravine through beech, poplar, and oak trees. Where the trail drops down into a second ravine, stay to the left to avoid crossing the stream at the bottom. Continue with the streambed to the right and a small ridge sloping up to the left, blocking the sound of traffic on the pike. End at the long set of wide, wooden steps leading down a steep hill to the big parking lot.

MORE INFORMATION

Both parking lots are often full on weekends, so arrive early. Swimming or wading is prohibited. In times of heavy or sustained rain, dangerous flash flooding can and does occur; use caution and common sense. For more information, visit fairfaxcounty.gov/parks /scottsrun or call 703-759-9018 (the Riverbend Park office, which oversees the preserve).

NEARBY

For a longer hike, combine a circuit at Scott's Run with an out-and-back trip on the Potomac Heritage Trail, either west toward Riverbend Park and Great Falls Park (Trip 45) or east toward Turkey Run Park (Trip 48), Potomac Overlook Regional Park (Trip 49), and Theodore Roosevelt Island (Trip 27). Meadowlark Botanical Gardens (Trip 44) and Washington and Old Dominion Trail and Gerry Connolly Cross County Trail (Trip 34) are also nearby.

47 HUNTLEY MEADOWS PARK

Huntley Meadows Park is a 1,400-acre natural oasis in the heart of suburbia, less than a mile from the hustle and bustle of US 1. A prime birding location, it contains a large freshwater marsh that supports more than 200 species.

Features 🧍‍♂️ 💧 ⛺

Location Alexandria (Hybla Valley), VA

Rating Easy

Distance 2.1-mile loop

Elevation Gain Minimal

Estimated Time 1 hour

Maps USGS Alexandria, USGS Mount Vernon; map available at park's visitor center; online: fairfaxcounty.gov/parks/huntley-meadows/trails

GPS Coordinates 38° 45.611′ N, 77° 05.736′ W

Contact Huntley Meadows Park, Fairfax County Park Authority, fairfaxcounty .gov/parks/huntley-meadows, 703-768-2525

DIRECTIONS

From I-95/I-495 (Capital Beltway), take Exit 177A to US 1 (Richmond Highway) south. Travel 3.0 miles through a series of traffic lights and then turn right onto Lockheed Boulevard. Go 0.7 mile to the intersection with Harrison Lane. At the intersection, turn left into the park's main entrance. The visitor center parking lot is ahead.

TRAIL DESCRIPTION

The trails at Huntley Meadows Park do not cover great distances but feature scenic boardwalks traversing a 50-acre freshwater marsh. Managed by the Fairfax County Park Authority, the park is in Hybla Valley, between Old Town Alexandria and Mount Vernon. The lowland area, formed by an ancient shift of the Potomac River, hasn't always been a nature lover's paradise. Human endeavors—farm fields and dairy pastures, a prospective airpark for zeppelins, a federal public roads test zone, a National Guard antiaircraft site, and a Naval Research Laboratory radio communications test facility—previously held sway. In 1975, President Gerald Ford authorized the transfer of the land to Fairfax County for $1. During the years, suburban development has increased surface runoff and, coupled with enterprising beavers, greatly expanded the park's wetlands.

Begin the hike at the Lockheed Boulevard parking lot and walk a short distance to the visitor center. Bird-watchers and photographers use the center as a rendezvous point.

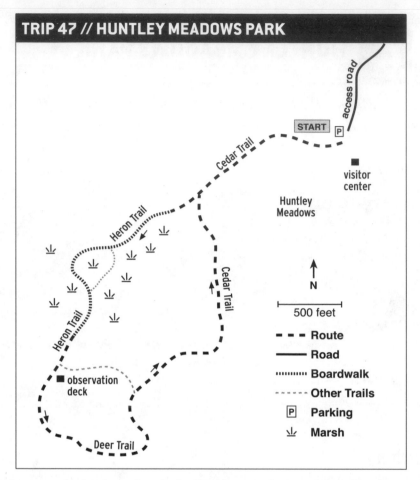

Check the nature logbook, peek at the bird feeder outside the window near the main desk, and visit the gallery for rotating photography exhibits about Huntley Meadows Park flora and fauna.

Exit the visitor center and start down Cedar Trail, a gentle avenue through the woods to the wetlands. Travel through young sweet gum and maple interlaced with shaggy-barked grapevines. This young edge habitat, preferred by marsh rabbits, house sparrows, and indigo buntings, soon gives way to mature, broad oaks. Arrive at the intersection with Heron Trail. Bear right onto Heron Trail and quickly reach the wooden boardwalk at the wetland's edge.

On the right side, a few feet down the boardwalk, stands one of the park's few sycamore trees, a stalwart sentinel over Barnyard Run—a small, lazy stream—as it enters the marsh. Take time to enjoy the watery ecosystem from the boardwalk. Dense stands of cattail, buttonbush, swamp rose, and lizard's tail thrive here, acting as natural filters for runoff from the surrounding suburbs and helping protect the Potomac River and Chesapeake Bay. Watch for animals that feed on these plants: beavers, otters, muskrats, frogs, turtles, herons, ducks, geese, and songbirds.

The boardwalk offers a broad exploration of the marsh and is dotted with benches that invite hikers to linger. As Heron Trail makes its way around the marsh, it splits. Stay to the right to enjoy the slightly longer path along the marsh's edge. Arrive at an intersection where the split ends, and turn right to continue. The boardwalk briefly pops back into the forest before arriving at a two-story observation tower. Forest in every direction ensures the tranquility of this spot. Past the tower, the serpentine boardwalk parallels the forest edge at the point where Barnyard Run exits the marshland and makes its way toward Dogue Creek (named for an Native American tribe known as Dogue, Doag, and Tauxenent) at the western edge of the park.

Both the boardwalk and Heron Trail end at the edge of the forest, where Deer Trail begins. Here, two informal trails break off in succession on the right—keep following Deer Trail forward.

Continue past a swale on the right where blue flag (a native iris) and rhododendron bloom as early as April, luring white-tailed deer. Farther along, dead pines and live gray-barked beeches surround a meadow with bluebird nesting sites. At the next intersection, bear right onto Cedar Trail. Follow this pleasantly flat trail through the woods and arrive at the intersection with Heron Trail. Turn right to keep following Cedar Trail to make the return trip to the visitor center (or loop around again to the boardwalk to enjoy another stroll around the marsh). Dead oaks in this area, felled in the early 1990s by a rare disease, provide nesting sites for barred owls and several types of woodpeckers, including the large

Boardwalks wend their way through the marshes, allowing visitors up-close views.

(and spectacular) pileated woodpecker. Upon returning to the visitor center, take a break, record any nature sightings in the logbook, and be sure to ask the resident naturalists about any unknown species you encountered.

MORE INFORMATION

Huntley Meadows is at 3701 Lockheed Boulevard, Alexandria, VA 22306; use this address to find the park on a global positioning system (GPS) device. Parking is free. Dogs on leashes are permitted except on the boardwalk. The park features a 1.2-mile dual-use hiking and biking trail that ends at a wetlands viewing platform, with access from the parking lot at 6901 South Kings Highway. Leashed pets are permitted on this trail. The park has excellent educational programs for the entire family, ranging from site-specific bird-watching to teen night hikes. Hours vary by season. The visitor center is closed on Tuesdays. For more information, visit fairfaxcounty.gov/parks/huntley-meadows-park or call 703-768-2525.

NEARBY

Restaurants, historical attractions, hotels, and parks are all plentiful in Alexandria and along US 1. Just a few miles south are George Washington's Mount Vernon and Gristmill, worth a day trip in their own right. A stone's throw from the park entrance, uphill along Harrison Lane, is Historic Huntley. Built in 1825 by George Mason's grandson, this house is now listed on the National Register of Historic Places, and the building and grounds are open to the public.

FROM THE POTOMAC TO THE ALLEGHENY HIGHLANDS

On any given day, Mount Vernon Trail hums with activity. Workers ride their bikes to jobs, runners train for their next race, and friends chat while taking a stroll. And, for some, these 18 miles are one of the many stretches that make up the hundreds of miles of the Potomac Heritage National Scenic Trail (PHT).

It might be surprising to learn that a long-distance route lies so close to the District of Columbia. Commuters along busy George Washington Memorial Parkway might see the trail's blue blazes—and might even spot a hiker or two on the side of the road.

As envisioned, the PHT was intended to follow a corridor from the mouth of the Potomac River in Virginia to the Allegheny Highlands area of Pennsylvania. It was created by Congress in 1968, when the National Trail System Act authorized studies for additions to the National Trails System, including this trail. A 1983 amendment to the act designated the PHT as a component of the National Trails System.

At that time, three sections existed: Mount Vernon Trail, the Chesapeake & Ohio Canal Towpath, and Pennsylvania's Laurel Highlands Trail. Today, the PHT is a multimodal, braided system that uses existing trails and corridors to form that route from the Potomac River to the Allegheny Highlands.

It is very much a work in progress, one that is being stitched together with hiking trails, biking paths, and water routes. Visitors can hike one section, bike another, and paddle a third. This trail endeavors to connect exceptional spaces. In the Washington, D.C., area, hikers can put together segments to form loops or explore certain locations. The PHT pops up in Riverbend and Great Falls parks and again in Turkey Run Park. D.C.'s Civil War Defenses (the ring forts) are part of the system. Its trail signs can be seen throughout Virginia and in southern Maryland.

The PHT also has its share of thru-hikers. Arlette Laan, a long-distance hiker who recently completed all eleven National Scenic Trails, finished a thru-hike of the PHT in 2020. She noted: "There are some lovely stretches of nature along the river. You're never too far from a town or city, but it's quiet and it feels like a nice getaway even if you just go for one overnight. I think visiting the PHT during fall foliage would be amazing. I enjoyed the tail end of the colors and it was gorgeous."

The PHT is evolving, pulling in existing trails and connecting them via road walks or other footpaths. Laan opted for a direct route based on the main intent of the trail—to follow the Potomac River from its start into the Allegheny Highlands. Her journey took her from the road walk in Point Lookout State Park to the Chesapeake & Ohio Canal Towpath and Great Allegheny Passage and concluded with Laurel Highlands Trail in Pennsylvania.

"I'm pleasantly surprised at how beautiful this morning's section is," she wrote when passing through the D.C. area. "Rocky shores and some lingering fall colors reflected in the canal which looks more like a pond here."

The PHT is managed by the National Park Service (NPS) in cooperation with a host of local partners—anywhere from 60 to 80 organizations. Although many sections of the trail are well established, the NPS is working with its partners to identify where gaps exist and then look for opportunities to connect or close those gaps. Roughly 820 miles of the long-distance route have been identified, and 100 more are planned to help connect existing gaps.

Laan's journey is just one of many that explore the PHT—think of it as a pick-your-path adventure. The NPS website (nps.gov/pohe/index.htm) offers several suggestions to help get the wheels turning and take advantage of the multitude of ways to experience the trail. In northern Virginia, for example, a trip could include Mount Vernon and Frank Lloyd Wright's Pope-Leighey House. Southern Maryland offers a biking, hiking, and paddling adventure. The options are nearly endless.

48 TURKEY RUN PARK

This enjoyable outing pairs an easy walk in the woods with an exciting scramble along the Potomac River.

Features

Location McLean, VA

Rating Easy to Moderate

Distance 2.3-mile loop

Elevation 200 feet

Estimated Time 2–2.5 hours

Maps Online: nps.gov/gwmp/planyourvisit/upload/Turkey-Run-Park-Map -508-21.pdf

GPS Coordinates 38° 57.863′ N, 77° 09.168′ W

Contact Turkey Run Park, National Park Service, nps.gov/gwmp/planyourvisit /turkeyrun.htm, 703-289-2500

DIRECTIONS

From I-495, take Exit 43 and merge onto George Washington Memorial Parkway (GW Parkway). Take the exit for Turkey Run Park, and turn left at the sign on the exit ramp to enter the park. Once in the park, proceed to the first parking lot to start the hike.

TRAIL DESCRIPTION

Turkey Run Park offers challenging trails and river views, all within a short distance of GW Parkway. The parkway itself includes 4,850 acres: it is home to at least 81 endangered or rare plants and animal species; in addition, 243 species of birds have been recorded and 99 species of trees have been identified. As for Turkey Run Park—well, the spring showing of wildflowers is one of the area's best.

From the parking lot (Area C), look to the east to spot a wide forest road with a "Service Vehicles Only" sign—this is the starting point for red-blazed Woods Trail. The trail quickly splits to circle around a restroom and water fountain. Veer left past a small amphitheater with benches. (A short path leads to an overlook platform just behind the benches.) Pass the benches, continuing to loop around, and arrive at an intersection. Go left to stay on Woods Trail.

The trail dips into the woods, staying mostly level. Pass a connector path that leads to Picnic Area B. Woods Trail works its way around this picnic area, crossing two small wooden footbridges. It climbs slightly uphill before passing the park headquarters and then turning left into the woods.

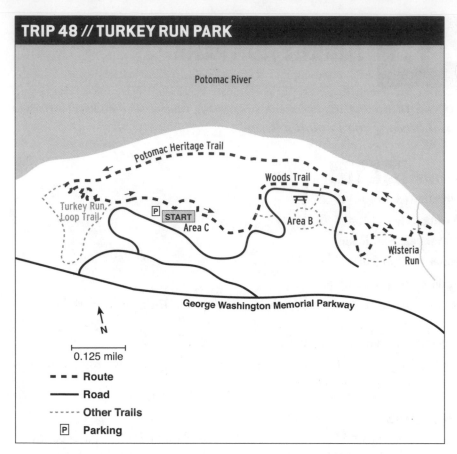

Potomac River

Potomac Heritage Trail

Woods Trail

Turkey Run Loop Trail

P START
Area C

Area B

Wisteria Run

George Washington Memorial Parkway

N

0.125 mile

- - - Route
──── Road
------ Other Trails
P Parking

At roughly 0.7 mile into the hike, arrive at a sign signaling that the Potomac Heritage Trail is 0.3 mile away. Traffic noise may be audible as the route nears GW Parkway—but that's about to change. The trail has been mild walking on a wide path up to this point, but now it gets serious, dropping 170 feet as it swings to the left. As the trail heads downhill, Wisteria Run comes bubbling into sight. At 1.0 mile into the hike, prepare for the first of two stream crossings—carefully traverse Wisteria Run and then resume the descent.

As Woods Trail nears the Potomac River and the junction with the blue-blazed Potomac Heritage Trail, it splits. Bear left to go downhill to join the Potomac Heritage Trail and traverse Wisteria Run again—use caution on this rocky (and often quite wet) crossing. Take time to look for the blue blazes to stay safely on track.

After the mild walking along Woods Trail, the Potomac Heritage Trail offers a more adventurous stretch with rocks to navigate around and over. It evens out for a bit, offering a respite to enjoy the views, but at 1.5 miles into the hike it gets quite rocky again, with some rock scrambling required. Do not rush through this portion of the trail.

Arrive at the intersection with yellow-blazed Turkey Run Loop Trail. This intersection is well signed, and a wooden staircase serves as a good marker (yes, the hike is about to rather quickly gain back all the elevation lost in the initial descent to the river).

When the trail has to go uphill, this well-placed staircase can help make it easier.

The staircase helps in navigating the steeper portion of the climb, and switchbacks gently assist with the final bit. Once at the top, the trail maintains a slight ascent as it returns to the parking lot.

MORE INFORMATION

The park is open daily from 6 A.M. to 10 P.M. Restrooms and water fountains are available from May to September; water is turned off from October to April. The site has three picnic areas, and charcoal and propane grills are permitted. Please use the red cans in each picnic area to dispose of ashes. Plan to pack out all trash; the park has no trash cans. Woods Trail is suitable for children, but the Potomac Heritage Trail has some rocky stretches that might prove challenging for young hikers.

Note that during high river levels (minor flood stage and above), sections of the Potomac Heritage Trail will be underwater and may become impassable.

NEARBY

The Potomac Heritage Trail spans the length of the Potomac River, connecting Theodore Roosevelt Island (Trip 27) with Scott's Run Nature Preserve (Trip 46). Four miles to the south is Fort Marcy Park, one of the ring forts that surrounded Washington, D.C., during the Civil War—this fort guarded the approach to Washington, D.C., via the Chain Bridge (see "Ringing Around the City" on page 106).

This small park packs in trails, interpretive nature displays, and even a raptor enclosure.

Features 🚶 🐕 ⬆️

Location Arlington, VA

Rating Easy

Distance 1.7-mile loop

Elevation Gain 200 feet

Estimated Time 1–1.5 hours

Maps Online: novaparks.com/sites/default/files/maps/Potomac%20Overlook%20Map%20FINAL%204-18.pdf

GPS Coordinates 38° 54.665' N, 77° 06.472' W

Contact Potomac Overlook Regional Park, Northern Virginia Regional Park Authority, novaparks.com/parks/potomac-overlook-regional-park, 703-528-5406

DIRECTIONS

From downtown Washington, D.C., take US 50 (Constitution Avenue) west, which becomes I-66. Cross Theodore Roosevelt Bridge, staying in the right lane. Follow signs to George Washington Memorial Parkway. Merge onto George Washington Memorial Parkway and head north for 1.3 miles. Use the left lane to take the Spout Run Parkway exit toward I-66 West/US 29/Arlington/Washington. Continue onto North Spout Run Parkway and make a slight right to merge onto Lorcom Lane. After 0.5 mile, turn right onto Nelly Custis Drive. Nelly Custis Drive becomes Military Road. Turn right onto Marcey Road. Enter the park and park in the first lot.

TRAIL DESCRIPTION

Potomac Overlook Regional Park is a slice of green space in northern Virginia's Arlington County. On just 67 acres, the park offers trails, interpretive displays on native flora and fauna, demonstration gardens, an interactive nature center, and a raptor enclosure. It also hosts a popular summer camp for children.

For hikers, it holds the perfect after-work adventure: leave the world of video conferencing behind and enter the world of nature. The area used to be farmland and is slowly transitioning—with tulip poplars coming in first—to the hardwood forest typically found in this region. Start on blue-blazed Blue Jay Way. The trail quickly splits—bear left.

Arrive at the intersection with Overlook and Red Maple trails. Turn right here to follow both these trails downhill, and then quickly turn left when they split to follow yellow-blazed

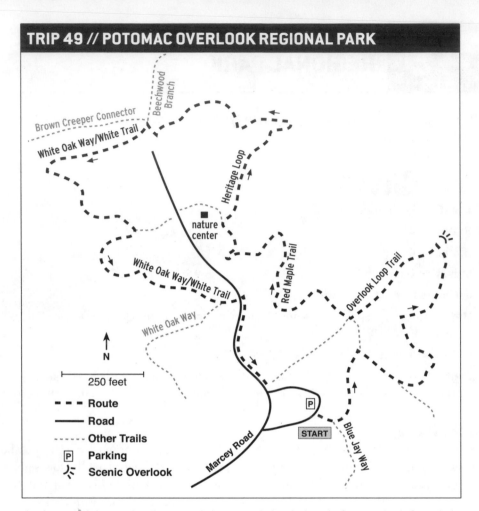

Overlook Trail. The trail rolls up and down and slowly bends first to the left and then to the right—passing a side path that connects from the neighborhood—as it makes its way to the overlook.

Or does it? Arrive at a sign with the question "What happened to the overlook?" When the park was created in 1971, it was reported that visitors could see the Potomac River throughout the year from this vantage point—and could even spot D.C.'s famed Fourth of July fireworks display. But as time passed, the trees surrounding the park grew, and their leaves now obscure the view during the spring and summer months. In late fall and winter, however, the overlook still lives up to its name.

After checking out the overlook, continue on Overlook Trail as it goes over a wooden footpath and meets Red Maple Trail—benches are here at this intersection. Turn right to start following this red-blazed route.

In about 0.1 mile, pass a connector path to the road—bear right to stay on Red Maple Trail. Rather quickly, the trail reaches an unmarked intersection—again, bear right. The trail now steeply descends to meet green-blazed Heritage Loop. Turn right here to start following the loop trail, which slowly bends to the right as it draws near the park boundary

While the Nature Center is a great spot to see wildlife, keep your eyes open on the trails as well. You never know what you might find! *Photo by Nova Parks, Creative Commons on Flickr.*

and then turns rather sharply left to climb uphill as it moves back into the park's center. Pass a sign marking the location of a seasonal Native American camp, used once in summer months for fishing and hunting, that dates from 500 BCE to 500 CE.

Heritage Loop comes to an intersection with several trails, but clear direction is provided by a sign indicating White Trail to the left and a path to Donaldson and the Potomac Heritage Trail to the right. Go left onto white-blazed White Trail (labeled White Oak Way on the map) and follow this trail, which has the slightest of inclines, for the final 0.4 mile of the hike. Two connector paths lead back to the park road. Pass the first connector and then turn left to follow the second connector to the road. Once on the road, turn right to return to the parking lot.

MORE INFORMATION

Potomac Overlook Regional Park, at 2845 Marcey Road in Arlington, Virginia, is open daily from dawn to dusk. The Nature Center is open Tuesday through Saturday, 10 A.M. to 5 P.M., and on Sundays from 1 to 5 P.M. It is closed on Mondays and on Thanksgiving Day and December 24 and 25. To be inspired for the journey, consider downloading Potomac Overlook's coloring pages—one of which features Twiggy, the park's resident barred owl (novaparks.com/parks/potomac-overlook-regional-park).

NEARBY

With George Washington Memorial Parkway nearby, it's easy to tie together more hikes in this area—both Turkey Run Park (Trip 48) and Theodore Roosevelt Island (Trip 27) are short drives away.

WALKING THROUGH BLACK HISTORY

Stroll down King Street in Old Town Alexandria on any given day, and crowds are bustling in and out of restaurants and shops. Many visitors are marveling at the old architecture and taking in the history. Two blocks south is Duke Street, not as bustling but also filled with history related to the African-American experience in the area.

The building that is now the Freedom House Museum once served as the headquarters for one of the nation's largest domestic slave trading companies. In operation from 1828 to 1861, the company sold more than 1,000 people annually from northern Virginia to the southern states before it became part of a hospital complex during the Civil War. Nearby is Alfred Street Baptist Church, Alexandria's oldest African-American congregation, which traces its origins to the early 1800s. The church sits within the vicinity that was known as "The Bottoms," one of the city's first free Black neighborhoods.

The 1790 Census, the first one conducted in the United States, showed that African Americans composed 22 percent of the population in the Alexandria area—90 percent enslaved and 10 percent free. In Washington, D.C., the 1800 Census documented that African Americans were 25 percent of the population, with the majority enslaved. Given the demand for labor as the new capital city was being built, African Americans participated in the construction of many of the federal buildings seen today. Some were permitted to earn money because of this work and in turn were eventually able to purchase their freedom.

Unlike other cities, D.C. did not have any laws in place requiring people to leave after purchasing their freedom. The Black community grew as a result, and by 1830, the number of free African Americans was higher than the number of those still enslaved. The growth of the free Black population also led to laws aimed at restricting their movement—for example, the "Black codes" issued in 1808 set curfews and charged fines for violating them. And while the freed population grew, slavery and the associated trade were still pervasive in the city. The "Retrocession Act" in 1846, which returned the area west of the Potomac River back to Virginia, led to fewer rights for the free Black residents who were now subjected to Virginia's harsher laws.

The Pearl Incident of 1848 further highlighted the presence of slavery in the nation's capital. Seventy-five enslaved adults and children from Maryland, D.C., and Virginia attempted to escape on the *Pearl,* a small schooner docked in Southwest Washington, D.C. The ship made it as far as Maryland's Point Lookout before it was captured; those trying to escape were jailed and then sold. Two teenagers—the Edmonson sisters—were eventually freed due to the advocacy of their father, who was born free, and they became vocal leaders in the abolitionist movement. A monument to them sits on Duke Street.

The Compromise of 1850 outlawed the slave trade in the District of Columbia but not slavery itself. It was not until April 16, 1862, when Congress passed the District of Columbia Compensated Emancipation Act, that slavery was ended in Washington, D.C. (This day is still commemorated annually by the city as Emancipation Day.)

Both during and after the Civil War, more than 25,000 African Americans moved to Washington, D.C. Communities grew, including many around the forts that made up the Civil War Defenses of Washington, such as Fort Ward in Alexandria. The city became a cultural hub, drawing Black leaders from across the country. These communities all can be explored on foot today. Head north, away from the National Mall, to Logan Circle to see the Mary McLeod Bethune Council House National Historic Site. This house served as the first headquarters of the National Council of Negro Women, founded by Bethune. Head southeast to explore the historical center of the Anacostia neighborhood and visit Cedar Hill, the house where Frederick Douglass lived from 1877 until his death in 1895. Head over to U Street in Northwest Washington, D.C., once known as "Black Broadway," which was home to more than 200 Black-owned businesses. Cab Calloway, Louis Armstrong, Miles Davis, Billie Holiday, and other talented musicians played in local clubs.

Walking through Black history is walking through the history of America, with all of its challenges and triumphs. These are important walks to take.

50
ARLINGTON NATIONAL CEMETERY AND U.S. MARINE CORPS WAR (IWO JIMA) MEMORIAL

This Metro-friendly hike passes through some of the most hallowed and lovely hills in the nation, offering classic vistas of the capital city.

Features 👨‍🦯 ♿ ⬆ 🚌

Location Arlington, VA

Rating Easy to Moderate

Distance 4 miles one way

Elevation Gain 600 feet

Estimated Time 3–4 hours, including sightseeing

Maps USGS Washington West, USGS Alexandria; brochure map at cemetery welcome center; online: arlingtoncemetery.mil/Portals/0/Docs/ANC-Map-2017.pdf

GPS Coordinates 38° 52.998′ N, 77° 3.946′ W

Contact Arlington National Cemetery, arlingtoncemetery.mil, 877-907-8585

DIRECTIONS

Take Metrorail's Blue Line or Yellow Line to the Arlington Cemetery station. Use either exit and proceed along Memorial Avenue to the cemetery's welcome center through a gate on the left side of the roadway. If you choose to drive to Arlington Cemetery, the garage has limited parking for an hourly fee, and you can take the Metro back to the parking garage from the Rosslyn station at the hike's terminus. Walk from the garage to the welcome center to begin your hike.

Arlington National Cemetery is an active cemetery hosting 25 to 30 burials a day, Monday to Saturday. Many individuals and families also come to visit the graves of loved ones here. Out of respect for those grieving, visitors are asked to yield the right of way to funeral processions and to refrain from taking photos of funeral services or graveside visitors. Appropriate conduct is requested at all times while on the cemetery grounds. Security screening was introduced in fall 2016.

TRAIL DESCRIPTION

It might seem unusual to include a walk through a cemetery in a day-hiking guidebook, but Arlington National Cemetery is a special case. Its iconic American symbolism, rich history, and sheer beauty combine to make this a walk everyone should take at least once, to absorb all the site has to offer. Think of this trip as a guided historical hiking tour. The route encompasses the cemetery's most visited points of interest (the Kennedy gravesites, the Tomb of the Unknown Soldier, and Arlington House), along with some less traveled

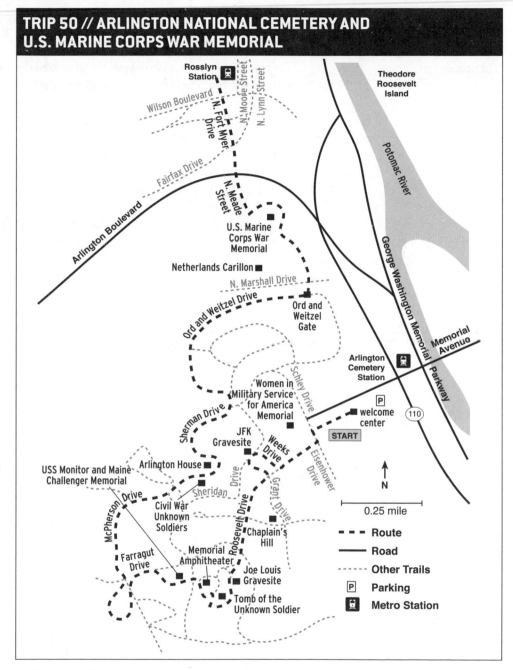

pathways and lesser-known landmarks, before moving outside the gates to the massive Iwo Jima memorial.

This hike keeps mostly to paved walkways and is suitable for older children who can understand the meaning of this place. The walk requires pedestrians to climb some steps and possibly step off the pavement onto grass or gravel in a few stretches. Be prepared for a few inclines steep and lengthy enough to get most people huffing and puffing.

Stop at the cemetery's welcome center to fill water bottles, to pick up a map, and, if applicable, to inquire about the location of a specific gravesite. A small exhibit hall offers rotating displays. Exit through the center's west doors (near the tram tour ticket window) and proceed straight ahead. When you come to a crosswalk, look to your right, toward the cemetery's gates, and note the golden seals of the branches of the U.S. military. Beyond those gates, glimpse the Women in Military Service for America Memorial, built into a hillside. The memorial hosts events, seminars, and exhibits exploring the experience of more than 2.5 million women in America's armed forces and support units, from the Revolutionary War through the present day. Of particular interest are the register inside the building (where visitors can find service data, photos, and other media related to individual servicewomen) and the rooftop arcade of glass tablets inscribed with quotations from some of those women.

From the crosswalk, proceed directly up Roosevelt Drive and into the cemetery. Pause for a 360-degree view of the headstones that stretch in silent, precise rows in every direction, representing the fallen of all ranks and branches who themselves once stood in ready formation. Here and elsewhere during your visit, you can begin to grasp how many men and women have participated in our armed forces during the centuries, especially when you consider that this is just one of more than 100 national cemeteries. Note the marble headstones, provided by the U.S. government, all bearing the same information: faith symbols; name, rank, and service branch; notations of decorations, such as the Medal of Honor or the Silver Star; and (on the back) the names of any spouses and dependent children buried with the service member. Due to the heightened meaning of an Arlington burial, service members interred here today must qualify for the honor under special rules. Active service members who die in the line of duty and any U.S. president, due to the commander-in-chief role, are automatically eligible. Two presidents—Kennedy and Taft—and three five-star generals to date have been buried here.

Turn right onto Weeks Drive and look toward Arlington House (the Custis-Lee mansion) atop the hill. You will visit the house later in the hike, but you won't see this view of it again. Note the flag in front of the mansion: if it's at half-staff, funerals are in progress in the cemetery. Proceed straight until you cross Sheridan Drive, toward the curving granite plaza at the gravesite of President John F. Kennedy and members of his family. Before mounting the steps or the circular ramp, look to your right, where the cemetery's section 5 contains the graves of several U.S. Supreme Court justices, including Thurgood Marshall, the court's first Black justice.

Walk up to the Kennedy graves, where an eternal flame, ignited at the slain president's burial on November 25, 1963, illuminates his resting place. Next to him is his widow, Jacqueline Kennedy Onassis. (Although she did remarry after the president's death, she was eligible for burial here because she was a widow again when she died in 1994.) Remains of two of their children, a stillborn daughter and a son, Patrick, who died as an infant, were brought here following President Kennedy's death. Turn around and face the Memorial Bridge to appreciate the vista along the National Mall. Several individuals who knew John F. Kennedy have claimed that, while touring Arlington House earlier in 1963, the president remarked, "I could stay here forever." Quotations from the young president's speeches, engraved on the memorial wall, enhance the experience. If you are here in spring, the tulip trees and flowering crabapples provide additional beauty.

Next, walk down the three steps toward the roadway but quickly turn right along the cobblestone path and approach the white wooden cross marking the gravesite of President Kennedy's younger brother, Robert F. Kennedy, who was also a U.S. attorney general. During his own campaign for the presidency in 1968, Robert Kennedy was shot as he exited through a back corridor of the Ambassador Hotel in Los Angeles. The white cross was installed at his particular request. Also here is a simple marker for the youngest brother, Edward "Ted" Kennedy (a U.S. senator from Massachusetts), who died in 2009. Pause to enjoy the peaceful meditation pool that lies beneath several engraved quotations from Robert Kennedy's speeches.

Take the steps out to the roadway and turn left, looking for the large headstone marking the grave of Michael Musmanno, a judge in the Nuremberg trials following the fall of the Nazi regime in World War II. Immediately turn sharply right onto Grant Drive, walk past the tram stop, and look to your right for the headstone of Daniel "Chappie" James Jr., a Tuskegee Institute alumnus, a decorated U.S. Air Force fighter pilot, and the first African American to reach the rank of four-star general. Then look left at the equestrian statue marking the burial place of Sir John Dill, a British field marshal stationed in Washington, D.C., during World War II. When he died during his tour, he was granted burial at Arlington in keeping with the British tradition of laying soldiers to rest where they fell. Dill's is one of some two dozen graves of foreign officers in the cemetery.

Turn right, back onto Roosevelt Drive, and look to your left toward Chaplains' Hill, where three identical tall stone markers standing side by side honor the military chaplains who died in the two world wars and in the Korean War. Take a moment here to notice the many shapes, sizes, and colors of grave markers provided by survivors of the deceased before you proceed up the hill. When you come to a Y intersection, keep left and then turn right onto a flagstone walkway. Now to your left, in section 7A, you'll see a tall, brown headstone with a bronze plaque for the world heavyweight-boxing champion Joe Louis. Louis's 1938 rout of former champ Max Schmeling of Germany humiliated the Nazis and helped make the "Brown Bomber" a favorite of U.S. GIs during World War II. Louis himself served in the war as a special assignment officer in a segregated unit and earned the Legion of Merit decoration. Turn left just past Louis's grave and continue uphill past a black headstone with U.S. Air Force wings. This is the grave of astronaut Michael J. Smith, a naval aviator and the pilot of the ill-fated space shuttle *Challenger*, which exploded shortly after its launch on January 28, 1986. Come to an elliptical lawn and proceed toward its far end, staying silent as you go. The Tomb of the Unknown Soldier is at the top of the steps to your right, and a ceremony might be in progress. Walk uphill under several large, old maples and then around to the right to approach the plaza in front of the tomb. Make sure no sentinels are approaching or exiting the enclosure, and when the way is clear, find a place on the marble steps from which to observe the changing of the guard (occurs every hour from October to March and every half hour from April to September).

The Tomb of the Unknown Soldier was established following World War I, when many American troops fell on foreign battlefields and were buried without identification. Grieving families thus had no closure. In 1921, the remains of one unknown American soldier were brought here to represent all service members who never came home from that war. On the face of the tomb's white Colorado marble are the words "Here rests in honored glory an American Soldier, known but to God." In the 1930s, an honor guard of soldiers from the Third U.S. Infantry was posted to the tomb. The remains of unknown soldiers from World War II and the Korean and Vietnam wars were later added, but the Vietnam unknown soldier's remains were later disinterred and identified with the aid of DNA testing technology as those of Lt. Michael Blassie of St. Louis. His former tomb will forever remain empty.

While on duty, the tomb guard sentinel performs a 21-step, 21-second walk before the tomb; turns to face the tomb; waits 21 seconds; turns again and shoulders rifle between tomb and onlookers; waits another 21 seconds; and repeats the walk in the opposite direction. With each step and pause, the soldier is intently focused, precise, and dignified in movement, mentally counting the seconds while pacing out an endless 21-gun salute to fallen comrades. Although the sentinel is prepared to defend the tomb if necessary, the primary purpose is to guard a memory and a standard, rather than a physical structure.

Be prepared to remain silent and standing for the solemn ceremony. Watch for the relief commander and the new sentinel to enter the enclosure. If weather allows, the commander performs a white-glove inspection of the new sentinel's rifle on the right-hand (south) end of the plaza. Following the guard change, wait for all but the newly posted sentinel to exit the enclosure before you attempt to leave the steps. Be advised that wreath-laying ceremonies often follow the guard change. It's worth remaining to observe one of these if you can; you'll get to hear an army bugler blowing "Taps" after the commander asks you to place your right hand over your heart.

Stroll through the Memorial Amphitheater, which hosts official ceremonies, such as the annual Memorial Day and Veterans Day observances, when the U.S. president usually speaks and places a wreath at the tomb. Walk out to the roadway, Memorial Avenue, and look across the road and to the left at a short walkway bounded by draped chains. This is the grave of Audie Murphy, the most decorated American soldier of World War II. As you move toward the tall, white mast of the USS *Maine*, pause to visit the memorials to the crews of the space shuttles *Challenger* and *Columbia* on your right. The USS Maine Memorial remembers the 266 sailors who were lost when the ship, anchored in Havana, Cuba, in 1898, exploded and touched off the Spanish-American War with the rallying cry, "Remember the *Maine!*" Many Americans jumped to the conclusion that Spanish forces, seeking to put down a Cuban bid for independence, had blown up the American vessel, but recent research suggests the explosion might have been caused by a coal-fired boiler malfunction aboard the ship.

Walk around the memorial's mast to the circular driveway and out to Farragut Drive. Turn left and look across the road into section 13 at the white headstones with the letters *U.S.C.T.* These stones mark the graves of soldiers in the United States Colored Troops, segregated army units dating to the Civil War and the Spanish-American War. (America's military wasn't fully integrated until the Korean War in the early 1950s.) At the

Facing page: Sunrise bathes the U.S. Marine Corps War Memorial—often referred to as the Iwo Jima memorial—and its six flag-raisers, whose figures are roughly five times life size. Carved into the stone base are the names of Marine military engagements since the Corps's inception in 1775. *Photo by Beth Homicz.*

intersection with McPherson Drive, turn left briefly to visit the Confederate Memorial and burial section. These 400 southern troops, mostly officers, were buried or reinterred here after Congress authorized a special section for the purpose in 1900. This section's complex legacy and history are detailed on the cemetery's website: arlingtoncemetery.mil/Explore /Monuments-and-Memorials/Confederate-Memorial.

Return to McPherson Drive and turn left, walking through several older sections with large, old trees (and several headstones engulfed in their roots). Continue around the circle at section 14 to the intersection of Meigs Drive; turn right here. Watch for a sizable marker on your left bearing the name Doubleday; that's Abner Doubleday, credited with inventing the game of baseball. Come to the overgrown Old Amphitheater on your right, bear slightly left onto Sherman Drive, and turn right on the gravel path to visit Arlington House. Before you walk around to the front porch, look to your right into a grove of shrubbery to see the marker for a mass grave holding the remains of 2,111 unidentified Union and Confederate soldiers recovered from Civil War battlefields. Stroll through the flower garden, noticing the ring of Union headstones around it, and look out to admire the vista over the Potomac. Notice a table-shaped grave marker in front of the mansion. This is the site of the reinterred remains of Pierre L'Enfant, designer of the city plan for Washington, D.C., who died as a pauper abroad but was later honored with a final resting place overlooking the city he created (see Trip 25: National Mall).

Pass Arlington House, the former home of Robert E. Lee, maintained by the National Park Service. The Park Service completed a major rehabilitation project in 2021 and added new interpretive exhibits to tell inclusive stories that bring in multiple and diverse historical perspectives.

Return to Sherman Drive, turning right and proceeding downhill past a heavily wooded area on your left. This is section 29, known as Arlington Woods and hotly defended by environmental groups as one of the best examples of old-growth, terraced gravel forest remaining in Virginia. Some of the old forest has been preserved as a buffer zone. Turn left onto Ord and Weitzel Drive, pausing to view the Vietnam War Memorial Tree, and stroll along the curving road past the cemetery's Millennium Project on your left. This extensive effort to provide for future burial space has consumed some of that old-growth forest.

Watch for small, block-shaped markers in this area and standard-issue headstones labeled "Civilian" or "Citizen." Many of these indicate the graves of residents of Freedman's Village, established on this site during the Civil War to resettle and educate formerly enslaved people. Turn left to exit the cemetery through the Ord and Weitzel Gate, carefully cross the roadway, and proceed uphill toward the U.S. Marine Corps War Memorial. Look left to glimpse the square tower known as the Netherlands Carillon, containing 57 bells that were a gift from the people of the Netherlands to the United States following World War II.

Now approach the largest bronze statue ever cast—and one of the most famous. Based on a Pulitzer Prize–winning photo by Joe Rosenthal of the Associated Press, the memorial depicts five marines and a navy medic raising an American flag atop Mount Suribachi on the Pacific island of Iwo Jima in February 1945. An initial amphibious landing on February 19, 1945 set off a brutal five-week push to secure the island as an Allied base despite the Japanese forces' entrenchments and hidden artillery. The photo—actually of a second flag-raising that day—was taken on February 23, five days into the battle. Three of the six men were later killed in action on Iwo Jima.

Walk around the circle to your right, watching to see if the flag seems to rise as you move—an optical illusion that has long delighted tourists. The piece's sculptor, Felix de Weldon, once scoffed at the urban legend suggesting that he had added an extra hand, possibly a hand of God, among the figures. He denied he would have executed such a travesty of his masterwork. The men's figures are roughly five times life-size, 32 feet tall, and their canteens would hold about eight gallons of water. Circle the statue to note all six figures and the names of major engagements of U.S. Marines since the inception of the corps in 1775.

When ready to call it a half-day, walk past the parade ground, cross the parking area, and scramble up the wooded slope to North Meade Street. Turn right and walk about four blocks to the Rosslyn Metro station, which contains one of the world's longest continuous escalators at 207 feet.

MORE INFORMATION

Arlington National Cemetery opens daily at 8 A.M. It closes at 5 P.M. from October to March and at 7 P.M. from April to September. Admission is free. The changing of the guard at the Tomb of the Unknown Soldier takes place on the hour year-round and also on the half hour April to September. Restrooms and water fountains are available at the welcome center, the Women in Military Service for America Memorial, the Memorial Amphitheater, and Arlington House. Visit the Arlington National Cemetery website at arlington-cemetery.mil or call 877-907-8585 for more information. The website also offers instructions for downloading and using the ANC Explorer smartphone app.

The park maintains services and accessible parking for visitors with disabilities and recently added an accessible ramp to the Memorial Amphitheater. Learn more at arlingtoncemetery.mil/Visit/Visitors-with-Disabilities.

NEARBY

Just outside the cemetery gates along VA 110 is the Pentagon, the headquarters of the Department of Defense. The 9/11 Pentagon Memorial features winglike benches in honor of each of the 184 souls lost here on September 11, 2001. Find more information at pentagonmemorial.org.

APPENDIX: FURTHER READING

HUMAN HISTORY

Blight, David. *Frederick Douglass: Prophet of Freedom*. New York: Simon & Schuster, 2020.
  This Pulitzer Prize–winning biography looks at the life of abolitionist and author Frederick Douglass.

Chambers, John Whiteclay II. *OSS Training in the National Parks and Service Abroad During World War II*. Washington, DC: National Park Service, 2008.
  Covers the creation of the Office of Strategic Service, how the parks were converted into spy-training facilities, and the details of training activities in camps as well as in local towns and businesses. Available online at nps.gov/articles/series.htm?id=16D749F1-1DD8-B71B -0B65F7F40FA87A5E.

Ewing, Heather. *The Lost World of James Smithson: Science, Revolution, and the Birth of the Smithsonian*. New York: Bloomsbury USA, 2007.
  A fascinating, deeply researched journey into Smithson's late-Enlightenment world and the optimistic spirit of its scientific vanguard; the greatest contribution to date to our knowledge of the Smithsonian's benefactor.

Henson, Matthew. *A Negro Explorer at the North Pole*. Montpelier, VT: Invisible Cities Press, 2001 (reprint).
  Henson's autobiography, originally published three years after the successful expedition to the North Pole, tells the full story that Peary wouldn't—or couldn't—such as the discrimination Henson faced for most of his long life.

Johnson, Dolores. *Onward: A Photobiography of Matthew Henson*. Washington, DC: National Geographic Children's Books, 2005.
  Tells a strong story and provides rare photos of Henson and Peary's expeditions and of the Inuit guides who helped them reach the North Pole. Geared toward young people, but worth a read by anyone.

Lapp, Joe. *Kenilworth: A DC Neighborhood by the Anacostia River*. Washington, DC: Humanities Council, 2006.
  This booklet charts a history of the Kenilworth neighborhood. Available online at planning .dc.gov/sites/default/files/dc/sites/op/publication/attachments/Kenilworth_Brochure.pdf

Mayer, Henry. *All on Fire: William Lloyd Garrison and the Abolition of Slavery*. New York: W.W. Norton & Company, 2008.

A powerful read about the abolition movement, especially noteworthy for its in-depth treatment of John Brown.

McIntosh, Elizabeth P. *Sisterhood of Spies: The Women of the OSS*. New York: Dell Publishing/Random House, 1998.

Although the female members of the Office of Strategic Service don't seem to have trained in Prince William Forest or Catoctin Mountain parks, this is a compelling, entertaining set of tales by a female OSS and CIA veteran.

McPherson, James M. *Battle Cry of Freedom: The Civil War Era*. New York: Oxford University Press USA, 2003.

An excellent in-depth, one-volume overview of the events leading up to, and the political and military conflicts of, the Civil War.

Rountree, Helen C., ed. *Powhatan Foreign Relations, 1500–1722*. Charlottesville, VA: University of Virginia Press, 1993.

One of the very few published books touching upon the Piscataway people and their lands, traditions, migrations, and relations with neighboring tribes.

Smith, Richard Harris. *OSS: The Secret History of America's First Central Intelligence Agency*. Guilford, CT: Lyons Press, 2005.

Considered by many to be the authoritative work on the OSS's creation and operations, it tells of interagency rivalries as well as behind-the-lines derring-do.

Stone, Robert, director. *American Experience: The Civilian Conservation Corps* (DVD). PBS Home Video, 2009.

Documents the reasons behind the CCC's creation, and the impacts on its members nationwide. Many interviews with CCC veterans.

Tayac, Gabrielle, and Edwin Schupman. *We Have a Story to Tell: The Native Peoples of the Chesapeake Region*. Washington, DC: National Museum of the American Indian Education Office, 2006.

An educator's guide geared toward high school students, with good depth and insight into the historical and current-day challenges faced by regional tribes.

NATURAL HISTORY

Allaby, Michael. *Temperate Forests* (Biomes of the Earth Series). New York: Chelsea House, 2006.

A general textbook on flora and fauna for grades 7 and up, with good, basic information on beavers, riparian zones, and more.

Choukas-Bradley, Melanie. *City of Trees: The Complete Field Guide to the Trees of Washington, D.C.* 3rd ed. Charlottesville, VA: University of Virginia Press, 2008.

Astonishingly in-depth and invitingly written, this guide spotlights the plants—and the larger-than-life personalities—that have made Washington the beautiful city it is today.

National Geographic Society. *Wild Animals of North America*. Washington, DC, National Geographic Society Book Division, 1998.

A beautiful pictorial look at beavers and other wildlife, with entertaining informational tidbits.

Reed, John C. Jr., Robert S. Sigafoos, and George W. Fisher. *The River and the Rocks: The Geologic Story of Great Falls and the Potomac River Gorge*. Washington, DC: United States Geological Survey, 1970.

The classic study of Great Falls geology, fascinating and not too technical. Available online at nps.gov/parkhistory/online_books/grfa/contents.htm.

Schlyer, Krista. *River of Redemption: Almanac of Life on the Anacostia*. College Station, TX: Texas A&M University Press, 2018.

This book, combined with photographs, offers a look at the history of this Washington, D.C., river.

INDEX

ABOUT THE AUTHORS

Growing up, **Jennifer Adach** frequently had her head in a book and eschewed any outdoor activities—that is, until she moved to Washington, D.C., for college and quickly fell in love with the city and its endless opportunities for recreation. Now, she is fortunate to combine her two passions: hiking and books. She is the co-author of *AMC's Best Day Hikes in the Shenandoah Valley*. Jennifer leads backpacking trips for DC Ultralight Backpacking, including women-only trips, and is a board member for the Capital Hiking Club. She's hiked extensively throughout the Mid-Atlantic area, section-hiked the Tuscarora and Mid State trails (Pennsylvania), and thru-hiked the John Muir Trail and Sweden's Kungsleden Trail. She enjoys discovering all the D.C. area has to offer, talking about hiking gear, and encouraging beginner hikers and backpackers to get on the trails. She lives in Alexandria, Virginia, with her partner, Michael Martin, and their two cats. When not on the trail, she can still be frequently spotted with her head in a book.

Beth Homicz received a Bachelor of Science in Language from Georgetown University in 1990 and qualified for her Washington, D.C., professional tour guide license in 1994. For seventeen seasons, she led some 15,000 visitors, from many nations and all walks of life, on lively, memorable, custom adventures among the cultural and historical sights of the nation's capital and the East Coast.

Beth has written for *The Washington Post*, penned a regular column for *Destinations* magazine, and published articles on topics ranging from political strategy to relationship-based marketing. She has created and delivered staff-development programs in effective writing for several federal agencies, including the U.S. Department of Defense, the Bureau of the Census (U.S. Department of Commerce), the National Credit Union Administration, and the Environmental Protection Agency.

Currently, Beth lives beside a creek in rural Virginia, works as an award-winning reporter for a community newspaper, and has a novel in progress about the Underground Railroad.

ABOUT AMC'S POTOMAC CHAPTER

Started in 1984, the Potomac Chapter is the southernmost of the Appalachian Mountain Club's eleven chapters. Its 2,400 members—mostly from Washington, D.C., Maryland, and northern Virginia—engage in various activities, including day-hiking, backpacking, paddling, biking, and social get-togethers. The chapter also organizes conservation initiatives and offers education and leadership opportunities.

To view a list of AMC activities in Washington, D.C., Maryland, northern Virginia, and other parts of the Northeast, visit activities.outdoors.org. To learn more about the Potomac Chapter, visit amcpotomac.org.

AMC BOOKS UPDATES

AMC Books strives to keep our guidebooks as up-to-date as possible to help you plan safe and enjoyable adventures. If we learn after publishing a book that relevant trails have been relocated or route or contact information has changed, we will post the updated information online. Before you hit the trail, visit outdoors.org/books-maps and click the "Book Updates" tab. While hiking, if you notice discrepancies with the trip descriptions or maps, or if you find any other errors in this book, please let us know by submitting them to amcbookupdates@outdoors.org or to Books Editor, c/o AMC, 10 City Square, Boston, MA 02129. We will verify all submissions and post key updates each month. AMC Books is dedicated to being a recognized leader in outdoor publishing. Thank you for your participation.

AMC's Best Day Hikes in the Shenandoah Valley, 2nd Edition

Jennifer Adach and Michael R. Martin

Bounded on the east by the Blue Ridge Mountains and on the west by the Appalachians, the Shenandoah Valley is a region of exceptional natural beauty, and an iconic location in American history. This guide offers 50 of the best hikes in the region for all skill levels, from easy walks of a few miles with little elevation gain to more demanding treks through challenging terrain.

$18.95 • 978-1-62842-107-1 • ebook available

Quiet Water Mid-Atlantic

Rachel Cooper

Discover 60 spectacular trips on 64 of the best flatwater ponds, lakes, and rivers for paddlers of all skill levels in New Jersey, eastern Pennsylvania, Delaware, Maryland, Virginia, and Washington, D.C. This title—brand new to the trusted Quiet Water series—features an at-a-glance trip planner, driving directions and GPS coordinates for parking, and turn-by-turn descriptions of the trip routes, with maps included.

$19.95 • 978-1-62842-087-6 • ebook available

AMC's Best Sea Kayaking in the Mid-Atlantic

Michaela Riva Gaaserud

This new guide features 50 coastal paddling adventures from the New York City Water Trail to beautiful Virginia Beach at the mouth of the Chesapeake River, with an at-a-glance trip planner, descriptions and maps of the routes, and information on launches, tide and currents, and nearby attractions. It's your indispensible guide to kayaking on the Mid-Atlantic seaboard.

$18.95 • 978-1-62842-031-9 • ebook available

This Wild Land

Andrew Vietze

Almost twenty years ago, Andrew Vietze made an unexpected career change: from punk rock magazine editor to park ranger at Baxter State Park in Maine. From midnight search-and-rescue missions to trail maintenance to cleaning toilets, Baxter rangers do it all…and over the decades Vietze has seen it all. In *This Wild Land*, Vietze tells his story with humor, action, and an eye for the compelling details of life as a park ranger, making it the perfect read for outdoor and armchair adventurers alike.

$18.95 • 978-1-62842-132-3 • ebook available

Find these and other AMC titles through ebook stores, booksellers, and outdoor retailers. Or order directly from AMC at outdoors.org/amcstore or call 800-262-4455.